CURRICULUM STUDIES
GONE WILD

A Book Series of
Curriculum Studies

William F. Pinar
General Editor

VOLUME 37

The Complicated Conversation series
is part of the Peter Lang Education list.
Every volume is peer reviewed and meets
the highest quality standards for content and production.

PETER LANG
New York • Washington, D.C./Baltimore • Bern
Frankfurt • Berlin • Brussels • Vienna • Oxford

Nathan Hensley

CURRICULUM STUDIES
GONE WILD

Bioregional Education and the Scholarship of Sustainability

PETER LANG
New York • Washington, D.C./Baltimore • Bern
Frankfurt • Berlin • Brussels • Vienna • Oxford

Library of Congress Cataloging-in-Publication Data
Hensley, Nathan.
Curriculum studies gone wild: bioregional education
and the scholarship of sustainability / Nathan Hensley.
p. cm. — (Complicated conversation:
a book series of curriculum studies; v. 37)
Includes bibliographical references.
1. Environmental education—Curricula. 2. Place-based education—
Curricula. 3. Curriculum planning. 4. Sustainability. I. Title.
GE70.H46   333.72071—dc22   2010046190
ISBN 978-1-4331-1296-6 (hardcover)
ISBN 978-1-4331-1295-9 (paperback)
ISSN 1534-2816

Bibliographic information published by **Die Deutsche Nationalbibliothek**.
Die Deutsche Nationalbibliothek lists this publication in the "Deutsche
Nationalbibliografie"; detailed bibliographic data is available
on the Internet at http://dnb.d-nb.de/.

The paper in this book meets the guidelines for permanence and durability
of the Committee on Production Guidelines for Book Longevity
of the Council of Library Resources.

© 2011 Peter Lang Publishing, Inc., New York
29 Broadway, 18th floor, New York, NY 10006
www.peterlang.com

All rights reserved.
Reprint or reproduction, even partially, in all forms such as microfilm,
xerography, microfiche, microcard, and offset strictly prohibited.

Printed in the United States of America

I DEDICATE this book to my dad, who taught me to enjoy, appreciate, and explore the curriculum of life while showing me how to be enchanted by its simple pleasures.

Contents

Foreword *by Richard Kahn* ix

Acknowledgments xiii

Introduction 1

1. A Call to Action 9

2. The Context of Curriculum Studies 25

3. A Material World: Education and Environmental Degradation 43

4. The Scholarship of Sustainability 95

5. Place and Education: Bringing It All Back Home 135

6. Trudging Towards Sustainability 176

References 221

Foreword

> Let the beauty of what you love be what you do. There are a thousand ways to kneel and kiss the earth, there are a thousand ways to go home again.
>
> Rumi, *The Essential Rumi*

IN HER much talked about recent bestseller, *The Death and Life of the Great American School System* (2010), Diane Ravitch argues that the key to actualizing a relevant and rewarding educational system at the start of the 21st century will be to move the general will from an accountability discourse to one focused upon curriculum. Are schools to be primarily about administratively managed outcomes, she wonders polemically, or about the best possible engagement with education's larger purpose: providing teachers and students the opportunity to experience a vital and philosophically informed curriculum of study? While the call for the latter seems altogether right in many ways, Ravitch's belief that we can rid ourselves of the worthless rituals associated with value-added approaches to teaching by fashioning a curriculum for learners modeled after the ideas of E. D. Hirsch or the national standards curriculum envisioned by *A Nation at Risk* seems highly problematic. After reading Nathan Hensley's provocative book, *Curriculum Studies Gone Wild: Bioregional Education and the Scholarship of Sustainability*, I now understand why.

As Hensley points out, a "curriculum" is literally a race. In Roman times, it was the race of chariots in times of war or in the bread and circuses spectacle of the coliseums. Now we have the Obama administration's Race to the Top. By contrast, Hensley's book counsels that today's foundational pedagogical moments move more appropriately toward the ground—that we must learn once again what it is to become Whitman's leaves of grass or Guthrie's wheat fields waving as a culturally relevant response to the planet's unprecedented Ground Zero of ongoing genocide, ecocide, and zoöcide. Moreover, if Ravitch wants Core Knowledge for all and a commitment to curricular standards, Hensley better suggests that we commit to the creative study of the panoply of places in which we stand (e.g., our backyards, communities, or watersheds) and that we stretch out a good long while with the vast world of unique experiences not already packaged for us as consumable commodities by the global capitalist culture industries.

"Curriculum" also shares a common linguistic origin with "current," as in the surge of water down stream. Thoughtfully, therefore, images of the river return time and again to *Curriculum Studies Gone Wild*, and the book itself seems to twist and turn in its approach to its subject, oxbow and eddy in defiance of a pipeline linear method, then become rapid for a brief moment until finally banking back into the deep trout pools and fecund tributaries of the reader's imagination. Notably, at various moments Hensley recounts his own formative experiences on the rivers he has been taught both by and on, finding therein a wealth of lessons (cognitive, affective, sociocultural, moral) into what it means to be an Earthling. Such opportunities are ontologically unavailable to even the most resource-rich classroom or Internet site. Thus, the mantra: "Go wild!" which, in this sense, means to flow into the reaches of untapped human potentials. Of course, not everyone has such easy access to rivers as of yet undone by the Army Corps of Engineers or to the ancient history alive and well in remote wilderness areas (yes, nature like all else is a *class* issue). But as William Blake (2008) spoke of a "World in a Grain of Sand," might not every common street corner and schoolyard be seen as likewise bustling with a myriad of wild encounters just waiting to erupt?

Bioregional education as Hensley champions distinguishes itself from today's banking pedagogy by being able to listen to the many voices of nature all too often suppressed by the digital chatter of our iPads and Blackberries. Crucially, *Curriculum Studies Gone Wild* reminds us that saving the world necessarily requires being able to hear and converse with it first—that we become ecoliterate in the poetry of, as Derrick Jensen (2004) puts it, "a language older than words." Indeed, what could be more central to our learning (or, after Freire, our "humanization") than this? Whether one lives in an industrial hellhole or a forest cabin, the fact that a great many—knowing a great many things mind you—now inhabit places in which they lack adequate names for the majority of flora and fauna that make up their everyday lives, or are without competency in how to live with integrity by the majority of their own hand, or are otherwise prevented from the knowledge of their region's ecological character and the way in which it serves to sustain life...all this is shocking evidence that we need both well-placed condemnation of what passes for acceptable education today as well as a restorative sustainability curriculum based in appreciating the resilient qualities of nature. This would be an education into what is both awful and aweful—an ecocurriculum for sustainability. As Hensley articulates it, this is not to be reduced to a sub-field or specialty certification, but is instead a learning web of learning webs that supports (and is the living expression of) all our various evolving human relations and convivial practices of fellowship.

When I first saw the title of this book, I will admit that I didn't quite fathom what sustainability education had to do with scholars of curriculum being objectified, getting drunk, or taking their tops off. Hensley is of course being playfully subversive in his theory that a non-dehumanized education into "natureculture" (Haraway, 2007) is the direct opposite of such formulaic pop media pedagogy as the infamous Girls Gone Wild series. Rather, an eco-curriculum for sustainability is multiplicitous, complex, and diverse. It breaks with and exists beyond the current paradigm of what Hensley terms a "carbon copy curriculum" that works for megamachinic technocrats and corporate industrialists all. In this, the eco-curriculum is pointedly political and counterhegemonic in its struggle—it is not simply Outdoor Education, but rather a "decarbonizing" of the curriculum through epistemological curiosity and rigorous criticality. In this respect, Hensley provides one of the most pointed intellectual thrashings of the Social Efficiency mode of curriculum that I have had the pleasure of reading in awhile. The point being that sustainability educators need to know the ideological nature of their opposition, just as they must be well-versed in forms of birdsongs, medicinal forms of plant life, or the crosscultural significance of biogeochemical cycles.

Curriculum Studies Gone Wild wants to open up the univocal pedagogy of the high stakes testing room to the polysemous encounters that populate people's direct experiences with the land (conceived broadly). But it remains staunchly within the tradition of reading both the world and the word in light of one another—what Hensley calls the "ecological text." Besides his attempt to integrate sustainability as a key form of advocacy into curriculum studies in the way that previous scholars have opened the field up to concerns based on race, class, gender, disability, heteronormativity, and other forms of social antagonism in previous decades, Hensley also joins with William Pinar's notion of curriculum as a "complicated conversation" by theorizing an eco-curriculum of place that dialectically synthesizes the claims made by/for theory and practice, self and other, culture and nature, human and nonhuman, and speech and silence. Therefore, this book should equally appeal to environmentalists interested in comprehending how a mountaintop represents a form of public sphere as well as those more academically interested in researching how the broad history of curricular theory offers numerous pathways and sources that inform the journey toward our present moment's catastrophic demand for an eco-curriculum for sustainability.

I congratulate my friend on his achievement.

Richard Kahn, Ph.D.
Core Faculty in Education
Antioch University Los Angeles

References

Blake, W. (2008). *The complete poetry and prose of William Blake*. David V. Erdman (Ed.). Berkeley, CA: University of California Press.

Haraway, D. (2007). *When species meet*. Minneapolis, MN: University of Minnesota Press.

Jensen, D. (2004). *A language older than words*. White River Junction, VT: Chelsea Green.

Ravitch, D. (2010). *The death and life of the great American school system: How testing and choice are undermining education*. New York: Basic Books.

Acknowledgments

THIS BOOK owes much to the support of my wife, Diana. Diana has been a continual source of inspiration, encouragement, and editorial insight. Her dedication and wisdom has enabled me to find balance and persistence in the task of creating this work. Additionally, it is important to note that the friendship and counsel of my brother Caleb, sister Shannon, and mother has enabled me to achieve the dream of bringing this project to the point of publication. Without the sense of community that comes with close family and friends this work would have not been sustainable. Lastly, it is important that I acknowledge William Pinar, Marla Morris, Ming Fang He, and Dan Rea for the ideas, feedback and guidance throughout the writing of this book.

Introduction

> The frog does not drink up the pond in which he lives.
>
> Sioux Proverb in *The Environmental Science of Drinking Water*

> Mystery creates wonder and wonder is the basis of [the human] desire to understand.
>
> Neil Armstrong in *Journey to Wholeness*

WHERE ARE you from *originally*? The first time I was asked this was my freshman year in college during a sea kayaking expedition near the Apostle Islands of Lake Superior. Because I never really thought about "originally" being a part of the question, I was taken by surprise. The question helped me realize the importance of remembering one's roots.

Originally, I come from a very close family of five in Pittsburg, Kansas—the southeastern part of the "Wheat State." We were and still are a very close family.[1] My parents instilled a love of nature in us children—taking us on frequent walks during all seasons to the nearby park to roll in the oak leaves, look for frogs, and to play on the tornado slide. On summer nights, we regularly set out a blanket in our yard and watched the stars as my twin brother Caleb, sister Shannon, and I would catch lightning bugs and place them in a big glass jar. Whenever there were meteor showers we would take a break from the lightning bug hunt and watch the shooting stars in awe.

Although we did not have great financial means, we had plenty of love and laughter. My family always found ways to share this love with others and had fun in the process. Since my parents were in the ministry, we were commonly serving in the community. We volunteered with programs that helped the underprivileged to get heat in their houses and spent a lot of time at the church—Open Door Fellowship. The name was the philosophy of our church, to keep the doors open to the community in times of need, times of celebration, and all times in between. Before I was born my mom and dad owned a Christian bookstore called the "Hosanna House" and the books left over from this business served as the foundation to my dad's extensive home book collection. My dad loved literature

---

1 Sadly, my dad, Charly Hensley, passed away in June of 2007, but his legacy lives strong in me, as he is the one who sparked my intellectual curiosity at an early age. He also instilled in me a unique sense of spiritual reverence, curiosity about the world, and a sense of humor.

and used words as his tools and his toys. He lived an intellectual life with humor at the foundation. He used words in creative ways throughout his preaching, writing, stories, puns, and anecdotes. He was the kind of preacher who infused humor into his sermons. One time, as he was leading a prayer before a church dinner, he said that "many think that a mind is a terrible thing to waste but for today a waist is a terrible thing to mind."

Life at home was good, but school helped me carve out my own intellectual journey. There were teachers who, like my father, inspired me to learn and to become more in tune with my unique strengths. It was these teachers who encouraged me to think critically, to have fun learning, and to appreciate the importance of developing lasting relationships within the surrounding social and ecological community. After working with these teachers, I found myself to be more invested in school and the learning process.

From an early age I was intrigued by the wild, simple, and sometimes intricate beauty found in nature. My modes of exploration included expeditions to the backyard, excursions to the school playground, canoe outings on nearby rivers, and journeys through the rolling hills, woods, and prairies that surrounded my grandfather's farm. These nature encounters cultivated a greater interest in seeking more outdoor adventures.

My passion to study place-based eco-curriculum and sustainability came from early encounters with the natural world. The open fields and grasslands of Kansas gave me ample opportunity to encounter a beautiful natural landscape at an impressionable age. My home in Pittsburg is part of the Spring River watershed.[2] Watersheds are important features in nature as they commonly serve as the boundary for various bioregions.[3]

Although I did not know it at the time, as a child I learned more about the Spring River watershed every day. By simply being present with the outdoors, by playing near Cow Creek and watching it ebb and flow with floods and drought, I began to learn the nuances of the ecosystems that made up the place in which I was raised.

---

2   A watershed (also called a drainage basin) is an area of land that drains into a common body of water. In other words, all of the rainwater that falls in Pittsburg eventually drains to the Spring River, thus I lived in the Spring River watershed.

3   A bioregion is a particular ecologically and geographically defined area. It is sometimes referred to as a slice of the larger biosphere (McGinnis, 1999; Thayer, 2003).

Cow Creek is situated along the border of Pittsburg and is a tributary of the Spring River watershed. My twin brother and I fished and swam in Cow Creek fairly often. The Cow Creek riparian[4] corridor was the first place where I saw a deer in the wild. My formative years spent in the outdoors enabled me to get closer to one of my greatest passions, the wild.

I will never forget the first time that I entered a designated "wilderness area." I was a high school student volunteering with the Student Conservation Association (SCA) on a summer conservation work crew. It was the Caney Creek Wilderness area located in the Ouachita Mountains of southwestern Arkansas. In preparation for the wilderness, our seven person crew worked on breaking in our boots, strengthening our backs, and sharpening our tools at the Shady Lake recreational area just outside of Mena, Arkansas. We were introduced to the natural world, outdoor skills, and the principles of sustainability in an experiential manner. We learned all about loading our packs, tying knots, group dynamics, weather patterns, flora and fauna and much more.

When we arrived at the Caney Creek Wilderness trailhead, I began to be transformed. Nature writer C.L. Rawlins (1993) observes that "[a]t first you're a stranger to the forest. It's too quiet. You feel as if your every move is seen and judged" but then "without noticing a difference, you feel more at home here than anywhere else" (p. 54). So I quickly transitioned from feeling "I'm not in Kansas anymore" to noticing that the further we went in to the wilderness the more I actually felt at home. It was a transformational experience that put me onto a path of promoting environmental stewardship in an educative context. John Muir (2001) once stated that "[t]he clearest way into the Universe is through a forest wilderness" (p. 312). I think Muir is right; my encounter with the wilderness opened up my universe. It was during my work with the SCA that I began to appreciate the outdoors even more.

Fromm (1992) describes biophilia[5] as the "passionate love of life and of all that is alive," adding that "it is the wish to further growth, whether

---

[4] The word riparian is derived from the Latin *ripa*, which denotes a riverbank. A riparian corridor is the interface between a body of water and the land through which it flows (riparian zone, n.d.). Characterized by their unique aquatic habitat, soil, and plant composition, riparian corridors serve several purposes. This corridor serves as a buffer that filters toxins out of the runoff that flows from the land into the waterway. Benefits of the corridor include water quality protection, living space for wildlife, and erosion protection (see Iihardt, Verry, and Palik, 2000).

[5] E.O. Wilson (1984) defines biophilia as "the innate tendency to focus on life and lifelike processes" (p. 1).

in a person, a plant, an idea, or a social group" (p. 406). For me the wilderness evoked an acumen grounded in biophilia. It served as an integrating context for my love of life and inspired me to pursue an education grounded in ecological experience. It was a much different education than what I was exposed to in the public school system. Instead of an emphasis on grades and test scores, the SCA program emphasized a form of expeditionary eco-education. Our expeditionary focus was to engage in conservation projects while building a cohesive team and learning more about ourselves as individuals. I found that working with nature can cultivate an interest in stewardship—I became a *biophilious* person. Fromm (1992) posits that a "biophilious person...prefers to see something new rather than to find confirmation of the old" (p. 406). Through this and other nature immersion experiences I developed an interest in seeing education as something new. When I am backpacking, climbing, or canoeing I feel most fully alive, connected, and in harmony with the universe.

Explorative encounters with nature fueled my passion to spend time outside and to look at life through an ecological worldview (Goldsmith, 1998; Sterling, 2001) which Fromm (1992) characterizes as seeing "the whole rather than only the parts, structures rather than summations" (p. 406). Nature immersion enhanced my reverence for life and propelled me towards becoming a more engaged and active steward of Earth. I am drawn to the spiritual connectivity embodied in outdoor exploration and adventure. Dwayne Huebner (1999) calls this the "lure of the transcendent" (p. xxi). By encountering nature, I developed a greater interest in protecting the outdoor world. I discovered there is inherent value to encountering wild places—that there is urgency in working as a steward of the natural resources that sustain us. It became clear to me that all life has unquantifiable value.

William Blake (1926) believed in the intrinsic value of life. He stated that "For everything that lives is holy, life delights in life" (p. 55). I resonate with this notion of life. While working in the outdoors I have found this to be true. When I bring students considered to be "at-risk" into the wilderness I notice that there is typically a qualitative shift in how they interact with one another. Instead of continually bickering or complaining about their home life, they begin to understand the importance of opening up to one another and working as a cohesive group. Also, I notice that students become more reflective in outdoor expeditions. During a canoe expedition that I was leading in Rhode Island, a student stated that "out here [in the forest] we are free to be who we really are." Wow, what a statement! She noted that in her school everyone had to wear a mask and act phony, but in the woods she felt more connected to who she really was. Her transformation showed through her words.

I believe that nature immersion can bring out a deeper sense of self. Additionally, I have found that nature experiences tend to foster a sense of wonder that promotes inquiry and interest in restoration—both ecologically and spiritually. Rachel Carson (1965) said that "[i]t is more important to pave the way for the child to want to know than to put him on a diet of facts he is not ready to assimilate" (p. 45). I agree with Carson. We need to light the spark and ignite the passion to inspire students to want to learn, to explore, and to wonder. Carson's encounters with the wilderness and intrinsic enchantment have sparked my passion for studying sustainability.

After high school, my passion to learn about other cultures and to live in new places led me to Northland College in northern Wisconsin, far from my Kansas home. Northland was located at the shores of Lake Superior. Here I got to live with the Ojibwea[6] on the Bad River Reservation. With the Ojibwea, I learned the importance of following my heart. Sacred ceremonies encouraged the process of learning about oneself. I participated in many ceremonies including sweat lodges and pow-wows. Participating in these events helped me realize how much I loved learning about other people. While experiencing other cultures and the outdoors firsthand, I also studied eco-social interconnectivity in the classroom. I earned a Bachelor of Science degree in Outdoor education. For one semester during my undergraduate years, I lived in a tent in the ravine on campus. I became attentive to the changes in the seasons and learned how to stay warm in subzero temperatures. Perhaps my desire to dwell in the woods is inherent. My last name, Hensley, means "dweller in the woods frequented by wild birds." There is truth to this, for I enjoy dwelling in the woods while encountering wildness in all its forms.

After college I went on to work in a variety of states with a number of wilderness programs, environmental education facilities, and alternative schools. It was through my work as an outdoor and experiential educator that I began to develop an interest in what I refer to as *an eco-curriculum of the wild*. I will discuss this more later in this book.

My passion for outdoor experiential education led me to actively and intentionally pursue alternative education teaching opportunities. Leading programs like Outward Bound enabled me to participate in a more holistic form of education. I worked with wilderness therapeutic

---

6   This is a Native American group located in the northern part of the United States.

programs, outdoor education schools, conservation programs, and alternative schools. As I worked with students who had been in juvenile detention centers, adolescents who were emotionally and behaviorally disturbed, and teens who were manipulative, I developed an even greater respect for the power of nature to facilitate intrapersonal growth and healing. On extended wilderness backpacking trips, I noticed that students began to develop a greater sense of place. They started to realize the value of spending time outdoors and encountering its wildness.

I believe that everyone needs to be given the opportunity to develop a greater sense of place. After we know *where we are*, we are better able to find out *who we are* (Shepard, 2003; Snyder, 1995). My interest in outdoor education as an approach to promote self-growth led me to work as an instructor with a variety of programs, settings, personalities, and ability levels. Working with outdoor programs has served as a profound educational experience. The outdoors has become my primary "classroom," where I am both an instructor and a student. For me, direct experience and intellectual exploration has replaced the more conventional "authoritative text" of the traditional school-based classroom. My personal experiences in the field gave me an even greater passion for exploring sustainability within the realm of education.

The conversation that represents ecological sustainability fascinates me. After researching for more than three years, I have found that there are many layers involved in understanding sustainability. But, there is also a relatively simple and intuitive aspect woven into the tapestry of it. The simplicity of sustainability is well articulated by the Sioux proverb which states that "a frog does not drink up the pond in which he lives" (Bourne, 2005). This means that nature inherently understands sustainability and will not act in ways to harm its own. Frogs, though they are not typically seen as such, are very important aspects of nature. I believe that it is important to turn to our indicator species, the frogs, the lichens, the wildflowers, even our children, to understand what we are doing to this planet.

Indicator species are the most fragile life forms that enable us to comprehend the anthropogenic (human generated) impact upon the biosphere. Reed (1990) writes that an indicator species "should be sufficiently sensitive to provide an early warning of change" (p. 357). By turning to these indicators we can begin to grasp the environmental consequences associated with our ecological footprint. There are several big questions that emerge when one tries to understand sustainability. But as Reed states, "Big questions require answers from several scales" (p. 357). It is these big questions that have put me on the trajectory that I am on—a trajectory towards advancing the project of building a more sustainable planet. It is the quest to better understand these big questions that has catalyzed my passion to work as an experiential educator.

The natural world is remarkable, and there is a multitude that we can learn from and through it. Biologist Janine Benyus believes that learning through nature can "take us aback, make us more humble, and put us in the learner's chair, seeking to discover instead of invent" (in McLennan, 2004, p. 43). She is touching on a fundamental shift in paradigm where we, as humans, embrace nature as a teacher. Learning from nature involves the reverential recognition of how simple and elegant nature's solutions to dauntingly complex problems are. I posit that it is through nature immersion and exploration that we can gain a more authentic sense of our role in the biosphere. Accordingly, it is crucial that we forge an education that will enable students to do as Edgar Morin says and "ecologize[7] everything" (in Gadotti, 2008, p. 39). That is, I argue that we must help students to realize the social, ecological, and interconnectedness between all phenomena. Realizing this interconnectivity involves appreciating the significance that one person can make in forging a more sustainable, a more habitable, and a more compassionate world.

---

7 Later, in this book, I discuss the notion of *ecologizing* in greater depth.

Chapter 1
A Call to Action

> To protect what is wild is to protect what is gentle...Wild mercy is in our hands.
>
> Terry Tempest Williams, *Red: Passion and Patience in the Desert*

> If we are to continue on the path of reconstructing and protecting the earth systems upon which we depend, it will be necessary to design an educational response to the ecological crisis.
>
> J. William Hug, *Learning and Teaching for an Ecological Sense of Place: Toward Environmental Science Education Praxis*

> If ever a species needed a survival plan, it will be homosapiens in the twenty-first century.
>
> Joseph Pelton in *The Future of Higher Education: Exploring and Creating the Future in Virtual Space*

THE LIVING systems that comprise this planet are simultaneously intricate and simple, sensitive and robust, and mysterious and transparent. A simple house plant sitting next to my desk illustrates the systemic multiplicity associated with being alive. The nutrients from the potting soil, the complexities of its cycles—including the continuous exchange of water and oxygen—sustain it. The plant is transparent—I know quickly if it is not doing well because its color changes and it starts to wilt. When we turn our attention to the greater natural world, we see the wild mercy that Terry Tempest Williams (2001) refers to. Instead of working towards our planet's restoration, we have lost touch with our sense of place and continue to generate an even greater rift between our view of progress and our effort to restore, maintain, and sustain ecological health. Many do not realize it, but the lifestyle that most Americans live is partially responsible for the current environmental crisis. By participating in the madness that we call consumerism, we are undermining the integrity of our life support system, Earth. The biosphere is overburdened by anthropogenic (human generated) carbon emissions, and the natural resource base is continually being diminished by our quest to advance what is now called progress.

As an outdoor and experiential educator, I have had the opportunity to see some of the effects overconsumption has on various ecosystems. I have found that there is an overwhelming amount of environmental degradation from which most of us are detached. I have witnessed firsthand the silence and emptiness of recently bulldozed forests, the radical deterioration of a river's aquatic habitat, and the suffering of animals that have lost their habitat. These encounters with nature under distress have made me painfully aware of the harm we are inflicting on the planet and have fueled my interest and urgency in studying ecological sustainability.

Also, while working as an outdoor educator, I have noticed a disturbing trend of student disconnection from nature. In some cases digital media is replacing human encounters with the outdoors. I am interested in finding ways of educating that can cultivate a more harmonious connection to the natural world. I argue that enabling students to get outside and encounter nature, through carefully chosen experiences that are supported by reflection, processing, and synthesis, will strengthen students' innate interest in living more sustainably. They will also benefit from the holistic and qualitative connectedness that is accessible when we go outside and explore nature firsthand.

In this book, I set out to explore the eclectic landscape associated with the sustainability movement while contributing to the project of ecological revitalization and mobilizing what I call the scholarship of sustainability. The *scholarship of sustainability* is a form of research intended to advance dialogue related to place-based environmental restoration. It is situated within the arena of curriculum studies and grounded within the field of education. In this book, I do not offer prescriptive solutions to the ecological crisis. Instead, I draw from the current body of literature that surrounds the field of sustainability and education in order to contribute to the formulation of a new paradigm that can further advance the ecological movement towards a more balanced and harmonious human-Earth relationship. It is a form of research that is dedicated to finding ways to save our ship, our Earth ship. I posit that we are receiving an "S.O.S" from Earth in many different forms. This includes global climate change, increase in disease, decrease in biological diversity, and reduced ecological resiliency. The planetary S.O.S. demands understanding and a well orchestrated educational response.

As a scholar devoted to advancing sustainability within the academic realm, I am also interested in advancing sustainability in my daily life. Some of the ways that I am doing this include frequent trips to the local farmer's market instead of the big supermarket, volunteering with agencies that are committed to reducing individual and collective ecological footprints, and talking with friends and family about living green. Also, my wife, Diana, and I are practicing "voluntary simplicity" (Elgin, 1993) by living in a small apartment and trying to keep our material possessions to a minimum. The less that we own, the less negative impact we have on Earth and the less we need to worry about protecting and maintaining.

My wife and I are trying to consume less and share more. We are sharing more by getting involved in our community and finding ways to engage in service for the environment and for social justice. One of the agencies that we enjoy volunteering with is Habitat for Humanity, an organization committed to eliminating poverty housing and homelessness from the world. By working with Habitat for Humanity, we help fight poverty and reduce the ecological footprint of inadequate housing. Houses that are not well insulated require more energy to heat and cool—resulting in a large eco-footprint (Wackernagel & Rees, 1996). When families are moved from inadequate housing to adequate housing, the ecological impact of that family is dramatically reduced and of course the family is in a much better living situation. Farmer's markets can also serve as excellent models for sustainable practices. The food at these markets is local and fresh, it is harvested in season, and people are drawn together in a festive setting to meet their farmer and get reconnected to the community.

Diana and I realize that there are several more steps that we can be taking to live more sustainably, and we plan to do something new every few years in order to reduce our ecological footprint. In the future, Diana and I would like to build and live in a straw bale house that will help educate others about the possibilities of using earth-based building materials to construct one's home. While writing this book, I have become even more interested in the prospect of building an alternative earth-based home.

When I was an undergraduate at Northland College in Ashland, Wisconsin, I had several experiences that affirmed my path as an experiential and outdoor educator. Outdoor experiences are inherently holistic—they encourage the use of all of our senses and help us to integrate cerebral learning with physical (and sometimes spiritual) learning. As a junior at Northland, I lived in a cabin located in the Bad River Indian Reservation twenty minutes from campus. The cabin was situated on an Ojibwea elder's property just off the shore of Lake Superior. It was a gorgeous location. My college roommate, Philip, and I frequently went walking on the sandy beaches and explored the breathtaking scenery of the lake. On the weekends we would spend full days walking along the beach and kayaking on the lake. One day we discovered some perfectly spherical rocks ranging from pea size to softball size. We started to play with these rocks and threw them hard, like baseballs, into the sand that had just been drenched by Lake Superior waves. After being thrown into the sand, the rocks would leave craters. When we returned from our explorations, in the evening, we excitedly told our friend, the elder and landlord, Joe Rose, about what we found. He said that these round stones were called grandfather stones and that they were very sacred, so sacred "we should treat them like we would our own grandfathers." Oops! We learned a big lesson that day...to treat nature with reverence. This is just one of the many experiences that helped me to gain a deeper respect for the natural world and put me on a path of stewardship.

The Call of the Wild

I am drawn to the primeval beauty of natural areas, the allure of the wild. This is why I have selected a career and research trajectory steeped in sustainability. I remember the feeling that I experienced when I visited the Sequoia grove at Sequoia National Park in northern California; it was a deep reverential sense of awe. This is the feeling that I get when I visit wild places. Wildness denotes wholeness and complexity—it has to do with fullness of being and is associated with actualizing one's potentiality. Carl Jung (2001) observed that "Matter in the wrong place is dirt. People got dirty through too much civilization." He added that "Whenever we touch nature, we get clean" (p. 1). We need to reclaim our connection with Earth by reencountering nature. What does Jung mean when he says that people got dirty through too much civilization? I think that he is referring to the way that too much time in manmade environments can affect our sense of self. When he says we get clean by touching nature, he is eluding to the notion that we need to visit wild places more to help us regain a deeper sense of union with our self, our community, and the ecosystem that we inhabit. We are getting dirty by spending too much time in socially produced artificiality. Jung (2001) saw natural life as "nourishing soil for the soul" (p. 1). To explore the wildness of nature and of our own soul is to reconnect to the "'feeling of primordiality' that is the beginning of all things" (Sabini, 2001, p. 5). Cultivating a feeling of primordiality is tied to the visceral propensity of advancing an ethic of stewardship.

By encountering wild places, places that convey an essence of original integrity, we get a more authentic picture of the universe. It is transformative to explore areas that are untrammeled by humans. How do we educate in a way that facilitates a feeling of primordial nativeness? A wilderness-based curriculum deals with restoring our connection to self and to our place. It involves reconnecting to our unique qualities, our subjectivities, and our affinity to contribute to making the world a better place. Without a sense of place we are rootless and mindlessly going through the motions of our lived experience.

The Journey Towards Sustainability

The purpose of this book is to explore—through the medium of autobiographical, theoretical, intellectual, and place narrative—the way in which encounters with our bioregion can clarify and expand our understanding of our role in advancing a more sustainable world, our link in the interconnected web of life, and the way in which we may, through experiential education, develop a greater sense of place and sense of self. This exploration is grounded in an ecological worldview—a view that embraces the integrality[1] of the environmental relationships that sustain us. I believe that the project of advancing sustainability is a continual process. It is this process that enables us to formulate creative responses to pressing issues of climate change and overconsumption.

It is my belief that an education grounded in place can enhance our ability to respond to the overwhelming burdens of the ecological crisis. Education that is experiential and place-sensitive embraces the nuances of the surrounding natural environment and social community to cultivate meaningful relationships between the student, the school, and the community, and between people and the planet. It is the robustness of these relationships that may help us to cope with the inevitable ecological stressors germane to the industrialism that guides today's economy. Healthy and vibrant relationships help us to respond to Earth's natural resources that are rapidly being ravished and degraded by humans at an unprecedented scale. The more depth that we have in our relationships, the more resilient we become. Building resiliency is fundamental to advancing sustainability (Hopkins, 2008). Resiliency denotes the amount of stress that a living organism or system can take before collapsing. It applies at social and psychological levels, ecological levels, and economic

---

1 Integrality is derived from the word integral and denotes a belongingness that is a "part of the whole" (integrality, n.d.).

levels. I argue that education, at its most fundamental level, must invoke an ethic of stewardship while building the student's capacity to function under unanticipated stressors. These stressors include, but are not limited to, rapid depletion of our food supply, coastal flooding, battles over natural resources, debates over water rights and responses to the peak oil crisis.[2]

I posit that human powered experiences in nature, such as backpacking, trail maintenance, riparian corridor restoration, and canoeing, have the capacity to educate, inspire, and empower people to embrace a symbiotic perception of the human-Earth relationship. Wilderness travel has the capacity to deepen our sense of self while expanding our sense of relatedness to the cosmos—it has both an ethereal and a material value to it. The ethereal value comes in the sense that we get closer to understanding our role from a cosmological perspective and the material value comes in that we can begin to understand the tangible essence of our role in the places that we inhabit. Nature-based experiences are an unmatched medium that can help us to forge an integral relationship with one another and the bioregion in which we live.

This book pivots on explicating a notion of what I refer to as an eco-curriculum conceptualized as a responsive, eclectic, and urgent field of study. Eco is derived from the Greek word for home, *Oikos*. An eco-curriculum, in this sense, has to do with a home curriculum. It is a curriculum that embraces the beauty and idiosyncrasies of the places in which we inhabit. Our home is our dwelling place. Our home has an inexorable impact on shaping our personalities, perceptions, feelings, and passions. When education embraces the inherent value of living well, in our unique places, there is a fundamental shift in epistemology, the way in which we learn. An eco-curriculum embraces an integrative and emergent form of inquiry aimed at advancing the field of curriculum within the context of the sustainability movement. The ability to unite previously disjointed perceptions of self and the environment is what makes an eco-curriculum integrative. An eco-curriculum is emergent because literature pertaining to education and ecology is beginning to expand in tempo with the ecological maladies that we face.

I set out to foster a broader, more environmentally integrated conceptualization of curriculum studies. Accordingly, this book aims to share how new generations can be educated to consider, foster, and understand sustainability. One way that I do this is by positioning sustainability within the context of what Schubert (1997) posits are the most basic

---

[2] The peak oil crisis is described in greater depth later in this book.

questions in curriculum studies. Later, I focus on exploring two of the three basic questions in curriculum. Schubert (1997) declares that these three questions are: "What knowledge is most worthwhile?[3] Why is it worthwhile? How is it acquired or created?" (p. 1). My hope is to foster a wider conceptualization of what it means to live sustainably in this world.

What I refer to as *curriculum studies gone wild* is a liberating process committed to nurturing authentic encounters with one's lived experiences and with nature. It is grounded in the cultivation of an eco-curriculum of place and the belief in our inherent need to experience the enchantment of the wild. I believe that we do not have to go into designated wilderness areas to experience the enchantment of the wild. The beauty of a curriculum gone wild is that it can be put into action in virtually any setting if it is facilitated well. In other words, we can promulgate a curriculum that enables students to move freely in an unconfined journey to self-realization. This is one aspect of a curriculum gone wild as it honors the possibilities that are tied to actualizing a deeper sense of self.

Curriculum Studies Gone Wild: Bioregional Education and the Scholarship of Sustainability is a book oriented towards resituating contemporary curriculum discourse into a bioregional framework while seeking ecological revitalization.

Statement of Originality

My work departs from what has already been done in the field of curriculum studies in several ways. I argue that we are stuck in what I refer to as a *carbon copy curriculum*, a curriculum primarily consisting of copying preceding educational approaches. Contemporary education simply embraces what has already been done in previous generations as the "best way" to educate. My conceptualization of a carbon copy curriculum is grounded in understanding the environmental ramifications of mindlessly duplicating the thinking, consumption habits, and attitudes towards nature that are partially culpable for perpetuating the ecological crises that we currently face. Grounded in perpetuating a business-as-usual approach and dismantling the human-Earth relationship, the carbon copy curriculum advances anthropocentric thinking. The carbon copy curriculum overlooks the environmental ramifications of an education that duplicates habits and behaviors that are oriented towards

---

3   Herbert Spencer (1860) also posed the question, "What knowledge is of most worth?"

advancing economic prosperity or other pre-determined indicators of "success." In other words, a carbon copy curriculum is oriented to maintain a form of education that puts today's human interests above the interests of future generations and other living beings. The emphasis is placed on advancing a top down transmission of "official knowledge" that is not to be questioned by anyone—it is only to be handed down. In the carbon copy curriculum we teach our children that success is tied to material possession without teaching them that materialism is fundamentally tied to resource exploitation.

Another point of departure from existing work in the field of curriculum studies is my discussion surrounding *de-carbonizing a carbon copy curriculum*. To de-carbonize, in this sense, means moving beyond the narrow focus of contemporary education, the quest for ceaseless monetary advancement, material acquisition, and the push to make education an arena that solely prepares children for the job market. Private possession and personal acquisition have become a dominant ideal in education and in virtually all other fields (Schubert, 2009a). Dewey refers to this focus on material accumulation as the *acquisitive mind*, the compulsion to own more, a mindset that has purportedly taken over the entire education system (Schubert, 2009a). De-carbonizing a carbon copy curriculum is an attempt to transcend the industrial paradigm, the thinking that adheres to the notion that "more is better." It is this thinking that takes an environmentally exploitive stance to economic development. In other words, the industrial paradigm—which drives a carbon copy curriculum—positions the value of economic development over ecological vitality.

De-carbonizing a carbon copy curriculum involves a move towards a form of education that is carbon neutral. Carbon neutrality refers to having a "zero net" carbon footprint (Martin, 2006). Carbon neutrality can mean that a particular process, person, institution, or organization emits no carbon throughout a lifetime. Carbon neutrality can also refer to the process of offsetting the carbon that is released by the person, process, machine, or group in question. One way to offset carbon emissions is to plant trees to help capture the carbon that is released by burning fossil fuels (Martin, 2006; Rogers, Kostigen, & Kostigen, 2007). To de-carbonize, in the educational sense, is to equip students with the knowledge, skills, and abilities to live carbon neutral lifestyles. In this book I argue that one of the most effective ways to teach children about living sustainably is to familiarize them with the ecological and social communities in which they live. By introducing them to their place and the interconnections of the relationships that sustain them, children will be more likely to want to explore and find out how they can work to protect their place.

Additionally, this book is differentiated by the focus on a place-based (bioregional[4]) discussion conceptualizing curriculum as a phenomenon deeply linked to place consciousness. I explore the notion of a place-based curriculum understood as ecological text. I seek to understand how curriculum studies can contribute to the survivability of our planet through a localization of education and stewardship effort. There is a dearth in existing curriculum studies-based scholarship that argues for viewing curriculum as bioregional ecological text.

A Note About My Approach

I cite other authors frequently in this book to acknowledge their contribution within the framework of a place-based eco-curriculum. This is in recognition of the fact that I stand on the shoulders of giants, and I acknowledge that the work that has been done on environmental education has created an important niche within the field of curriculum studies. Without the existing body of literature on education and ecology I would not have been able to write this book. Pinar argues that literature reviews are "[n]o longer warm-ups to the main attraction" instead, they should "become the focus" of the work (2007a, p. xxv). He adds that appreciating existing scholarship is paramount to honoring and emboldening the work of the theorists that have come before us. It is important to point out that this book is not one large literature review. I depart from the literature review format in several ways. For example, I employ autobiographical narrative, propose new ecologically oriented terminology, engage in a theoretical exploration of sustainability and place-making, and utilize an example of my surrounding bioregion to illustrate the importance of developing place-consciousness.

Reverence for Life

Cultivating a reverence for life is at the foundation of sustainable living. Gary Zukav maintains that "reverence is...the experience of accepting

---

4   Bioregionalism is a political, ecological, and social movement that is organized around the stewardship of naturally defined areas referred to as bioregions. A bioregion is comprised of a series of similar ecosystems that are defined by both physical and ecological features of a given landscape. These defining features include soil, plant communities, animal habitat, topography, and watershed boundaries.

that all life is, in and of itself, of value" (in Riley-Taylor, 2002, p. 20). It is the recognition of the sanctity of all life, and it encourages a shift towards sustainability. As Terry Tempest Williams (2008b) suggests, a commitment to sustainability honors all marginalized and mainstream life. This commitment tells others, human and non-human beings, that

> *We will be present with you. We will not turn our backs on the poverty of our brothers and sisters. We will not walk away from our commitment to face whatever the future may bring. We will watch, listen, speak, and act on behalf of a 'reverence for life.'* (Emphasis in original, p. xvii)

In order to affect lasting eco-social change, we must not walk away from our responsibility to act and reflect on behalf of an ecologically derived reverence for life. We must recognize and act upon the poverty within our communities. From this standpoint sustainability is solidarity. It is the standing together with others in an effort to restore environmental vitality that enables us to develop a stronger sense of purpose. A sense of purpose is integral to the formulation of an adequate response to the ecological crisis. I suggest that perpetuating a greater reverence for life should be central to fostering a place-based eco-curriculum.

A Call to Action

Hunter Lovins urges that "according to the UN millennium ecosystem assessment [compiled by climate specialists from many of the world's countries], we have polluted or exploited two thirds of the earth's ecosystems on which life depends to the point in which the ability of these ecosystems to sustain future generations can no longer be taken for granted" (PC, 10/28/08). I was surprised by this statistic; two-thirds of our ecosystems have been dramatically altered because of human activity. It is an overwhelming and inconvenient truth. What can we do as humans to mitigate this looming threat on our planetary habitability?

As Brown notes, "In almost all the natural domains, the earth is under stress—it is a planet that is in need of intensive care" (in Kahn, 2010, p. 1). This intensive care response must recognize that natural areas have been commoditized, manipulated, and destroyed, impacting wilderness, prairies, forests, and wetlands. We need to institute a form of planetary health care that will prevent Earth's "fever" (Gore, 2006) from getting worse. Even more urgently we must implement strategies for preventative planetary health care. This is a call to action at political and curricular levels.

Overconsumption has led to the extinction of several species (Broswimmer, 2002). In the realm of education, the marketplace mentality and patterns of uncritical consumerism have become commonplace, and intrinsic motivation has been usurped by material incentive, contributing to patterns of ecological degradation. Rachel Carson (1962) posits, "Future generations are unlikely to condone our lack of prudent concern for the integrity of the natural world that supports all life" (p. 13). We must honor future and present generations through working to understand a curriculum for sustainability. In this book, I argue for cultivating a more sustainable mode of living grounded in place and rooted in stewardship, democracy, and justice. I explore how education can cultivate an ethic of stewardship and create opportunities for transformation within the context of sustainability. Accordingly, this book is framed by an ecological worldview (Capra, 2002; Shiva, 2004; Sterling, 2001). This ecological orientation honors the interdependence and interrelatedness found in the "web of life" and employs an ecological approach (Bateson, 1972) to uncover and recover the intersections between sustainability and education. One approach to exploring sustainability is place-based education, which will be discussed in Chapter 5.

Setting the Stage

Sustainability is inherently a transdisciplinary and emergent concept. Accordingly, it is important to utilize a transdisciplinary mode of inquiry in researching sustainability. The prefix "trans" in the word transdisciplinary means to go beyond or to span. Accordingly, to move towards a more sustainable human-Earth relationship, we need to be willing to go beyond what is currently happening or to connect the dots between seemingly unrelated disciplines. It is only through collaboration that we can work through, reduce, and transform the perils of the ecological crisis.

Understanding sustainability's far-reaching nature provides curriculum theorists with the contextual tools for transforming education. These tools surface when scholars recognize and understand the importance of what I refer to as *eco-contextualization*. Eco-contextualization requires the pragmatic consideration of what threatens the diversity of our geographic place and the uniqueness of our personal conceptual space. The diversity of our geographic place refers to the health of the bioregion that we inhabit. A bioregion is the section of the biosphere, the unique ecosystem, in which we live. If there is not diversity in our bioregion, the habitat may not be able to adequately serve as a home for the flora and fauna that natively reside within it. A bioregion that primarily contains monocultures lacks the diversity necessary to adapt to any form of ecological stress (disease, climate change, etc.). This lack of resilience can lead to the collapse of a species because it lacks the assortment of food, community, and shelter necessary for organism health. The uniqueness of our personal conceptual space is essentially the identity that defines us. We struggle to go within and cultivate our "interiority" (Pinar, 2004, p. 23). Our personal conceptual space, our identity, is encapsulated by the nuances, predisposition, and character that separate one person from others. So, eco-contextualization hints at the unique effort necessary to re-inhabit the personal space that makes us who we are.

Each eco-social context is slightly different and requires a distinct combination of thought and action to restore balance. The notions of restoring balance and embracing the world's complexities is central to promoting sustainability. In the following research, I examine the theoretical underpinnings of sustainability while embracing the traditions of curriculum scholars and educational philosophers. I maintain that humankind has reached a critical point where we must transform existing modes of educational discourse and inquiry into that of "greening the curriculum" (Klohr, 1971). As we face the ecological crisis, it is interesting to look at how the Chinese culture views the word crisis.

The Chinese ideograph for crisis (pronounced *wei-ji*) is composed of two characters that illustrate an important point (Capra, 1982, p. 26). One of the characters means "danger" and the other means "opportunity" (Lydon, 1992, p. 76; Capra, 1982, p. 26; Fox, 2006). We stand at the convergence of great ecological opportunity and great danger. In order to promote sustainability, we must promote educational practice and scholarship that generate deeper awareness and understanding regarding human influence on the environment. This is the form of understanding that helps us to recognize the opportunity to respond to the dangerous mode of living associated with the contemporary Western education paradigm.

I submit that the field of curriculum studies is uniquely positioned to help protect Earth and advance the sustainability movement. Within the framework of curriculum studies scholarship, we can advance the study of the relationships that sustain us. As I will discuss in a later chapter, curriculum studies is replete with opportunity to facilitate a return to the "homework" of restorative ecology. The human and non-human relationships that sustain us are interconnected. Pinar (2007a) notes that "Environmental, sustainability, and other ecological studies have exploded [in the sphere of education] since the early 1990s" (p. xxvii). However, compared to the totality of scholarship in the field, the body of work pertaining to sustainability within the arena of bioregional curriculum studies is limited. Noel Gough (2003) maintains that sustainability has been under-theorized within the sphere of environmental education. He suggests that as curriculum theorists we need to focus more on sustainability. I intend to help fill this gap in the literature.

By seeking to fill the gap between sustainability studies, place studies, and curriculum studies, we honor the capacity for ecological revitalization that each person and group embodies. I argue that we need to critique the notion of "resources" embodied in today's consumer culture. That is, I believe we need to reconceptualize what it means to view a person as a "resource" and work to treat human and non-human life with greater respect. This potential for transformation is located in the urgent task of becoming better stewards of the resources that we have and ultimately learning to use less.[5]

Thomas Berry (1999) maintains that in order to survive we must enter an *Ecozoic* era in which "humans will be present to the Earth in a mutually enhancing manner" (p. 55). The importance of being present to Earth in a 'mutually enhancing manner' is central to my forthcoming discussion. Invoking a deeper understanding of sustainability, Berry (2006) generates an enlivened "orientation for a new ecological period for the human-Earth community" (p. 10). Viewing Earth from an ecological lens compels us to understand and subsequently reduce the negative impact that we have on Earth. The survival of the human species depends on equipping the next generation with the knowledge, skill, and ability to live in a more sustainable way with virtually all other living beings. We must address the ecological crisis that has been recognized as a greater threat to security than terrorism (Reason, 2007).

If we attempt to forge sustainability alone, we will perish. At this point in time, the job is too large for individuals to tackle alone. We have reached the tipping point of ecological well-being and we need to respond rapidly, cohesively, and purposefully (Gore, 2006; 2009). Generating a more humane and environmental discourse necessitates a coalition of eco-advocates. Thus our youth must be empowered and enabled to "work strategically across, as well as within...boundaries to advance common democratic projects" (Carlson, 1998, p. 118). Democratic projects generate a more profound respect for one another, a deeper commitment to interpersonal and interdisciplinary alliances. I see common democratic projects as miniature and large coalitions for advancing ecological

---

5   Using less is a fundamental principle of sustainability. This concept is also referred to as "voluntary simplicity" (Elgin, 1993). In essence, voluntary simplicity encourages us to use and buy less so we can learn to share and reuse more.

harmony and the celebration of biophilious behavior. Adding a more refined picture of democracy, Dewey gives us a framework from which to move forward. Dewey maintains that the democratic process is "a search procedure in which we look for policies, laws, and administrative techniques that will allow us to continue a common life in a way that all of us can find fruitful and fulfilling" (Ryan in Evans, 2000, p. 319). Developing a common life that we all can find fruitful and fulfilling requires deep thinking and collaborative action. In the context of sustainability, our consideration must be extended to all living beings.

Seeing ecological revitalization as a common democratic project adds to our understanding of what is necessary to affect a more sustainable human-Earth relationship. To invoke a sense of democracy in the process of advancing sustainability means to take participatory dialogue seriously. A common democratic project involves freeing the "self to relate with others" while cultivating a "language of difference and thus...a unique perspective that enters into the public dialogue across differences, that is democratic community" (Carlson, 1998, p. 118). In the spirit of Carlson, I argue that advancing the sustainability movement requires a cohesive, locally derived, and participatory effort. Ecological sustainability is an effort to harmoniously coexist with other humans and nonhumans while advancing intergenerational solidarity.

Intergenerational solidarity is the collective effort to honor the ecologically salient behaviors of our ancestors while mitigating the behaviors that deteriorate the environment. Also, intergenerational solidarity involves an understanding of how our choices impact the current generation and future generations. This understanding keeps in line with the Earth Charter's[6] call to "Manage the use of renewable resources such as water, soil, forest products, and marine life in ways that do not exceed rates of regeneration and that protect the health of ecosystems" (in Sanders, 2008, p. 85). It is common sense to purposely conserve resources in a way that enables future generations and our current generation to live lastingly and amiably with the land base for many decades to come.

An emphasis on balance and wholeness adds to the book's conceptual framework and advances the restorative dialogue inherent to situating

---

6   I talk about the Earth Charter later in this book. According to the Earth Charter Associates (n.d.), the Earth Charter is "a declaration of fundamental ethical principles for building a just, sustainable, and peaceful global society in the 21st century. It seeks to inspire in all people a new sense of global interdependence and shared responsibility for the well-being of the whole human family, the greater community" (n.p.).

sustainability education into curriculum theory. I argue that the consideration of wholeness and balance is tantamount to valuing democracy and justice. Accordingly, the transition into a more sustainable world entails a "common democratic project" that transcends political, racial, class, gender, and geographical boundaries.

Introduction to the Chapters

In Chapter 2, "The Context of Curriculum Studies," I explore the intersections among ecology, sustainability, and curriculum studies. Accordingly, I pay homage to the work that has been done in the field and expose some of gaps that appear in the literature. I unpack the scope of various scholars' work while articulating the possibility for further investigation. The overarching theme in this chapter is the exploration of sustainability within the context of curriculum studies.

In Chapter 3, "A Material World: Education and Environmental Degradation," I investigate the connection between education and environmental degradation. I argue that the Western tendency to over-consume is predicated by traditional education models steeped in social efficiency and factory style "production." I explore the reality and impact of perpetuating a mechanistic worldview. I unpack the social efficiency paradigm and its role in generating a less sustainable world. I discuss how today's educational discourse is a "carbon copy curriculum." This chapter describes unsustainable patterns in the educational context.

In Chapter 4, "The Scholarship of Sustainability," I study the literature surrounding sustainability both within and beyond the field of education. I explore the history of the sustainability movement within the context of educational discourse. I continue this chapter by exploring emerging themes and topics within the scholarly work pertaining to sustainability. Also, I investigate the literature pertaining to education and ecological sustainability. I discuss the connections among the concepts of sustainability, sustainability education, curriculum studies, and an ecological worldview. The concept of sustainability education is explored and serves as a response to the unsustainable, mechanistically derived curriculum (discussed in Chapter 3). I conclude this chapter by offering a description of an ecological worldview.

In Chapter 5, "Place and Education: Bringing It All Back Home," I explore the ways that curriculum studies can help generate a sense of place. I discuss the importance of place consciousness in a globalized world that is rapidly colonizing the ecological and cultural heritage of the places we know and love. Thus, I explore place-based education within the context of mobilizing a bioregional eco-curriculum for sustainability. In particular, I explore the notion of understanding place as a framework for grounding educational discourse in practical and theoretical applications of relevant inquiry and action. This notion of bioregionalism is contextualized in a watershed-oriented approach to educational inquiry. This inquiry serves as a foundation situated to inform an environmentally derived quest to cultivate sustainable living, ecologically grounded experience, and democracy in the realm of education.

In Chapter 6, "Trudging Towards Sustainability," I explore the journey that is involved in creating a more sustainable planet. I recognize that the process of achieving a sustainable society is not one that will happen overnight and use the metaphor of a journey accordingly. This metaphor addresses the process-orientation that is associated with advancing sustainability. This journey is like a *trudge towards sustainability* which is identified as an arduous yet necessary trek across a vast, complex, and at times, a contested and tumultuous landscape. An exploration of the steps towards what I refer to as *decarbonizing a carbon copy curriculum* reveals that there is great potential for eco-social educational transformation. I discuss how the process of infusing sustainability into one's life is a "prayerful act" (Macdonald & Macdonald, 1995). Also, I propose suggestions for the implementation of an integrated eco-curriculum for sustainability. A discussion on integrated thinking weaves together the themes of the book in a way that provides opportunity for future "complicated conversation" (Pinar, 2004).

CHAPTER 2

The Context of Curriculum Studies

> This heart of mine knows the world is alive and full of purpose.
>
> David Jardine et al., *Curriculum in Abundance*

I WILL never forget the first time I went to the *Bergamo Conference on Curriculum Theory and Classroom Practice* in Dayton, Ohio. It was in the fall of 2007. At Bergamo, I got to see curriculum theory in action. Scholars from all different parts of the field and country attended, presented, conversed, and celebrated. There was a true sense of community that permeated the culture and the climate of the gathering. Meaningful and "complicated conversations" (Pinar, 2004) took place in the sessions, in the hallways, and outside on the forested and rolling terrain of the spiritual retreat center.

While at Bergamo, I found out firsthand that fall in Ohio is gorgeous—the leaves were changing, the air was crisp and cool. For my accommodation, I chose to save money and enjoy the great outdoors by camping at a nearby state park. The first night that I camped, I neglected to check the weather and later found myself in the midst of a major tornado warning. It was late, almost midnight, and I had just set up my tent when I heard the sound of the tornado siren followed by powerful winds that violently began to shake the trees. The powerful wind was followed by intense lightning and booming thunder. After a bolt of lightning hit the ground a few miles away, I decided to pack up my tent and find a hotel. Luckily, I was not picked up by a funnel cloud and involuntarily relocated to Lake Erie. The next day, I was able to integrate this story into my conference presentation.

I remember leaving the three-day conference feeling inspired and ready to tackle the world. Also, I recall being excited that the curriculum field was so diverse and that it embraced a wide variety of disciplines in order to understand educational experience. For me, as an experiential and outdoor educator, it was a confirmation that I had selected an appropriate field for my doctoral studies.

What does the field of curriculum studies have to say about ecological revitalization? Is there work that has already been done on this topic? There is significant work that has been done in the field of education and environmental sustainability. In education's subfield of curriculum studies, there is also an existing body of literature that addresses topics such as environmental restoration, ecological revitalization, and Earth-friendly living. The scope of existing curriculum studies-oriented and environmentally based education research has provided a strong foundation from which I can build. It is important to note that the watershed-oriented bioregional education (which I will explore in this book) has not been addressed in curriculum studies. In this chapter, I explore the existing curriculum studies-oriented literature pertaining to ecology and curriculum. This chapter serves as a conceptual foundation enabling me to further demonstrate how my work departs from what has already been done in the field. Also, this chapter enables me to build a framework in which I will expand upon throughout the rest of the book.

William Pinar has addressed the importance of advancing curriculum in a way that is more environmentally friendly. He posits that the field of curriculum studies needs to extend beyond conceptualizations that are anthropocentrically oriented. He says, "Appreciating that the biosphere subtends the species on whose behalf we must now conduct our educational labor... [requires] subjectivity expansive enough to welcome what is foreign, including the non-human" (Pinar, 2007b, p. xxi–xxii). Pinar suggests that curriculum studies has an important role in fostering sustainability. His notion of welcoming what is foreign, including the non-human, is central to advancing the field through an ecologically conceived formulation of educational labor. In an ecological perspective, curriculum scholars expand their conceptual framework to embrace all living beings. No longer are ecosystems ignored—instead they are studied. Pinar et al. sounded a call for "education to accept full responsibility in addressing global survival issues" (in Gough, 2003, p. 54), adding that "ecological problems become educational problems" (p. 54). It is time to recognize the possibilities for environmental revitalization within the context of education. We have a lot to learn from nature, from the non-human living beings.

One of the most important lessons from nature is the value of community. We can learn a lot from the interconnectivity that makes up a healthy ecosystem. The symbiotic (mutually beneficial) relationships in nature illustrate an important point. Life does not exist in a way that is fragmented and isolated; rather it is nurtured through an interdependent and dynamic interchange and exchange of food and waste. In nature, one being's waste becomes food for another being.[1] Beings within an ecologi-

---

1   This is a fundamental principle of sustainability—the importance of one being's waste becoming another being's food. For an intriguing discussion on this see Jensen and McBay's (2009) book entitled *What We Leave Behind*.

cal community support one another. This support is manifested in providing food, shelter, and water for the various life forms within the system. For example, in northern Wisconsin, wolf scat decomposes and serves as fertilizer for the plants that surround it. Understanding sustainability takes time—it is a process, not a fixed goal.

Sustainability invokes a complex conversation that is founded on an ecological perspective. I contend that it is important that we work to understand curriculum as ecological text. Understanding curriculum as ecological text involves a reconceptualization of the role of educational theory and practice. Triche (2002) notes that through the reconceptualization[2] of the curriculum field,

> [C]urriculum theorists hope to disrupt the accepted theory-practice relationship, which suggests that theory exists only to serve the practical effectiveness of classroom teachers. Instead, curriculum theorists have the responsibility to inform everyone engaging in education (students, practitioners, and administrators) that the practices traditionally associated with efficiently implementing bureaucratically determined educational objectives and activities are not the only possible curriculum practices. (pp. 31–32)

I argue that it is our role as curriculum theorists to transform the predominately efficiency-based schooling approach to education for sustainability. This transformation demands a great deal of intellectual labor and reflective practice. It is a lifelong task that must carry on to future generations and dynamically evolve in a way that can best respond to the environmental problems at hand with an emphasis on understanding. Learning towards sustainability is a pragmatic endeavor because it needs to be situational and contextually adaptive.

Curriculum Theory, Conversation, and Sustaining the Field

What can curriculum theory do to contribute to the sustainability movement? Does a topic like greening education fit within the realm of curriculum studies? I submit that curriculum theory is well situated to address the ecological crisis. Based on the seriousness of the ecological

---

[2] The reconceptualization of the curriculum field is a movement that was initiated in the late 1960s and early 1970s. It involved a reconceptualization of curriculum theory, shifting the emphasis from *developing* curriculum to *understanding* it. The reconceptualization of curriculum studies was a response to the Tylerian paradigm. The Tylerian paradigm emphasized education as a place for management, efficiency, and pedagogical standardization (see Pinar, 1997 and Pinar et al., 2004).

crisis, the work to green the planet rests on the shoulders of every academic discipline. I submit that education is one of the most vital places to begin the work of ecological revitalization. The far-reaching influence of education situates educational work as fundamental to precipitating the changes in perception that are necessary to living in harmony with Earth.[3]

Curriculum theory[4] is a unique subfield of education. Pinar (2004) states that "curriculum theory is a distinctive field of study, with a unique history, a complex present and uncertain future" (p. 2). The distinctiveness of the field is exemplified by the range of topics that it covers related to engaging in the interdisciplinary study of educational experience. These topics range from understanding curriculum as historical text, racial text, political text, autobiographical text, aesthetic text, postmodern text and much more (Pinar et al., 2004).

Curriculum theorists help us to re-imagine the possibilities for democracy (Dewey, 1916), ecological wellness (Bowers, 1993, 1997, 2006), and reclaiming our subjectivity (Pinar, 2001, 2006). Pinar (2004) points out that it is the interdisciplinary structure of the field that "makes curriculum theory a distinctive specialization within the broad field of education" (p. 2). In this sense, curriculum theory is discursive. Pinar notes that not "every instance of curriculum theory is interdisciplinary" (p. 2). Since there is not just one way to understand curriculum, it is best described as a "complicated conversation" (Pinar, 2004). The conversation is complicated because it embraces such a broad intellectual landscape. The fact that curriculum theory is conversational and not preset or deterministic is the beauty of it.

The political scientist Michael Oakeshott theorizes that conversation is an "unrehearsed intellectual adventure" (in Pinar, 2004, p. 188). A conversation is unrehearsed because it is not scripted. Of course, one can prepare for a conversation, but I think the notion of being unrehearsed is valuable in the context of education. In conversation we can respond to questions, improvise, and spontaneously engage in transformative understanding. Ted Aoki notes that the "conversation is not 'chit-chat,' nor is it...a conveyor belt of 'representational knowledge'" (in Pinar, 2004, p. 190). Aoki (2005) likens conversation to jazz improvisation—I think he is on to something with this. There is an organic and aesthetic quality in conversation. In this sense, conversation is an intellectual adventure—it

---

3   See Counts (1978) for a more in depth discussion on how education is situated to facilitate cultural change.

4   Used interchangeably with curriculum studies here.

is a tantalizing journey that involves study and exploration. I am drawn to the notion of education as a conversation—there is an intuitive organicity in the interchange between a student, her peers, and her instructor(s). My work within the field of curriculum theory has certainly been an ongoing conversation and an intellectual adventure. The conversation has been manifested through reading, interpreting, and unpacking the writings of the scholars who have helped to construct the theoretical space that I explore in this book. It is an intellectual adventure because I never knew what to expect in the conversations. This adventurous aspect is perhaps one of the reasons why I was drawn to curriculum studies— the field matched well with my background as an adventure educator.[5] Working to infuse sustainability into curriculum studies is also an adventure. We must begin the process of infusing sustainability into education by understanding the range of disciplinarity embodied by curriculum theory.

The Present and the Past

Recognizing the need to embrace the disciplinarity of curriculum studies, Pinar (2007a) maintains that we need to situate our work in a way in which the field can be sustained. In particular, Pinar discusses the importance of contributing to *horizontality* and *verticality* within the sphere of curriculum studies. He notes that horizontality "refers not only to the field's present set of intellectual circumstances...but as well to the social and political milieus" (Pinar, 2007a, p. xiv). Horizontality, in the context of sustainability, seeks to understand and advance the political and social conversation surrounding critical ecological issues such as anthropogenic climate change. Social and political milieus play a critical part in the scholarship of sustainability. The social arena is the place where grass roots action happens, and it is the place where some of the most important work is currently taking place. Horizontality is an important aspect of ecological revitalization—it encourages democratic participation in ecological revitalization.

According to Pinar, verticality deals with "the intellectual history of the discipline" (Pinar, 2007a, p. xiii). Verticality is the struggle to create

---

[5] Adventure education is a branch of experiential education that focuses on the development of interpersonal and intrapersonal skills while embracing experiences that typically include elements of "excitement, uncertainty, real or perceived risk, effort, and interaction with the natural environment" (Raiola & O'Keefe in Medina, 2009, p. 78).

an intellectual space that emboldens the work that has shaped our field. It emboldens the historical conversation by drawing from the rich intellectual past of curriculum studies. From the standpoint of verticality, Pinar believes that curriculum scholarship needs to testify "to the future by protecting the past" (p. xxv). Doing so involves critiquing the work that has been done and moving the conversation forward by forging a more sustainable planet for this and for future generations. As I will discuss later, being able to testify to the future is an import aspect of eco-curriculum. If we are unable to recognize the impact that today's decisions will have on future generations, we are living unsustainably.

I propose that there are no "easy" one-size-fits-all solutions offered to address the educational and ecological "nightmare" (Pinar, 2004) that we face today. This book seeks to add to the Scholarship of Sustainability in a time of intensified environmental disequilibrium. I believe that the field of curriculum studies enables us to fortify the effort of greening education. Curriculum studies is a vehicle for social transformation because it enables us, as scholars, to pose questions and to grapple with the theoretical spaces that may facilitate renewed interest in sustaining the planet. I propose that curriculum studies can help us to see sustainability as more than celebrating Earth Day or driving a hybrid vehicle—sustainability is a way of life. When we recognize sustainability as a way of life, there is a shift in the way in which we view the world.

The field of curriculum studies is robustly situated to make advancements in the political and the pedagogical arenas. Pinar (2007a) argues that the field of curriculum studies "is not moribund. It is intellectually very lively, complex, variegated" (p. xxv). In the context of protecting the biosphere, curriculum studies becomes even more enlivened. I propose that sustainability must work towards promoting an ecologically derived disciplinarity. In the spirit of Pinar, I propose that working towards sustainability involves a "comprehension, critique, and reconceptualization" (p. xxv) of the status quo. Thus, what I term *eco-disciplinarity* is a relational field of inquiry that elicits a form of understanding that is contextualized in the effort towards promoting biospheric wellness. We need to formulate a framework of eco-disciplinarity to address the questions surrounding the survivability of our planet.

Decolonization and Reinhabitation

In the context of curriculum studies and sustainability, decolonization and reinhabitation (Gruenewald, 2003) are important concepts and processes to consider in the formulation of an educational response to the ecological crisis. Decolonization and reinhabitation are two fundamental aspects inherent to reclaiming the places in which we live (Gruenewald, 2003). They help us to conceptualize what we need to do in order to live in a way that honors the nuances of our place. In essence, to decolonize is to reject the forces that prevent us from being connected to our bioregion, our life place. Reinhabitation involves becoming native[6] to the places in which we live. Becoming native to our place takes time—it necessitates a reconnection to our surrounding natural and social communities. It is through reinhabitation and decolonization that we move towards a deeper appreciation of place both as an idea and as a physical space. Curriculum studies for sustainability is an effort to both reinhabit and decolonize. By decolonizing and reinhabiting we facilitate democratic participation within the places we inhabit. This concept of returning to place is appropriately called *sense of place*. I will talk more about this in Chapter 4. We begin to not just take up space, but to truly inhabit our place and have a more holistic understanding of what our role is in this world. It is through a study of place that we can begin to have a greater appreciation for the *currere* of lived experience.

Currere and Ecology

Pinar and Grumet reveal that *currere*[7] is the Latin infinitive of "curriculum," meaning:

> To run the course: Thus *currere* refers to an existential experience of institutional structures. The method of *currere* is a strategy devised to disclose experience, so that we may see more of it and see more clearly. With such seeing can come deepened understanding of the running, and with this, can come deepened agency. (p. vii; in Pinar et al., 2004, p. 518)

---

6 To become native to the places that we live involves living in ways that are more place-conscious and ecologically sensitive. In this context, living like a native means recognizing and celebrating the fragility and resiliency of the Earth by adopting a more environmentally friendly way of living. Also, living like a native has to do with increasing one's environmental literacy and overall sense of place. These concepts are further explored in later chapters.

7 This section on *currere* and ecology serves as one of the frameworks in which this book pivots upon—the notion that the fundamental task of curriculum theory is to work from within while transforming the world in which one lives. We must begin our work autobiographically in order to take the necessary steps for living more sustainably (Pinar & Grumet in Pinar et al., 2004).

As I will discuss in Chapter 4, seeing our experiences more clearly and cultivating a deeper understanding of the running of our own course are central aspects to a curriculum studies for sustainability.[8]

Grumet states that "Currere is a reflexive cycle in which thought bends back upon itself and thus recovers its volition" (in Pinar et al., 2004, p. 517). Currere has a restorative quality that lends itself to revitalizing one's sense of self. A process of unfolding, currere enhances the move towards excavating our interiority and understanding what is going on inside oneself. It is through reinhabitation and decolonization (Gruenewald, 2003) that we are better equipped to forge an experiential understanding of how we can draw out (educe) a greater mode of participation with this world. This leads us to unpack the idea of enabling our children to think intergenerationally. Next, I explore how today's decisions will impact future generations.

Sustainable Growth of Human Beings

William Schubert (1986) purports that educators and curriculum theorists are "entrusted with the most serious work that confronts humankind: the development of curricula that enable new generations to contribute to the growth of human beings and society" (p. 423). I would like to add the notion of ecological sustainability to Schubert's conceptualization of the essential theoretical and practical aspects of the educational enterprise. Thus, I contend that the task of education and curriculum theory is to enable new generations to contribute to the *sustainable* growth of human beings and society. This involves attentiveness, a critical awareness of how the choices we make today may compromise the regenerative capacity of our biosphere to meet the needs of future generations.

An eco-curriculum for sustainability[9] inquires into environmental problems through a lens of critical literacy. Critical literacy involves asking deeper questions and advancing a more reflexive form of inquiry. Triche (2002) observes,

> In doing so, curriculum theorists are attempting to restore thoughtful or critical inquiry to classroom activities. They want to enable teachers and

---

8 In *Currere and the Environment*, Marilyn Doerr (2004) investigates the notion of an environmental currere—which situates Pinar's notion of currere within an ecological context.

9 Please note that I use the terms curriculum studies gone wild, curriculum studies for sustainability, and an eco-curriculum for sustainability synonymously.

students to begin questioning the kinds of underlying organizing structures presented by Tyler's curriculum principles, which "practical activity silences." (p. 32)

It is the critical thinking emerging from sustainability studies that moves us to question inadequate models of education such as Ralph Tyler's efficiency-based schooling model.[10] When education operates within the contemporary paradigm, students are "educated in disconnectedness— subject from subject, the present from the past and future, the knower from the known, the mind from the body, the heart or ethics from action, humans from the natural world, and individuals from the collective group" (Good, 1998, p. 78). What are the ramifications of educating in a way that promotes disconnectedness?[11] Students are becoming more and more alienated from one another, from the outdoor environment, and from themselves. This alienation prevents people from building a community of support. We need to respond to the isolated and atomistic approach affiliated with the Tylerian Rationale. In contrast, an ecologically conceived paradigm bridges the conceptual gaps that exist in the traditional fragmented curriculum design.

Curriculum Scholarship and Ecology: Looking at the Existing Conversation

From the scope of exploring the intersection between curriculum studies and ecology, it is helpful to look at the curriculum theorists who have

---

10 Curriculum development, from a traditional standpoint, has been concerned with Professor Ralph Tyler's four basic questions: 1. What educational purposes should the school seek to attain? 2. How can learning experiences be selected which are likely to be useful in attaining these objectives? 3. How can learning experiences be organized for effective instruction? and 4. How can the effectiveness of learning experiences be evaluated? (Slattery, 2009). Contemporary education has been dramatically impacted by his questions because education now focuses on test scores more than they do educational experiences. Tyler's approach holds efficiency and predictability as the highest goods. His approach has affectionately been named the Tylerian Rationale. Slattery (2009) notes that the Tylerian Rationale has "dominated the study of curriculum for the past fifty years" (n.p.).

11 William Pinar notes that it is also important to consider the "ramifications of reducing nature to a means to an end" (PC, March, 2010). For example, Pinar cites George Grant (1986), stating, "Nevertheless at a simple level it must be said that there is some connection between what we think other species to be (let alone our own) and how we treat them" (p. 65).

already done work on this topic. Pinar indicates that "the present day [curriculum] is one of scarcity, demanding of us 'sure-fire methods', the success of which is measured by regularly administered standardized examinations" (in Jardine, Friesen, & Clifford, 2006, p. ix). David Jardine, Sharon Friesen, and Patricia Clifford (2006) indicate that there is a transformative level of opportunity for revitalizing educational discourse in a way that generates a multitude of meaning and an abundance of rich educational experience. They dedicate their book to "the teachers and children who are suffering in the confines of a form of schooling premised on scarcity and impoverishment" (p. xxviii). Working in the confines of scarcity and impoverishment is a difficult and sometimes grueling task. How can we restore a conception of abundance in curriculum discourse? Children naturally know and recognize the plentiful range of experiences that are available in the real world. There is so much to be learned from the places in which we live, where the beginning of recognizing the abundance should take place. To study our place and to learn how to live well within our place is central to the curriculum of abundance that Jardine et al. discuss. They (2006) recognize the irony that exists in the discrepancy between the modern structures of efficiency used by the schools to create a scarcity of educational opportunity. The abundance surrounds us, yet we still operate from a perspective of scarcity.[12]

From an educational perspective, enabling people to experience "the abundance of things must be cultivated" (Jardine et al., 2006, p. 10). How can we help students to recognize, experience, and celebrate the abundance of the areas which they inhabit? David Jardine asks, "What would happen if we imagined children not as consumers and producers of constructed products of our own making, but as inhabitants in a world that is more abundant than I make of it?" (p. 147). When we conceive of students as not mere consumers, then we can begin to honor and build upon their capacity to be agents of eco-social change in this world. However, the attitude of impoverishment seems to prevail. Curriculum needs to be recalibrated and aimed at advancing sustainability. Situating curriculum into the context of sustainability invokes an ecological consciousness.

The notion of cultivating an ecological consciousness is a powerful one—there is a transformative quality associated in the project of seeing through an environmental lens. In "Ecological Consciousness and Cur-

---

12 Pinar notes that "'Abundance could be a counterpoint to 'disconnectedness,' less logically than ontologically, as being 'nature-full' e.g., ecological consciousness" (PC, March, 2010).

riculum," Morris (2002) investigates the significance of ecology within curriculum discourse. She indicates that "An ecological paradigm recognizes our integration with the world and others" (p. 571). Viewing the world ecologically allows us to see the interconnectedness of all living beings. Capra (1996) refers to this interconnectedness as *The Web of Life*. Human beings are *part of* the ecosystems that make up the biosphere, not *separate from* them. This interdependence with nature is critical to human experience. Morris observes that "[a]n ecological consciousness hopefully re-integrates us back into the wilderness" (p. 581). A return to wilderness is seen as a critical component to an education centered on sustainability. It is the return to wilderness that enables us to re-inhabit our place. *Curriculum Studies Gone Wild* is an effort to encourage ecological consciousness by seeking out and celebrating the environmental relationships that sustain us.

Going back to the key questions present in curriculum studies, Morris addresses the first question of what knowledge is of most worth? She responds, "The knowledge that will save the planet from complete destruction is of most worth" (Morris, 2002, p. 583). I agree with Morris but would add that it is highly important to find hope and joy in the process of working to save the planet from complete destruction. Without a healthy planet, it would be hard to have healthy people. The planet maintains and sustains us. Everything we do happens on the planet—but we must not forget the cosmic connectivity. I discuss the connection of spirituality to sustainability in a later chapter.

Cultivating the knowledge that will save the planet from complete destruction is a pretty serious task. At first, it may seem overly dramatic, but if you think about it, it means that schoolchildren need to have meaningful experiences in nature. While in nature, children are enabled to participate in imaginative and meaningful ecological experiences (Louv, 2005). Morris agrees, saying that "the tumbling streams and feathered birds have everything to do with lived experience, with life in schools" (Morris, 2002, p. 583). The text that emerges from the biosphere is inextricable from our educational experiences. When we are able to see from an intergenerational perspective, we position sustainability-related discourse at the forefront of education. Morris (2002) urges, "[f]or the sake of children, animals and the earth, teachers must educate to heal" (p. 583). Later in this book, I discuss how educating to heal is central to working towards sustainability. More specifically, this process of ecological restoration needs to be focused on healing the "bruised and tattered planet" (Callicott in Morris, 2002, p. 583). How do we initiate the healing of our planet? It begins in our own backyard.

Morris (2001) explores the notion of curriculum as ecological text. In this brief article, Morris tells us that "'[e]cological' doesn't only signify rats and snakes, etcetera, it also concerns our complex inter-relations with one another, with our everydayness and scholarly pursuits and the complex inter-relations of reading, writing, and thinking" (p. 4). The complexity of understanding associated with viewing curriculum as ecological text recognizes the value of study. The art and practice of study is how we participate in the inter-relations of reading, writing, and thinking. But, to study well is not an easy task. Morris asks, "What do we learn when we study?" (p. 5). With the abundance of educational possibility in ecological text, the answer is "[n]ot enough, never enough" (p. 5). Morris (2002) suggests that ecological text is a complex conversation. Striving to advance comprehension of the complex interrelations of reading, writing, and thinking are paramount to a curriculum founded on ecological sustainability. Advancing knowledge about interrelations is at the center of an eco-curriculum for sustainability. When people understand the interrelationships they can work towards ecological revitalization. Revitalization is a theme that runs through much of C.A. Bowers' work.

Bowers has contributed over 90 articles surrounding issues including ecology, sustainability, eco-justice and education. He writes often about revitalizing the commons and understanding the root metaphors that guide our cultural and educational assumptions.[13] Another theme that Bowers frequently explores is that of intergenerational equality. Bowers (2006) critiques that even the most progressive educational agendas undermine "the sense of intergenerational responsibility so essential to the commons" (p. 127). He attributes the erosion of intergenerational sensitivity to the overemphasis on "high-status" knowledge. He argues that it is science-focused educational reform that compromises ecological intelligence. He believes we have "created a generation of rootless individuals easily shaped by the hundreds of thousands of media commercials" encountered over a lifetime (Bowers, 2001a, p. 81). In other words, according to Bowers, education is driven by the marketplace. Students are enamored with commercials—the overwhelming presence of commercialized media is undermining students' abilities to develop a passion for living environmentally friendly lives. As a result, people are starting to see the planet more as a commodity than as a community (Majora Carter, PC, 2010). Building community takes time, whereas

---

13 Bowers is a prolific writer in the field of education, curriculum, and sustainability.

treating Earth like a commodity is fast and efficient. The commodity-based mindset is making people feel rootless, disconnected, and alienated from their home ground. The alienation from our place is beginning to compromise planetary habitability. Planetary habitability is compromised because we treat Earth as an object that is easily replaceable. Sadly, we could not be further from the truth.

Bowers notes that the root metaphors upon which modern society is built are not sustainable. There is urgency in the unchallenged levels of anthropogenic-Earth destruction.

> In effect, the cultural message systems that sustain the images and values upon which the consumer-oriented society rests continue unchallenged to reinforce the taken for granted attitudes toward material progress and individual opportunity—[this continues] even as the evidence mounts that the destruction of the environment now puts the entire technological/economic infrastructure at risk. (Bowers, 1995, p. 1)

The jeopardy of the entire technological and economic infrastructure goes unnoticed in the current system of economically driven discourse. Bowers adds that

> The schizophrenic condition that now characterizes people's lives, where concern about the immediate impact of degraded environment on health and economic well-being is kept separate from the critically important existential and cultural questions relating to 'how much is enough?,' to quote Alan Durning's fundamental question may very well continue until it is too late to affect the necessary cultural changes. (Bowers, 1995, pp. 1–2)

The question "how much is enough?" in terms of consumerism and environmental degradation is central to a curriculum built upon ecological sustainability. However, as Bowers indicates, we face a "schizophrenic condition" that obfuscates our ability to understand the level of degradation that is generated through anthropocentric consumption and production. We are in effect "ecologically autistic" (Berry in O'Sullivan, 1999, p. 95), and therefore we are unable to listen to and attend to the needs of our planet.

Bowers teaches us the importance of reconnecting to our environment. He heralds the value of maintaining intergenerational wisdom and encourages us to examine the root metaphors that guide our thinking and our teaching. He maintains that there is an overemphasis on constructing new knowledge in today's educational model. In contrast to constructing new knowledge, if we draw from the wisdom of our elders and ancestors, we can, according to Bowers, build a more adequate educational response to the ecological crisis. The response would be more adequate because we can learn how to live closer to the land and to avoid the mistakes that have led us to where we are today. Avoiding the mistakes that have led us to where we are today is something that Noel and Annette Gough address.

The work of curriculum scholars Noel and Annette Gough (Gough & Robottom, 1993; Gough & Gough, 2004, in press; A. Gough, 1997, 2005; N. Gough, 1994, 1989, 1999, 2006, 2009, n.d.) grapples with the overwhelming influence of globalization and industrialism on the vitality of our planet. Taking a critical stance, they challenge the fundamental assumptions that guide contemporary educational discourse. Noel Gough (1989) made a significant contribution to understanding the "ecopolitical" aspects of sustainability. He argues that the "materialistic and atomistic world view" still dominate "formal education in Western society" (p. 226). He proposes a theoretical framework for sustainability conceptualized around "the re-emergence of more practical and more holistic subjects for study" (p. 232). His work situates sustainability within political and the pedagogical contexts. His discussion surrounding the ecopolitical offers a deeper understanding to a curriculum studies for sustainability by arguing for more activism at the ecopolitical and educational levels.

Another shift in curriculum is explored by Annette Gough and Ian Robottom (1993). They discuss the notion of a "socially critical environmental education" while illustrating "ways in which students may be empowered to participate in transforming society democratically" (p. 314). This notion of transforming society democratically is a central feature to my conceptualization of curriculum studies for sustainability. If we embrace a participatory approach to sustainability, we are better situated to respond to the unanticipated problems of the ongoing environmental crisis. As with the other curriculum theorists mentioned in this introduction, this is not the space to highlight all of their scholarly work. The Goughs' involvement in advancing the literature pertaining to sustainability and education is profound. They both frequently write from a framework of critical theory and interrogate the mechanistic impact of industrial thinking and consumer culture.

Recognizing the multidimensionality inherent to curriculum inquiry, Noel Gough and Annette Gough (2004) posit that "[r]esearch is a textual practice, a process represented in language and performed through acts of writing, textual production and reading" (p. 410). They suggest that there is an aesthetic dimension to the research process. Instead of being rote or scientific, research (according to the Goughs) can be meaningful at the personal level. Moving beyond the mindless recapitulation of information (affiliated with traditional research modalities), the form of research proposed by the Goughs offers a transformative paradigm to curriculum scholarship. The Goughs intimate that in the "dominant traditions of the modern Western academy, research texts are positioned as objects with which authors enlighten readers through a single, literal reading" (p. 410). It is this commitment to the unilateral and convergent meaning produced through convergent thinking that Gough and Gough examine in their writing. They work towards providing an alternative narrative that includes "multiple framings" of their reflections in order to advance more pluralistic scholarship.

When we teach towards ecological sustainability we aim to change attitudes, behaviors, and participation within the sphere of stewardship. It is a form of education geared towards initiating environmental restoration efforts. In this sense, the Goughs contribute to the scholarship of sustainability within a context of educational discourse. Angela Lydon (1992) unpacks the possibility for curriculum theory and sustainability, stating:

> If [an ecologically oriented] mode of theorizing curriculum can disclose the order and balance present in the imperfect and flexible principles of nature, then education can reflect the stability and resilience present in natural systems as well as the diversity. As a result, an integrative context between human-earth relations can be envisioned. Such a mode recognizes that balancing individual interest with the welfare of the whole is the design of natural systems. (pp. 73–74)

When education reflects the diversity, stability, and resilience found in nature, it will be a wonderful advancement in the culture and climate of formal curriculum and pedagogy. There is abundant pedagogical possibility and plentiful theoretical opportunity for integrating ecology into all modes of education.

The existing body of literature that surrounds ecology and education is expanding daily. Even within the subfield of curriculum studies, the topic of ecology has been addressed by a number of theorists with themes such as: the eco-political (Gough & Gough, 2004), ecopedagogy (Jardine, 2000), revitalizing the commons (Bowers, 2006); ecology and curriculum (Morris, 2002), ecotones (Krall, 1994), transformation and sustainability (O'Sullivan, 2007, 2008). These curriculum scholars have made important additions to the study of sustainability in educational contexts. Through their help, we are better equipped to see a strong association between sustainability and curriculum. It is important that we pay homage to the work that has been done surrounding curriculum and ecology. This work has enabled me to enter the conversation in a way that is more informed and passionate. I am more passionate about this work because these authors have helped me to understand the urgency of the ecological crisis and have helped me to realize the possibility for curriculum studies to facilitate an educational response to the crisis. The work that has been done is crucial to the advancement of ecological discourse in curriculum. Although I draw on my predecessors, my scholarship diverges from what has already been done. I offer a unique perspective of sustainability and education mostly because curriculum theory enables me to explore the intersections of several disciplines. The multidisciplinary quality of curriculum theory allows me to construct a new form of inquiry, an inquiry oriented to advancing the theoretical spaces pertaining to ecological integrity and bioregional attunement. The existing body of literature does not explore the historical and contemporary conversation related to a watershed-based bioregionalism while infusing curriculum studies and sustainability into the explorative framework.

There is great opportunity within my notion of bioregional education inquiry and the ecological text in which I am theorizing. Viewing education as ecological text includes the study of place and the exploration of lived experience in the natural world. Understanding curriculum as ecological text involves being situated in place while studying the interdependence of all beings and the significance of the human-Earth relationship. The task of this book is to forge a more specific counter-narrative that responds to the prevailing industrialized and mechanized mode of educational acquisition and production. In this inquiry I seek to enter the existing conversation while adding to the discussion. Accordingly, this book offers an alternative to the mainstream scientific management paradigm with a discussion of an eco-curriculum for sustainability. A curriculum grounded in place and ecological revitalization seeks to cultivate a more harmonious human-Earth relationship.

Three Basic Curriculum Questions

As previously discussed, Schubert (1997) declares that three fundamental questions for curriculum studies are: "What knowledge is most worthwhile? Why is it worthwhile? How is it acquired or created?" (p. 1). Let us take a look at two of these questions within the framework of sustainability.

What knowledge pertaining to sustainability is most worthwhile? It is critical to appreciate the significance of developing an ecological worldview. Accordingly, I seek to understand the existing body of literature pertaining to ecological sustainability and curriculum. One approach to deepening the understanding of this literature is through viewing curriculum as ecological text. In this sense, the inherent interconnectivity that exists between past, present, and future is recognized from the perspective of advancing environmental well-being. Reviewing the existing scholarship of sustainability enables the reader to advance his or her ability to navigate sustainability studies while emboldening a deeper attentiveness to the integrality of lived experience.

The next question is *why is it worthwhile?* Equipping students, educators, and other scholars with the tools to restore and preserve the integrity of our biosphere is, as Wendell Berry states, "our most ancient and most worthy, and after all our most pleasing responsibility" (1997, p. 19). So, not only is sustainability education extremely relevant, it is a "pleasing responsibility." Berry's claim that sustainability is an ancient responsibility shows that it is a pleasing process that has been stifled through the dominant, consumer-driven paradigm. It is the task of education to awaken the instinct to be active stewards of this planet. Elaine Riley-Taylor (2002) observes that the word "steward" draws from Old English meaning "watchful" or "awake," emerging from the Greek, "'revere,' and from the Latin it means 'to respect' or 'to feel awe for'" (p. 7). "Unfortunately" Riley-Taylor adds, "those humans demonstrating respect or reverence for the earth stand in the minority compared with the many people who ignore, apathetically, the fact that we are part of a social and biological matrix" (p. 7). This lack of reverence for Earth serves as the pre-text to the ecological crisis that we face today. Thus, it is this realization that helps us to further conceptualize the relevance of working towards sustainability.

Complicated Conversation Towards Conservation

There is much terrain within the realm of curriculum studies and sustainability that is yet to be explored. In this book, I enter into the conversation and contribute a different perspective, a perspective that has become attuned to the natural world through multiday expeditions in the backcountry and through regular outdoor forays including day hikes and day paddling trips. My attunement has been shaped through intellectual inquiry and the adventure of the academic exploration associated with being a scholar in the field of curriculum studies. I have gained the tools necessary, through my educational journey, to identify gaps. It is the gaps in the literature that I intend to theorize upon throughout this book.

Theorizing around the scholarship pertaining to curriculum studies and sustainability is a *complicated conversation* (Pinar, 2004). It is complicated because of the many layers that make up the area of investigation. The layers of discourse include: understanding the energy crisis, comprehending the concept of resiliency, identifying potential points of intersection between curriculum and ecological restoration, and much more. It is a conversation that contributes to conservation efforts. The emphasis, in this context, is on deepening and expanding the academically oriented discussion pertinent to greening education while advancing ecological and bioregional understanding. This sustainability-oriented conversation advances conservation because it expounds upon protecting and celebrating the precious natural resources that remain. It is a conversation that explores ways to mitigate the unremitting epidemic of species extinction and heavy carbon dioxide production. The dynamic nature of the scholarship of sustainability is what makes theorizing upon ecology and curriculum more of a process than a stagnate mode of inquiry. This is how we must approach the scholarship of sustainability, as if it is a breathing field of theorizing that depends on the subjectivity of the authors and the readers to become more robust and better situated to face the uncertainties that lie ahead. We can become better situated to face future uncertainties by understanding what it means to live in a way that is Earth friendly and by attempting to understand the role that education has in this process.

CHAPTER 3

A Material World: Education and Environmental Degradation

> Our kinship with Earth must be maintained; otherwise, we will find ourselves trapped in the center of our own paved-over souls with no way out.
>
> Terry Tempest Williams, *Finding Beauty in a Broken World*

> With devastating force, the industrial way of life has invaded every aspect of human existence, including its political, legal, educational, and religious functioning. So extensive is this control that we must now speak of ourselves as living in an industrial civilization.
>
> Thomas Berry, *Evening Thoughts: Reflecting on Earth as Sacred Community*

AS A result of the industrial way of life described above by the ecotheologian Thomas Berry, we are in the midst of an ecological crisis that challenges the habitability of the planet. Individualistic-industrial[1] minded expansion removes the originality from our lives and replaces it with a conventionalized emphasis on uniformity. One of the hallmarks of this industrial mindedness is the labor of big business to control, commoditize, and direct the trajectory of one's lived experience. This labor of control works to domesticate and cultivate a "monoculture of mind" (Shiva, 1993). A monoculture of mind is a form of thinking that is entrenched in tunnel vision—it prevents us from seeing the big picture. Instead of seeing the world pluralistically, a monoculture of mind promotes a rigid mode of interfacing with one's surroundings, one's community, and one's self.

---

1 Here I am referring to the kind of individualism that Bowers (2003) describes, a "view of individualism [that] ignores the many ways the individual is dependent on a human community" (p. 61). An individualistic-industrialism views the natural world as a "commodity not a community" (PC, 2010, Majora Carter) while focusing on economic advancement and development as an ultimate goal. Accordingly, industrial expansion and increased monetary status is seen as more important than the relationships that can advance sustainability (the kind of relationships that are discussed in Chapter 5).

The industrial way of life has infiltrated virtually all levels of human experience. It is not just compromising the ecological integrity of the planet, it is eroding the human capacity to understand and respond to the ecological crisis. I propose that this far-reaching crisis should take precedence over all other enterprises academically, economically, politically, socially, and environmentally. A cascade of events has precipitated this crisis—including poor resource management, non-sustainable waste production, overconsumption, loss of wild places, and separation from nature. In this chapter, I explore the intersections between unsustainability and education. I address the rift between contemporary education and the natural world. While looking through the lens of curriculum studies I work to understand the impact of mechanistic thinking on our ability to connect in an ecological way with our surrounding bioregion. This exploration prepares a foundation for a deeper inquiry into the concept of sustainability. Additionally, I employ a metaphorical narrative that associates the industrial growth paradigm with the straightening of a river and a carbon copy curriculum.

Also, in this chapter, I offer a mosaic of what is unsustainable, thereby making it much easier to articulate the concept of sustainability. In subsequent chapters, this mosaic will serve as a conceptual backdrop while I formulate a transdisciplinary conception of sustainability. Terry Tempest Williams (2008a) states that a "mosaic is a conversation between what is broken" (p. 6). Our ecological crisis indicates that there is brokenness in the human-nature relationship. This brokenness extends into all levels of human experience including the spiritual, physical, social, emotional, and mental. Just as pristine natural areas are subjected to the destructive forces of today's industrial growth paradigm so is the "wildness" of human spirit. By *wildness* I am referring to the natural interests, proclivities, and interiority of the individual.

I argue from an educational standpoint that the current mode of educational discourse grounded in social efficiency is preventing students from undergoing the process of self-realization. In other words, I believe that we are not enabling our students to develop their full potential. I posit that contemporary American education at all levels is domesticating the inherent wildness of the human spirit. It is this domestication that promulgates our brokenness, fragmenting our experience. Also, it is obfuscating our ability to understand and respond to the *crisis of self-realization*. The industrial growth paradigm is intertwined with the social efficiency movement entrenched in today's educational discourse. The ramifications of industrial- and efficiency-mindedness are far reaching—we are experiencing a brokenness of unparalleled proportions.

This chapter seeks to understand this brokenness and enter the conversation from an educational perspective. By exploring the brokenness, I intend to advance an "agenda of good questions" (Davison in Bawden, 2004, p. 21) and engage the dialectic that occurs between sustainability and unsustainability. I maintain that the concept of advancing an agenda of good questions is powerful and timely. Good questions emerge from inquiry that is oriented towards addressing the immediate needs of communities and individuals. They are questions that explore how we can reduce the amount of fossil-fuel carbon emissions that humans generate throughout their lifetime. For it is only through good questioning that we can cultivate good answers. We must question the fundamental assumptions and the root metaphors (Bowers, 2006) that guide Western thinking and education. Thus, one theme in this chapter is to interrogate the role of social efficiency (one of the fundamental assumptions) in education and to understand its impact from a perspective of ecological sustainability.

How Can Curriculum Help Us Understand the Ecological Crisis?

Pinar (2004) asks "[h]ow can the school curriculum help us understand...the ecological crisis [and] globalization?" (p. 32). It is curriculum theory that invites these types of questions. Instead of focusing narrowly on one field of study, curriculum theory "[r]eject[s] colonization by the hegemonic disciplines such as psychology [and economics]...curriculum theory explores and constructs hybrid interdisciplinary constructions, utilizing fragments from philosophy, history, literary theory, the arts, and from key interdisciplinary formations already in place [such as human ecology]" (Pinar, 2004, p. 33). An eco-curriculum for sustainability offers a widening of our worldview that embraces the integrality of multiple disciplines in forging a more adequate scholarship of sustainability. As Pinar indicates, "curriculum is where we might understand the crisis" (PC, March, 2010). Grounding educational discourse in place enables us to think in ways that are new. It is time that we start trying to do things differently and break free from the patterns of globalized and industrialized ecological destruction that diminish biospheric health and integrity. As Schumacher (1973) posits in *Small Is Beautiful*, "Modern man does not experience himself as a part of nature but as an outside force destined to dominate and conquer it" (p. 14). How can we begin to see ourselves as a part of nature once again? We must start small—even in our own backyards—in order to address the ecological crisis.

Gustavo Esteva and Madhu Suri Prakash (1998) posit that it is impossible to think globally.[2] They believe that it is impossible to think globally because it is beyond the scope of the human mind to think at such a large scale. Again, small is beautiful. Grounding curriculum discourse in place enables us to think in ways that are new and more fecund. Curriculum that emphasizes a sense of place values lived experience. Place-consciousness transcends the boundaries of mono-disciplinarity. Place-consciousness serves as the common ground for integrated scholarship. It is time that we start trying to do things differently and think from a more local standpoint.

An Endangered Eco-Curriculum

In today's mechanistic and managerialistic education there are several forces that erode the integrality of lived experience. These forces endanger the promulgation of an ecologically oriented curriculum. John Dewey's (1934) conception of "having an experience" is helpful in terms of discussing the integrality of lived experience. Dewey posits that an experience "is one in which the material of experience is fulfilled or consummated, as for example when a problem is solved, or a game is played to its conclusion" (Leddy, 2006, n.p.). A consummated experience contains parts of an "enduring whole" without "holes or mechanical dead spots" (n.p.). There is a sense of wholeness in a consummated experience—an enlivened sense of belonging to this world. Dewey contrasts the undergoing of a whole experience with that of an inchoate experience. He suggests that an inchoate experience is one in which "we are distracted and do not complete our course of action" (n.p.). Contemporary American education appears to operate under a curriculum model that leads to inchoate experiences. Inchoate experiences in public schools are exemplified in the fragmented pedagogical approaches steeped in efficiency and time on task. Today's curriculum is bound to a standardized and automated realm of pre-determined trajectory. When there is an overemphasis on completing a pre-selected content standard, it is likely that the student is not given the opportunity to undergo an integral experience. In

---

2 Esteva and Prakash (1998) also posit that thinking globally is narrowly restricted in scope. They state that "[g]lobal proposals are necessarily parochial: they inevitably express the specific vision and interests of a small group of people, even when they are supposedly formulated in the interest of humanity" (p. 27). This is a powerful statement—that global thinking is parochial. For some it may be counterintuitive.

this chapter, I explore how the social efficiency model and the mechanistic worldview obfuscate the integrality of lived experience.

Educational theorist Thomas Leddy notes that "[i]n integral experience[s] there is a dynamic form that involves growth" (n.p.). Growth is central to undergoing an experience. In contrast, education that emphasizes a mechanical approach is mis-educative; it does not educe growth. As Mathew Fox tells us "Miseducation is education that fails to *educe*, to lead out of individuals their best and noblest capacities—our capacities for joy and wonder; awe and sharing; biophilia, justice and compassion" (Fox, 2006, p. 27, emphasis added). Mis-education is a by-product of the heterogeneous approaches of pre-determined, myopic, market-oriented education.

I propose that an education that embraces the integrality of lived experience is an education that promotes self-realization, interiority, wonder, biophilia, and contemplation. I submit that promoting the integrality of lived experience is equivalent to promoting a "wild" curriculum. A "wild" education encourages direct interaction with the curriculum, an unhindered exploration of an idea, argument, or phenomenon. It is wild because it is in lieu of a "controlled," pre-determined, fragmented, and de-contextualized education which is grounded in boosting standardized knowledge for passing tests. When an organism is wild it is given an opportunity to showcase its strengths and to develop its own niche. A wild curriculum enables the student to unfold and to work towards self-realization. A wild curriculum promotes an uninhibited guided exploration of our environment, in this sense it promotes what I call an eco-curriculum. An eco-curriculum is an ecologically derived curriculum that seeks to enliven the relationships that exist within lived experience and educational discourse. It recognizes the interdependence between all living beings and encourages the exploration and stewardship of our own environment. An eco-curriculum helps us to view ourselves as implicated members of the living community. David Orr (2001) insists that we need to recognize our implicated role in the web of life and not view ourselves as "isolated, self-maximizing individuals" (p. 8). Accordingly, an eco-curriculum invokes compassion and a comprehension of the "web of life."

Since ecology is the study of relationships that exist in a particular context, an eco-curriculum advances one's ability to recognize and not hinder the fragile relations that exist in one's bioregion. An eco-curriculum is built around an organic[3] conception of education. It is a

---

3   Brian Goodwin (2007) forms a discussion about taking a more organic attitude towards the natural world. According to O'Sullivan (2007), Goodwin "fosters a

curriculum that values the ecological and cultural nuances of the surrounding environment and community. It does not acquiesce to the dominant discourse that is associated with consumerism, industrialism, and social efficiency, but rather it works against the homogenizing forces of globalization. These forces include the hyper-consumerism (propounded through corporate influence in education), colonization, and rootlessness. Another aspect that I will explore in this chapter is how current educational approaches fit into what I refer to as a "carbon copy curriculum," which stifles an eco-curriculum.

A Carbon Copy Curriculum

John Dewey noted in one of his speeches that education is not equipping students with the necessary skills to face the future.

> The world is moving at a tremendous rate, no one knows where. We must prepare our children not for the world of the past, not for our world, but for their world. The world of the future. (Dewey in Richter, 1945, p. 110)

In terms of ecological sustainability, what does the world of the future hold? It is hard to tell, but from an educational perspective the current model of curriculum and pedagogy does not meet Dewey's challenge. Instead, American education has been perpetuating what I refer to as a "carbon copy curriculum" throughout the last century. This carbon copy curriculum compels schools to reproduce archaic and mechanical educational approaches. By reproducing outdated educational approaches we are obfuscating the possibilities for embracing educational transformation (O'Sullivan, 1999) and perpetuating an even greater dependence on fossil fuels. Instead of preparing our children for the world of the future, we are inadvertently "preparing" them for the world of the past and nurturing citizens with progressively larger carbon footprints. The myopic, reproduction-minded, and mechanistic thought processes associated with the current educational model are becoming less sustainable. From an ecological perspective, schools have become factories that inculcate environmental degradation by promoting inadequate notions of progress (Wessels, 2006; Bowers, 2002; Capra et al., 1991; Morris, 2008, p. 140; Orr, 1994).

'feeling' of the organicity within all aspects of the 'web of life'" while working towards a postmodern science "based on a dynamic open systems framework that is organic and holistic and in the more inclusive Earth context" (n.p.).

Mary Aswell Doll urges that we need to recognize that the Westernized compulsion to move forward, step up, and step on is compromising our ability to think critically. She argues,

> Progress has polluted our waters both in the environment and in our selves. Progress has endangered our species both in the wilderness and in the wild places of our selves. Chemicals have been abused both against the bugs and against what bugs ourselves. We have extended our notion of progress so that we have forgotten our selves, rooted in a collective past. (In Slattery, 1995, p. 183)

When we lose our rootedness we also lose our sense of place. It is time to put value in *soil* over *oil* (Shiva, 2008) and embrace the ecological connectedness available through knowing the nuances of our surrounding bioregion.

I argue that contemporary education perpetuates unsustainability through a carbon copy curriculum. This is to say, American education is stubbornly clinging to a pattern of reproduction that duplicates previous modes of curriculum and pedagogy. By replicating pre-existing modes of education, a carbon copy curriculum is static. The duplicative characteristic of today's education system is founded on the industry-oriented principles of efficiency and consumerism (Gadotti, 2008; Prakash, 1994, 1995). This outdated form of education emerges from a mechanistic paradigm that views the schools as factories that "produce" workers and consumers—not individuals who are capable of thinking critically and participating in the collaborative revitalization of our ecosphere. The mechanistic paradigm embraces an epistemology that reduces learning to a fragmented enterprise founded on standards and test scores. Instead of encouraging creativity, originality and self-realization, mechanization is geared towards the promulgation of predictability, control, and pre-determined learning standards. In this section I unpack the notion of a carbon copy curriculum and discuss its impact.

In attempting to understand the quagmire that characterizes today's educational discourse, I have employed the metaphor of a carbon copy curriculum. Carbon copies are "comparable...[meaning] one thing which closely or essentially resembles something that has already been made, produced or written" (Gove, 1984, p. 685). The tendency to replicate previous versions of education is what I refer to as a "carbon copy curriculum." In this "carbon copy" conception of schooling, public education reproduces antiquated modes of curriculum in order to maintain the status quo. Students are viewed as products that graduate with pre-determined attributes which include attitudes of consumerism, conformity, and efficiency. Stephen Sterling (2001) notes that education continues to advance in a way that conforms to the "philosophy and perceived needs of the market, and the managerial influence may now be seen in most Western and Westernized education systems across the world" (p. 12). A carbon copy curriculum does not encourage originality—it is a transmissive approach that replaces individuality with robotic duplicity. It gives students a false sense of purpose in this world because it pushes the idea that bigger is better. A carbon copy curriculum encourages material advancement in the form of bigger houses, bigger bank accounts, bigger cars, bigger fences, and bigger egos. Material advancement is only one of the ecologically compromising features of a carbon copy curriculum.

In a carbon copy curriculum, approaches to education from previous generations are carbon copied and mindlessly mimicked to perpetuate the industry-oriented schooling approach. The industry-oriented schooling approach emphasizes training, uniformity, and conformity. It is a plasticized approach to education because it "covers" everything—from subject matter to pedagogy—with an artificial "protective" veneer. This protective covering is present because the information (official knowledge) that the students are to learn is imported from a far off place (the curriculum experts), then transmitted into the students by the quality control officer (the teacher). As Leopold quipped, "...our educational system is headed away from...an intense consciousness of land" (1989, pp. 224–225). The carbon copy curriculum is one lens in which we can begin to understand how education has headed so far away from land consciousness. Students are not *transformed* in the carbon copy approach to education—they are *informed*.

In a carbon copy curriculum students are told what to do and must repeat this educational command by filling in the appropriate circle on the multiple choice test—learners are not given the chance to make their own educational choices. This means that students are not educated in a way that helps them to realize that overconsumption is tied to unrelenting carbon emissions—or that it is the same mindset that advances racism that also advances ecological destruction.[4] Thus, students gradu-

---

4   The mindset that I am referring to here is the individualistic mindset that is associated with the industrial mind. The individualistic mindset advances solipsism by positioning one's selfish needs over the needs of anyone or anything else, thereby creating an even greater rift between humans and the natural world. We can see how individualism is affiliated with the industrial mind, because both emphasize personal advancement and material success.

ate from a carbon copy educational experience with an increased likelihood to contribute to environmental degradation and participate in the fossil fuel economy. This destructive land ethic is a result of consumer-based educational experiences. When students learn to think that material possession is critical for success, the message is sent that the health of the planet is secondary to personal advancement. It follows that within the carbon copy curriculum paradigm, students graduate with a likelihood of uncritically generating an even greater carbon footprint through attempting to become "successful" in the contemporary sense. In his recent documentary about global warming, Robert Krulwich (2009) observes that as "more people become rich on Earth—the more we use carbon. Carbon is the atom that equals success" (n.p.). What Krulwich is suggesting here is that extensive carbon use is tied to economic prosperity. Accordingly, a bigger checkbook typically results in a greater carbon footprint. How does education's commitment to the status quo impact climate change? It is the tendency to teach in a way that encourages passive receptivity to information and not critical consciousness that takes us off the track of restructuring our economy in a way that promotes sustainability. In terms of getting a better grasp of the problems that we face it is helpful to look at organizations that are dedicated to investigating the impact of carbon on the environment. The Intergovernmental Panel on Climate Change maintains that the burning of fossil fuels is a major contributor to today's climate crisis (Lynas, 2008). We perpetuate the burning of fossil fuels through an education that embraces a carbon copy mentality—replicating petroleum-oriented consumption patterns that propound the climate change crisis that we currently face. In order to better grasp the human contribution to global warming it helps to understand the science of climate change.

Carbon dioxide (CO_2) is the atom that is responsible for climate change. The greenhouse effect is one of the factors that makes life on Earth possible (Gore, 2006; Hopkins, 2009). For it is the green house effect that traps the necessary heat to make the biosphere inhabitable to humans. Gore (2006) notes that greenhouse gases (which is composed of carbon dioxide and other[5] molecules) "allow light from the sun to come into the atmosphere, but trap a portion of the outward-bound infrared radiation and warm up the air" (p. 28). It is important to note that without greenhouse gasses "the average temperature of Earth's surface would be right around zero degrees Fahrenheit" (Gore, 2006, p. 28). The

---

5 Some other greenhouse gasses are methane, nitrous oxide, ozone, and water vapor.

problem occurs when there is too much greenhouse gas that gets trapped in the atmosphere. A surplus of CO_2 in Earth's atmosphere can create a problem—excess CO_2 molecules form a thicker blanket of greenhouse gases, thereby trapping more and more heat.[6] We have reached a tipping point where we can make a remarkable improvement on our level of carbon emissions. This is where education can make a difference. As I discuss in subsequent chapters, education has the capacity to reduce our carbon emissions by increasing our ethic of ecological stewardship.

The Running of a Course

In this section I employ a metaphorical discussion of a waterway to highlight the impact of education on the life journey. From the lens of curriculum studies, I explore the notion of a free-flowing river in juxtaposition with that of educational experience and lived experience. This metaphorical inquiry aims to deconstruct the hegemony of the social efficiency paradigm in association with the industrial growth model. I situate this discussion in both the physical and the conceptual framework of a Georgia-based watershed. A physical watershed is defined as an area of land that drains to a common body of water. Ecologist Donna Seaman says that the term watershed refers to "the higher ground—the line, ridge, or summit—that separates two drainage basins" but more recently it refers to "the region drained by such a divide, and an area through which water is drained into a particular watercourse or body of water" (in Lopez & Gwarteny, 2006, p. 387). A watershed commonly serves as the boundary for a bioregion (McGinnis, 1999).

For the purpose of this book, I view the bioregion that one lives in as one's place. This is why I added the term bioregionalism to the title of the book. According to Kirkpatrick Sale (2000), a bioregion is "any part of the

---

6 Because it is such a small part of the overall atmosphere, CO_2 is measured in parts per million (ppm). We are currently at 385 ppm and this number is reportedly increasing (350.org, n.d.) at a rapid rate. Scientists have determined that we need to return to 350 ppm of CO_2 to restore climactic equilibrium. Our carbon emission rates have increased just within the last 100 years. Hopkins (2009) shares that "[p]re-industrial levels of carbon were 278ppm, but by 2007 they have reached 385ppm...[this increase] has already had significant effects, disrupting the delicate balance of planetary climate" (pp. 31-32). A full exploration of climactic science is well beyond the scope of this book—the main point is that we have exceeded the safe amount of CO_2 and that we *do* have the capacity to reduce our collective and individual carbon footprints in ways that are more compatible with maintaining and sustaining life on this planet.

earth's surface whose rough boundaries are determined by natural characteristics rather than human dictates" (p. 55). These bioregions are "distinguishable from other areas by particular attributes of flora, fauna, water, climate, soils, and landforms, and by the human settlements and cultures those attributes have given rise to" (p. 55). They are commonly organized around water basins and watersheds. Frequently, smaller watersheds are nested within each other. It is important to note that the boundaries of a bioregion are typically fluid in that there is a dynamic interchange between one watershed and another. In other words, bioregions breathe.

What can we learn from our bioregions? How can the knowledge that we glean from exploring our places help us? By studying how nature accomplishes various tasks we can find answers to human problems. For example, if we could make solar panels as efficient as a leaf in converting sunlight into energy we would dramatically increase the possibility for photovoltaic energy production. Janine Benyus (1998) refers to this idea (the notion that we can learn a lot from mimicking nature) as "biomimicry," a concept which she describes as innovation inspired by nature. In this section I draw a parallel between the flowing of a river and the flowing of our life course. I will explore how a model of a free–flowing river can cultivate meaningful conversation surrounding the notion of sustainability.

I live near the Ogeechee River in southeastern Georgia. The Ogeechee begins in northern Georgia and travels in a southeasterly manner 245 miles to where it empties in the Atlantic Ocean. It is one of the few "untamed" rivers in North America (Lenz, 2008). Untamed rivers are rivers that have not been trammeled by humans. These rivers have not been impeded, rerouted, or restrained by humans—they are still wild. Unfortunately the number of untrammeled rivers is dwindling. Therefore, the Ogeechee is one of the most wild, pristine, and scenic rivers on the Eastern seaboard. This wildness results in high water quality. The river is a compelling metaphor for the educational journey.

To educate is to educe, to draw out, a bringing forth of the student's natural pathway. It is to facilitate the forward momentum of a person's life course. When we view curriculum and pedagogy as a mode of educing student passion—to explore their interests and engage in the public discourse for solving ecological problems—we recognize the importance of encouraging students to follow their natural pathway. That is, instead of telling students to get on a path of predetermined and engineered outcomes, a more sustainable mode of education is one that enables them to forge their own educational journeys. Enabling students to engage in their unique educational journeys involves helping them to develop a sense of place. Cultivating a deeper sense of place is a process of engaging the student in hands on, heads on, and hearts on experience. Developing a sense of place in students evokes a need to instigate reflexive activity with their surrounding bioregion. I call this intellectual environmental inquiry *eco-disciplinarity*.

Eco-disciplinarity refers to the process of gaining attunement to the particularities of place. When we work to get to know our home ground better, we are participating in a form of eco-disciplinarity. This process includes outdoor exploratory excursions getting out into the community, meeting people, and hearing stories about the local region. For example, I have learned through direct experience that the Ogeechee River is a black water river. Also, the water from a black water river tastes bitter and acidic because of the naturally occurring tannins. These tannins are leeched out from surrounding organic matter and drain into the river making the water tea like in appearance. I learned this—firsthand—by taking a canoe trip on the river. I noticed the water's darkness, and bitter taste after I tasted a sample of it. I guess you could say that it was full immersion learning. The water tasted bitter because of the tannins that have leeched into it. When I returned home I was able to research the phenomena a bit more by calling a friend who specializes in hydrology (water-based science).

Eco-disciplinarity involves getting to know our surrounding ecosystems by encountering, studying, and trying to understand them. When we notice seasonal changes that happen in nature we become phenologists. Phenology[7] is the study of cyclical plant and animal life events in relation to the influence of seasonal fluctuations in climate. From my excursions in wild places, I can resonate with Edward Abbey's (1990) claim that "wilderness is not a luxury but a necessity of the human spirit" (p. 169). Many people are writing off wilderness areas and other natural places because of the epidemic and widespread emphasis of economy over ecology. Before we write an epitaph for the remaining wild places, we must recognize that they sustain us and nurture our spirit. We need to encounter wild places and cultivate bioregional ecological wisdom.

Watersheds are fundamentally interconnected—"we all live downstream" (Macoskey in Good, 1998, p. 170; Lohan, 2008, p. 8). The notion that we all live downstream is significant because it illustrates the fact

---

7   Bill McKibben (2008) explores phenology in a compelling series of stories about his direct encounters with the natural world.

that human wellness is not simply a product of our own choices; it is also reliant on other humans. Our drinking water is dramatically impacted by those that live "upstream" of us. If we live downstream of a conventionally farmed soybean crop it is likely that we will have high levels of fertilizer in our water supply. We are all interconnected. The interplay that exists between bioregions is similar to the interplay that occurs between local and global social systems. This is a fundamental component of advancing ecological sustainability. We need to allow virtually all living beings to run their course.

The root of the word curriculum is derived from the Latin word *currere,* which means the "running of a course." Educational experience involves a running of a course, and all institutions that purport to educate and identify education in their mission and vision can have an influence upon this "course." Unfortunately, American education has fallen prey to the "audit culture" (Slattery & Edgerton, 2009; Taubman, 2009, p. 196). Slattery and Edgerton (2009) state that "In an audit culture, the language of accountability pervades social institutions which are being forced from 'the commons' into a market mode through a process some have called the 'new managerialism'" (n.p.). The audit culture compromises the "natural flow" of human lived experience. It replaces organic experience with the mechanistic purpose of marketing and management. Not only is the oppressive force of the audit culture eroding the vitality of our social spheres and civic squares, it is compromising our ability to relate to Earth and to ourselves.

As educators, theorists, and engaged citizens, it is our duty to initiate the healing of the brokenness associated with the "nightmare" that characterizes today's educational situation (Pinar, 2004). This brokenness represents the disconnectedness affiliated with social efficiency. I argue that environmental degradation threatens our liberty. It is crucial to note that there is no education "to be done on a dead planet." We cannot do anything on a dead planet because we depend on the planet for our own well-being. We are wrecking our planet. As Adrienne Rich states, we need to get busy "diving into the wreck" that comprises contemporary educational discourse (in Morris, 2008, p. 194). Educational discourse is a wreck from an ecological standpoint and—as ecological citizens—I submit that it is our duty to become involved in Earth's stewardship. Before we are able to dive into this wreck we need to study it and strive to understand our own unique contribution to the conversation of healing. To invoke the healing process one thing that we need to do is to explore the contradictions. The contradictions (Ayers, 2009) between profit and people, development and preservation, spiritual growth and efficiency, and more need to be investigated.

From the realm of understanding human experience it is important to note that our lives are fraught with contradictions. For example, we have empirical proof that burning fossil fuels generates the carbon that eventually forms a thicker atmospheric wall which leads to a greater greenhouse effect (Lynas, 2008). Despite the global atmospheric assault generated from burning fossil fuels, humans continue to burn gas without thinking twice (Monibot, 2007). Why is this happening? Again, we must dive into this wreck.

The Natural Course

Diving in is where we can begin to develop a greater understanding of our role on this planet. When one is able to identify her own niche she is[8] more likely to thrive. A river that is allowed to run its natural course is more likely to maintain its ecological integrity. However, when one's course (educational experience) is predetermined by external forces it is unlikely that she will be equipped to pursue her own interests. Intellectual curiosity can fade when it is not cultivated. A river that is managed and artificially redirected loses its ecological integrity and resilience. In many parts of the United States, industry has attempted to straighten rivers by redirecting their natural curves and meandering pathways into straight paths. I will next discuss how, from a hydrological perspective, a "straightened" river is less likely to thrive.

Historically, man has foolishly attempted to "control rivers" in various ways (Pearce, 2005). The effort to "control" rivers is epitomized by river straightening (also called channeling), rerouting, and damming. Channeling rivers and waterways is a method employed by humans to reduce the unpredictability of the river and make travel quicker between points. It was once believed that river channeling would mitigate flooding problems and "free up the floodplain for development of various types" (Inyo, 2001, n.p.). Waterways are channeled to make them more navigable, less chaotic, and faster flowing. Inyo states that when a river is channelized it is dredged and straightened which virtually eliminates all of its natural curves and bends. Nicola Surian (2003) explains that "The most common purposes of channelization are flood control, land

---

8 A note on the pronoun usage, *he* and *she* are used interchangeably throughout this book. In virtually all cases please assume that the pronoun includes both sexes.

drainage improvement, creation of new spaces for urbanization or agriculture, maintenance or improvement of navigation, and reduction of bank erosion" (n.p.)

Developing a river by straightening it commonly results in less-than-desirable consequences. Surian (2003) observes that "channelization [often] has induced severe effects on the environment" (Surian, 2003, n.p.). The river dynamics, water quality, and aquatic and riparian ecology can be heavily impacted by this process. Ironically, most rivers that are channelized generate more erosion and flooding (Surian, 2003). It follows that when people become more aware of the impacts that channelization has it generates "changes in the attitude about stream management" (p. 1). As a result of mankind's influence on waterways, Pearce (2005) notes that the "untamed rivers of the world are rapidly becoming extinct" (p. 10). I maintain that the effort to tame rivers is analogous to the school's effort to train students through scientific management and social efficiency.

In an educational context there are a number of factors at work that channelize and straighten the human lived experience. This educational culture is steeped in accountability and assessment resulting in an overwhelming presence of literalism. Shoaf (2001) insists, "Literalsim stops life by stopping the quest and questioning for meaning; it replaces the question with a premature answer, which is all too often a law" (p. 82). In an educational sense, there is a tendency to replace direct experience and inquiry with a predetermined answer. The predetermined answer exists in the form of standardized knowledge tied to a state mandated curriculum. Literalism is the close adherence to the "exact representation or portrayal, without idealization" (literalism, n.d.). Literalism is a product of homogeneous and uni-lateral thinking associated with today's educational system, a corporate juggernaut aimed at reproducing the status quo. A carbon copy curriculum is typically literalistic because it simply takes what already exists within educational discourse and repeats it without question or thought.

I submit that the effort geared towards testing and efficiency is a method of "straightening the course" of lived experience for students. This straightening is a channelization of curriculum and pedagogy, reducing risk and spontaneity in an effort to stabilize unpredictability and to impose a pre-established sense of authority on students. What happens to the ethereal or the ineffable in a literal curriculum? When we remove the mysterious we remove aesthetics—because art is created from the subjective mystery and conveyed in ways that are original. There is no room for original thought in literalism. In education, the culture of efficiency reduces any "wasting of time." In the schools, students are not given the opportunity to explore an idea on their own time; they are given a pre-specified amount of time in which they are required to retain the information that is transmitted to them. Resultantly, education has turned into what James Hillman refers to as a "single track obsession" and a "monotheistic literalism that follows one prospect only" (in Doll, 2000, p. 3). A single track obsession? Wow! What are we doing when we emphasize standards and uniformity? Are we truly trying to eliminate the innate human desire to explore? Educational literalism is rampant, and it is rapidly undermining the citizenries' ability to be informed and productive decision makers.

Ventriloquism Not Intellectual Exploration

Pinar (2004) points out that in today's educational model "teachers are forced to 'instruct' students to mime others' conversations, ensuring that countless classrooms are filled with forms of ventriloquism rather than intellectual exploration, wonder, and awe" (p. 186). Students and teachers are treated like marionettes, and the puppeteers (curriculum specialists, content experts, and policy makers) are off in some far-removed location. Dewey (1931) maintains that traditional education methodology consists of "[students] who stand at the end of a pipeline receiving material conducted from a distant reservoir of learning" (p. 34). This is the great disconnect in today's education system. Not only is education removed from the school's surrounding community and environment, it also embraces an imposed curriculum from far off places. Decontextualized curriculum is not the most palatable—it is usually not relevant and sometimes alien. For example, most textbooks have images of places in them that children have never visited. Imagine a textbook that highlights the specific neighborhood in which the school that is using it is situated. How do you think that students would respond to this kind of curriculum?

Instead of encouraging students to undergo their own direct experiences teachers are told to transmit other people's experiences and to force memorization. When schooling adopts literalism, it is closer to training than to actual education. Nancy Fenn (n.d.) quotes Joseph Campbell who stated that "literalism kills" and the "imagination quickens" (n.p.). In this case, education becomes an enterprise aimed at creating ready-made workers for the job market. In literalism there is commonly an over-analysis of ideas and a quantitative emphasis on linear progression.

There is a mechanistic structure in literalism that focuses on task outcome and utility.

The tendency to over-generalize and adhere to only one basic frame of reference is a symptom of literalism. This rigid adherence to a singular way of thinking is akin to Britzman's notion of a "conceptual fortress" (in Doll, 2000, p. 73). A conceptual fortress is a fancy term for entrenched thinking patterns that are hard to transcend. When we get stuck in the thinking associated with a conceptual fortress our understanding of that particular topic becomes law. The thinking that has gotten us into the ecological crisis that we are currently facing is a product of a narrowly accepted *conceptual fortress*—economic development is valued over ecological renewal. Those who develop conceptual fortresses struggle with finding their own sense of self. Instead, they identify with externally derived existences while shunning the interiority associated with a healthy self-awareness. Materialism commonly follows literalism...sometimes the reverse of this is also true. But, the point is that we are "losing ourselves" in the noise and distraction affiliated with the consumer culture.

Like the channelization of rivers, literalism pervades discourse and encourages the reduction of direct experience in favor of reliving, duplicating, and copying other people's experiences. Ultimately, in a carbon copy curriculum, efficiency is improved as risk is minimized. The loss of risk in learning can result in the loss of challenge. When we are not challenged we get bored. Thus the cultivation of student agency is sacrificed for increased test scores and dialogue is replaced with scripted instructional cues. Literalism in education is not sustainable. It is not sustainable because student curiosity is exterminated and replaced with preprogrammed thinking models. Students who are immersed in a carbon copy literalistic curriculum are not equipped to deal with the rapidly changing pace of the evolving world. Outdated educational approaches are inadequate when it comes to solving the problems associated with anthropogenic antecedents of climate change. Mary Doll (2000) suggests that we need to undergo a "greening of the imagination," which means "to turn it in new directions that reconceptualize the damaging ideas of progress" (p. 203). How can we turn towards new directions that enable us to reconceive progress? It begins with the recognition that current modes of education are inherently flawed. Part of this transition into more adequate educational models can be found in aesthetics.

The Poetry of Lived Experience

Song of the Builders

On a summer morning

I sat down

on a hillside

to think about God—

a worthy pastime.

Near me, I saw

a single cricket was moving the grains of the

hillside

this way and that way.

How great was the energy,

how humble its effort.

Let us hope

it will always be like this,

each of us going on

in our inexplicable ways

building the universe.

—Mary Oliver (2005, p. 92)

The natural curves and meandering paths that untamed rivers take is alluring. Similarly, human experiences are filed with meandering paths that compose the non-linear aesthetic aspects of the human life journey. In the above poem, Mary Oliver is touching on the profundity of a single cricket's work, drawing a metaphor for the inexplicability of each individual's life journey. Poetry is one form of art that offers enchanting and numinous experiences. It is an avenue that can allow us to reawaken the "elemental awe [that] starts things over for us, [and] brings us back to our origins, connects us to the beginnings, makes us young again" (Fox, 2006, p. 28). It is this elemental awe that enables us to transcend the impacts of a carbon copy curriculum. How do we reawaken this elemental awe? One way is to get back out into nature and develop a more grounded sense of place. Reconnecting to our beginnings allows us to become more receptive to new ideas and to be better situated for the unexpected. As

Ranier Maria Rilke (1993) urges, "Resolve to be always beginning—to be a beginner" (p. 25). Looking at life through the eyes of a beginner helps to restore the wonder and excitement of learning things for the first time. Beginners' eyes are amazed by the intricate beauty found in nature and enthralled by the wonders of life. Being a beginner offers us an opportunity to deepen our experience in ways that honor the sacredness and depth of human agency. In aesthetic experiences, we are more likely to authentically encounter life in non-linear positionalities.

Mary Doll (2000) maintains that the newness that aesthetic experiences provoke does not come easily. "[N]ewness cannot emerge without a conflict, which necessarily also involves suffering...a way of actively making one's self anew, rather than passively being begotten" (p. 55). The growing pains, associated with newness, are a close relative to fecundity. Thus, novelty works as a fertilizer for new growth, a by-product of fecundity. In the realm of education, David Jardine (et al., 2006) suggests that suffering is sometimes involved:

> Yes, educational experience involves suffering; it involves opening ourselves to the open-ended sojourn of things, their ongoingness and fragilities and sometimes exhilarating, sometimes terrifying possibilities and fluidities. (p. xxi)

The open-ended sojourn associated with life is found in the very texture of educational experience, which is associated with aesthetic inquiry. It is interesting to point out that the fertility of poetry has been associated with the foundation of human existence.

There is opportunity for delight associated with direct experience. In *Art as Experience*, John Dewey (1934) discusses the possibility for delight and states that art "quickens us from the slackness of routine and enables us to forget ourselves by finding ourselves in the delight of experiencing the world about us in its varied qualities and forms" (p. 110). Appreciating the various qualities and forms of life is at the core of living aesthetically. Living aesthetically also involves developing a stronger sense of self through autobiographical exploration.

Understanding the nuances of our personal idiosyncrasies is fundamental to understanding who we are as individuals. It is not, as some Marxists argue, narcissistic to deepen the attunement with oneself. As Silverman indicates, a focus on autobiographical inquiry—studying oneself—is "not an exercise in narcissistic solipsism, but rather as the extension in ever new directions of [one's] capacity to care" (in Pinar, 2004, p. 246). What does it mean to participate in autobiographical reflection? Autobiographical reflection is a process of exploring the experiences that have helped to shape us and allowing these experiences to change us. It is important to process how our experiences have shaped us. Berends claims that "Everything that happens to you is your teacher. The secret is to learn to sit at the feet of your own life and be taught by it" (in Luckner & Nadler, 1997, p. 8). Imagine what it would look like to sit at the feet of our own experiences. We would begin to see the way that our experiences shape our perception and how our perception shapes our experiences. There is much to be learned from each encounter we have with new ideas, new people, and new opportunities. We need to reengage with life to live freely and explore the elemental aspects of our experiences.

It is time to return to the pathway that makes up our own and unique life course and move away from the predetermined pathways that are disseminated in modern day educational approaches. As Doll (2000) quips, we as curriculum theorists should "seek to distinguish curriculum as a 'running' rather than a course" (p. xiii). When we see curriculum as a running of a course we honor the organic qualities of lived experience and move away from more mechanized versions of our personal life journey. But, how do we engage in a type of reflection that enables us to seek out our own life journey? As Carl Frederick urges:

> Take a look at your natural river. What are you? Stop playing games with yourself. Where's your river going? Are you riding with it? Or are you rowing against it? Don't you see that there is no effort if you're riding with your river? (In Stewart, 2000, p. 58)

Fredrick asks these questions to prompt us to comprehend our role in this universe. We must figure out where our natural river is flowing and find a way to realign with it. A person who tries to "literally" answer the questions will struggle because there are not definitive answers in our life journey. Aligning with our personal river is a process that is organic and dynamic. It is through aesthetics that a person is best situated to address these questions. Aesthetics, the study of beauty, give us another lens in which we can view our life course.

Today's educational system, which is steeped in literalism, inhibits people's ability to find their "river." People's rivers become obfuscated by imposed uniformity and the carbon copy curriculum. When we are stuck in a recursive cycle of educational duplication and replication we can almost eradicate originality. As Cornel West insists, "there are too many copies, we need more originals" (PC, 2008). Think about it this way, what does a copy of a copy of a copy look like? There is a dramatic loss in quality from the original to new copies. This loss in quality also happens in a carbon copy curriculum—because so many copies have been made we have a hard time knowing what is original and what is of most importance.

Art is one way to go back to the original. Schiller (1965) reminds us of the liberative capacity associated with the arts. "Art is a daughter of freedom, and must receive her commission from the needs of spirits, not from the exigency of matter," and we "must indeed...follow the path of aesthetics, since it is through beauty that we arrive at freedom" (pp. 26–27). From an educational perspective, it is important that we understand what it is that inhibits us from "riding with our river." Next, I will explore how our worldview inhibits our connection with nature, ourselves and with others.

I have employed the metaphor of a river to illustrate the importance of finding our own life journey and tapping into the originality that makes up our unique identities. I posit that it is only through self-reflection that we can best find our own river. My notion of realigning with our personal river is similar to Pinar and Grumet's (1976) notion of *currere* (the root of the word curriculum), which is described as the running of a course. I am not arguing that there is only one "correct" way to live our lives; instead I am arguing that we must seek out a more authentic sense of self. As Doll (2000) posits:

> It is the purpose of curriculum...to engage the imagination, such that it is possible to think more metaphorically, less literalistically, about one's world and one's presuppositions about that world. (p. xi)

Engaging the imagination, thinking more metaphorically, and collaborating with others in a participatory project of reclaiming our identity is at the essence of what I refer to as an eco-curriculum for sustainability. There is an emphasis on subjectivity. Subjectivity does not necessitate isolation and disconnection. As Pinar (2004) notes, the "significance of subjectivity is that it is inseparable from the social," for "it is only when we—together and in solitude reconstruct the relations between the two can we begin to restore our 'shattered faith in the regeneration of life'" (Lasch in Pinar, 2004, p. 4). I am passionate about restoring our shattered faith in the regeneration of life, and I maintain that this restoration must begin with understanding ourselves. When we have a stronger and more genuine sense of self we are better positioned to make unique contributions to advancing ecological sustainability. The sustainability movement needs more passionate people to move it forward. If the collective will and passion of a small group of people can move a mountain, imagine what can be done to protect that mountain. Each person has a distinctive perspective that can enhance the project of making this planet more inhabitable. Curriculum studies is uniquely situated to help guide the transition from a carbon copy curriculum to a de-carbonized eco-curriculum.

The Mechanistic Worldview: Robots in the Wal-Mart Parking Lot

The myth of control that pervades today's educational model is not sustainable. The root metaphor that guides the human-nature relationship is founded on a mechanical conceptualization of life. In this section I unpack the notion of the mechanistic worldview (used synonymously with the term mechanism) and its implications. I discuss how the mechanistic worldview compromises our ability to see the environmental impacts that we generate as a human species and resultantly impairs our ability to examine curriculum and pedagogy from an ecological standpoint. Because of this mechanistically derived root metaphor, humans are "treating the earth like dirt" (Unsoeld, 1974). I argue that a majority of the destruction we have done to the planet is associated with seeing Earth and all of its life forms as machines. When we treat the earth like dirt we miss out on the many lessons that it can teach us.

The mechanistic worldview is characterized by the argument that all natural phenomena can be explained by laws of nature. When living organisms are viewed as machines, they are reduced to the status of being an "object" to be mastered. Mechanism suggests that nature can, with little effort, be controlled, measured, and modified like a machine. In the subsection title I use the phrase "robots in the Wal-Mart parking lot" to depict how mechanism has infiltrated education. Students are being treated as if they are programmable robots unable to come up with their own unique thoughts. These students are taught in ways that encourage copious consumption and many trips to Wal-Mart. The corporate influence has infiltrated our schools. Education is characterized as a top-down transmission process[9] with zero input from students. The mechanistic worldview relies on the assumption that all natural phenom-

---

9   See Parker Palmer's (1998) discussion and illustration about the objectivist myth. He argues that contemporary education operates from a top-down model in which information is fabricated from anonymous experts "who are *qualified to know* truth" (italics added, p. 101). Next, this official knowledge is "passed down [to] amateurs who are *qualified only to receive* truth" (p. 101). Palmer's objectivist myth is similar to Paulo Freire's (1970) notion of banking education in which students are treated as piggy banks and knowledge is simply deposited into them to be withdrawn from them at a later time.

ena are easily explained by deterministic laws. Nature, within the mechanistic worldview, is considered to be easily predictable, similar to the cogs in a big machine. Mechanism implies that nature is easily controllable. In this view, everything that is broken in nature is seen as something that can be fixed like a machine. A fundamental assumption of the mechanistic worldview is that we can, as humans—with our advanced technology—repair any damage that we do to the planet. We see Earth as a timepiece that we can manage. Each part of nature is reduced to an individual component of the larger machine.

Carl Jung (2001) warned that "America was at risk of being devoured by its machines" (p. 13). In other words, we are allowing the convenience of the mechanized world to take over our sense of collective and individual identity. Willi Unsoeld (1974) says that we are alienated from ourselves, others, and Earth. The energy we put into making machines is consuming us. We rely on machines to do tasks that at one point defined us. For example, we rely on the automatic bread maker to mix, knead, and cook our bread. How is this affecting us? We, as humans, are becoming more and more disconnected from the natural world. We see nature as something to be conquered and are not compelled to protect the environment. We don't care about ecological well-being when we see the natural world as a machine.

When machines do all of the work for us we are disconnected from the processes that sustain us. For example, if we never take the time to cook our own food, then we are alienated from the processes that it takes to prepare it. There is an aesthetic quality in preparing our own food—when machines do it we miss that experience. Slattery (1995) observes that mechanistic thinking heralds that the universe is "a giant clockwork mechanism" (p. 613). A clockwork mechanism is not living. We objectify the sanctity of life when we embrace a mechanistic worldview.

Viewing the world as a machine suggests a sense of power over the biosphere, implying that not only can humankind control nature but that we can change it, like we can a clock. In this context, nature is seen as a "variable to be controlled, managed, or manipulated" for the purpose of advancing economic prosperity, commercial interests, and human comfort (Slattery, 1995, p. 612). According to Rachel Carson, "The 'control of nature' is a phrase conceived in arrogance, born of the Neanderthal age of biology and the convenience of man" (Carson, 1962, p. 297). This arrogance is what has brought us to the level of ecological destruction that we currently face. We believe that we "know" what is "best" for nature and thus we attempt to create a pre-determined infrastructure in which we can manipulate and manage nature and its features. There is danger in treating the natural world like a machine. We miss out on its beauty and we lose touch with ourselves. Fritjof Capra further explores the implications of a mechanical worldview.

Capra is an educational theorist and practitioner who is well versed in the discourse about sustainability and schooling. His understanding and analysis of Rene Descartes is poignant. In particular, he discusses the Cartesian impact upon our thinking:

> To Descartes the material universe was a machine and nothing but a machine. There was no purpose, life, or spirituality in matter. Nature worked according to mechanical laws, and everything in the mechanical world could be explained in terms of the arrangement and movements of its parts. The mechanical picture of nature became the dominant paradigm in science in the period following Descartes....Descartes gave scientific thought its general framework—the view of nature as a perfect machine, governed by exact mathematical laws. (Capra, 1982, p. 60; in O'Sullivan, 1999, p. 86)

Viewing the universe as a machine has profound ontological implications. Wendell Berry (1987) considers that life founded on mechanism is not only dangerous but becomes "[evil] when [mechanism] becomes the ruling metaphor and is used to describe and to organize fundamental relationships" (p. 70). Berry recognizes the inherent danger of mechanistic thinking. Morris (2002) states that mechanistic metaphors "for human consciousness are problematic" (p. 577). She adds that "[h]uman beings are not machines and to mechanize human beings is a way to devalue the very stuff that makes us human" (p. 577). Instead of viewing life as unique and beautiful, the mechanistic worldview reduces it to a controllable enterprise that is governed by deterministic and mathematical laws.

Instead of enabling students to learn through direct experience, today's predominant education model is factory-like. It is founded on a conceptualization of schools as factories and classrooms as machinery. Within this paradigm, schools become corridors of conventionality and squares of superfluity. We must realize that the incessant whirring of machinery and the monotonies of working in a factory are now invoked upon our children. Our machine-like focus on efficiency and standards is creating fragmentation and division. Poet William Blake understood this mechanical division to be evil and described it as "Satanic wheels and Satanic mills" (in W. Berry, 1987, p. 69). This type of education is characterized as "Moving [each other] by compulsion" (p. 69). It is a curriculum of compulsion, one that fragments, emphasizes uniformity, and turns

A MATERIAL WORLD 67

intellectual development into a vacuous place for replication of the status quo.

We are inundated with hundreds of commercial messages every day. These messages urge us to buy more and suggest that consumption leads to happiness. A number of ecological thinkers maintain that the mechanistic worldview is culpable for the consumption mindedness associated with globalization (Gray-Donald & Selby, 2008). The pervasiveness of mechanistic thinking is overwhelming. Stephen Sterling (2001) notes that today's educational model is "still informed by a fundamentally mechanistic view of the world, and hence of learning" (p. 13). This mechanistic view results in "uncritically reproducing norms, fragmenting understanding...rewarding dependency and conformity, and by servicing the consumerist machine" (p. 15). It is the education-based encouragement of consumerism, dependency, and conformity that is unsustainable. It is this instantiation of a carbon copy curriculum that deepens our reliance on a fossil fuel economy. Although we may not realize it, by purchasing more stuff, we become more dependent on fossil fuels. From the production, to the packaging, and to the transportation of products the more stuff we buy, the bigger our carbon footprint becomes. A carbon copy curriculum does not just replicate previous generational education habits, but it also advances the epidemic of compulsive consumerism. This epidemic of consumerism leads to greater greenhouse gas emissions—which are integral to the carbon copy curriculum.

One consequence of the carbon copy curriculum is that we are losing our ability to identify how we as individuals are degrading the biosphere. The carbon copy curriculum advances anthropocentric thinking. Accordingly, we have on human-centered blinders that prevent us from seeing the bigger picture. Education is not embracing a holistic or ecological worldview. Instead, the focus is on advancing the industrial-minded consumer culture. Sterling (2001) posits that education is "largely ignorant of the sustainability issues that will increasingly affect all aspects of people's lives as the century progresses" (p. 13). Ultimately, education is "blind to the rise of ecological thinking which seeks to foster a more integrative awareness of the needs of people and the environment" (p. 13). The notion of integrative awareness is central to advancing dialogue grounded in sustainability theory.

Mechanical Drawbacks to Mechanistic Thinking

Mechanism leaves us with a sense of isolation from the rest of the biosphere. Pinar posits that we are informed by a corporate factory mode in which "variable organizational forms and 'knowledges' are employed for the sake of the bottom line, test scores" (Pinar, PC, November 2009). In both Pinar's and Sterling's conception, schooling is not sustainable. Arguably, the notion of servicing the consumerist machine is one of the most distinguishing characteristics of a mechanistic worldview. Servicing the consumerist machine is reductionary because it prevents us from seeing a fuller picture of our actions and thoughts.

Reductionism is rampant in the mechanistic worldview. Human thoughts and actions are reduced to computation and robotic movement. Callicott elaborates on reductionary thinking explaining that:

> Mechanism and its view of how we know things, reductionism, are informed by the idea that the world is made up of entities that are outside of and discrete from each other. The world is like a machine that can be understood by identifying, hence knowing, its constituent parts. (In Gray-Donald & Selby, 2008, p. 3)

Therefore mechanism obfuscates the uniqueness and beauty inherent to life and explains it away as something that is trivial and marketable.

The mechanistic worldview sees reductionism as cutting edge. According to Wilson, nature is organized by simple universal laws. He says,

> [Reductionism tends to] fold the laws and principles of each level of organization into those at more general, hence more fundamental levels. Its strong form is total consilience, which holds that nature is organized by simple universal laws of physics to which all other laws and principles can eventually be reduced. (Wilson in W. Berry, 2001, pp. 38–39)

From a Cartesian perspective, we are more likely to assign an attitude of indifference to machines. This form of thinking has seeped into our everyday thinking, and we miss out on the aesthetic qualities of nature. As previously mentioned, mechanism leaves people with a false sense of control over nature and all its phenomena.

Robin Good (1998) states that we have a tendency to look at "nature as an object to be controlled and manipulated so that more growth and development can occur." It follows that we base our "ecological 'solutions' on scientific, technological, and economic expertise" which "replicates and perpetuates the modern developmental paradigm" (p. 81). This developmental paradigm is what motivates us to straighten our rivers. It is for the sake of convenience and speed that we want to eliminate the curves and bends in wild rivers. Whose interest does it serve to eliminate the curves, the passages, and the pivot points from educational experience?

The short answer to this is that it really does not serve anyone's interests to eliminate the processes that enable us to become who we are.

From a short-term perspective, eliminating these processes of becoming may serve the interests of the elite, because when the natural course is obfuscated, people do not think critically. Accordingly, no one will question the hierarchy and hegemony that make up modern modes of social status and decision making. Can it be sustainable to proceed within the paradigm of mechanistic control? I would argue that it is not sustainable to proceed with the usual. A paradigm of mechanistic control erodes the capacity for individuals and groups to respond to the ecological crisis. I argue that the interest of the student is not considered within a mechanistic paradigm. Even if it is inadvertent, we are robbing our next generation from fostering a healthy sense of place, self, and community. We are compromising the strength that can surface through the process of attaining self-identity. The overemphasis on development, speed, and efficiency is a hallmark of today's industrial thinking. Perhaps this developmental paradigm can better be understood from the perspective of how we perceive different phenomena.

Capra (1982) maintains that the mechanistic worldview is at the core of our environmental crisis (p. 60). He tells us that the sustainability crisis "must be seen as just different facets of one single crisis, which is largely a crisis of perception" (in Bergea, Karlsson, Hedlune-Astrom, Jacobsson, & Luttropp, 2006, p. 1431). We are oppressed by the tunnel vision of mechanism. Instead of being able to see the "entire" picture of something, or how a phenomenon is a sub-system of a larger system, mechanistic thinking locks us into a narrow field of vision. We only see how something operates on its own, not how it is a critical part of a larger system. This crisis in perception originates within an educational realm. Similarly, David Orr (1994) states that the

> ...disordering of ecological systems and of the great bio-geochemical cycles of the earth reflects a prior disorder of thought, perception, imagination, intellectual priorities and loyalties inherent in the industrial mind. Ultimately, the ecological crisis concerns how we think and the institutions that purport to shape and refine the capacity to think. (p. 2; also in Smith & Williams, 1999, p. 28)

The crisis of perception and conception explicated by Orr and Capra is one that is promulgated in contemporary American education. It is an education that subscribes to modern notions of success that are not tenable from a perspective of cultivating critical eco-education in an era of biospheric uncertainty. It is posited that the educational commitment to mechanism is cultivated through the industrial mind. Unpacking the influence of the industrial mind is a daunting task, as its influence is far-reaching. I argue that understanding the industrial mind's influence, in relation to precipitating a "disorder of thought, perception, and imagination," is paramount to "learning our way out" (Milbrath, 1989) of the ecological and educational crises.

A number of writers discuss the ecological crisis in the context of potential human extinction (Vitousek et al., 1997; Lehman, 1998; Matheny, 2007; Ackerman, 1997). Edumund O'Sullivan (1999) tells us that "the terror here is that we have it within our power to make life extinct on this planet" (p. 6). Diane Ackerman further explores the notion of human extinction. She states, "It is possible that [humans] may become extinct, and if we do, we will not be the only species that sabotaged itself, merely the only one that could have prevented it" (in Maffi, 2001, p. 1). As Ackerman points out, we are the only (known) species capable of recognizing and circumventing extinction. Recognizing and avoiding human extinction is a delicate and pragmatic process. O'Sullivan points out that "Because of the magnitude of this responsibility for the planet, all our educational ventures must finally be judged within this order of magnitude [increasing the vitality of the biosphere]" (1999, p. 7). O'Sullivan's measurement of educational success is an important consideration in this time of apocalyptic environmental collapse. How can we reorient educational discourse to focus primarily on increasing the vitality of our biosphere? Can we refashion our educational discourse to take into account extinction patterns and the planetary climate crisis? We need to *re-wild*[10] educational discourse and restore the natural bends and curves into educational and lived experience. To help understand why we are still trying to manage and control educational experiences by focusing on testing and pre-determined content, it is important to identify the

---

[10] To re-wild educational discourse is to turn to the organic pre-industrial modes of learning and living. This is the kind of learning propounded by Mathew Fox (2006) in his discussion regarding Ancestral Wisdom Education. Fox (2006) posits that we need to embrace the elemental awe that "starts things over for us, brings us back to our origins, connects us to the beginnings, [and] makes us young again" (p. 50). It is also a form of learning similar to what Dewey (1916, 1938, 1902) proposed. Re-wilding education is returning to direct experience as a means of engaging in our learning. This is reengaging and participating in our education—not being a mere spectator. Re-wilding parallels my argument for returning one's river to its natural course. In other words, to re-wild is to return to a more ecologically intelligent way of interacting with the natural world.

paradigms that direct Western education. The ecological crisis that we face demands political and pedagogical action.

The Industrial Mind

Industrialism is affiliated with the industrial revolution. It is an economic system that is "built on large industries rather than on agriculture or craftsmanship" (industrialism, n.d.). Industrialism is built upon a selfish desire for advancing big business—it sees the world as a commodity and not a community. Industrialism is driven by mechanistic thought. Industrialism values the development of infrastructures that place economic development over the value of everything else. As I discuss later, industrialism is a paradigm that has had a large influence on American education. When I think of industrialism, I think of whirring machinery, smokestacks, and large factories surrounded by tall fences. I think of the images in Dr. Seuss's (1971) *The Lorax*, where fish are swimming in polluted streams filled with "Gluppitty-Glup...[and] Schloppity-Schlopp" (n.p.). When we recognize the level of destruction that is happening around us and how it is associated to industrial thinking, I believe that we will work towards living in ways that are more ecologically harmonious.

Humans are not designed to move at the pace of industry, but we have created an industrial system that is self-perpetuating. It perpetuates itself through the mode of rapid growth affiliated with modern conceptions of success. It is not my intent to articulate the full landscape of industrialism here; my hope is to paint its picture, using broad strokes. Bowers posits that the industrial model of production is the "most powerful cultural transforming force [in history]" (in Jucker, n.d., n.p.). It is through industrialism that the United States has become what it is today, a world superpower. But there are negative consequences associated with this success. Humans focus more on monetary gain than on the community development that existed in pre-industrial times. The forty-hour workweek has invaded our day-to-day life, and family time is taking a back seat to career time. Industrialism has leaked into our educational system (Berry, 2006).

Industrial thinking is the thinking that is aligned with industrialism relying on a mechanical paradigm. Roy Morrison (1995) tells us, "industrialism as technique is more than just the adoption of the factory system based upon mass production and facilitated by the division of labor, standardized and interchangeable parts, and specialized technologies. [It] is [ultimately] a system for maximizing production and consumption" (p.

30; p. 25). This statement makes me think about the rapid expansion of "industrial parks" in towns across America. They are the parts of a community that no one wants to live near because of the pollution from the smokestacks, the austerity, and the run-off of chemicals into the drinking water.

In a recent talk that environmental activist and green leader Majora Carter delivered at Georgia Southern University she discussed the overwhelming industrial presence that exists in Detroit, Michigan. Detroit is a great case study for people interested in studying ecological justice because of the environmental inequalities that the residents experience. Poor people in Detroit are either on the streets or live near environmental dumping sites. Carter stated that there are virtually no grocery stores in the city of Detroit—residents have to drive out of town to purchase groceries. According to Carter, there are several thousand acres of vacant lots strewn throughout the city. The lots exist because city officials wanted to easily do surveys of standing buildings, so they knocked down uninhabited buildings to ease the surveying process. A similar (but to a lesser extent) phenomenon exists in Chicago. When I think of industrialism I think of the empty residential buildings strewn throughout inner city of Chicago. When my sister lived in the Windy City I used to travel through Chicago on a fairly frequent basis to visit her. Whenever I saw the poor condition of the inner city, I experienced shock and disappointment. Industrialism perpetuates vacant living complexes and lots because the industrial emphasis places profit over people.

Industrialism is strictly aligned with increasing productivity and advancing material wealth. Thus, it emphasizes market-oriented growth over personal growth. Maximizing the industrial mind is dangerous from an educational context. Consumption-based education promulgates the "product" over the "process." This is a streamlining that places economic prosperity over humanization. Lewis Mumford refers to this industrial revolution as movement framed by the advancement of the "megamachine." Viewing life as a machine has profound implications. Again, we tend to channelize lived experience and work from the perspective of being able to control nature. Channelizing lived experience entails straightening the educational pathway for an individual. A channelized educational model is built upon pre-determination and standardization, eliminating personalization and what I refer to as ecologization. Ecologization is the work of connecting people to their place by teaching them about the relationships that sustain them. When we ecologize and personalize we recognize the fact that the world is as Alan Watts once stated "a wiggly place" (in Schubert, 2009a, p. 26). Lived experience is not something that should be nailed down and held into place. Schubert (2009a) notes that "the great mistake humans make is to try to straighten things out in order to understand them!" (p. 27). Again, we must be careful to not straighten people's life rivers—when we do, we sterilize and plasticize the texture of lived experience and insulate the student from engaging in the process of self-actualization. Channelizing people's life rivers also prevents them from connecting with their home ground and developing a strong sense of place. To put it simply, we need more green and less machine, less "megamachine."

The megamachine is the mechanized conglomerate of industrial interests that continues to grow at exponential rates. It is a collective of mechanistic-oriented discourse aimed at perpetuating "a more dehumanized system, with greater productive efficiency" (Mumford in Morrision, 1995, p. 33). Morrison comments that "industrialism is our way of life, a machine of such scope that the unindustrialized vestiges of the living world are now strange and exotic, to be confined in parks and reserves for their own protection" (1995, p. 32). He saliently adds that the industrial megamachine "is an evolving global system of interacting hierarchical orders—which include material and informational domains—that seek integration in both political and economic realms" (p. 33). The megamachine overlooks the social or ecological ramifications hidden in the rapid expansion of an economic agenda. In a world dominated by the megamachine, we attempt to nail down the wiggly-ness that characterizes lived experience.

The focus on the megamachine is referred to by Gadotti as the technozoic era, which is a reliance on technology with the belief that it has the capacity to solve all of our environmental problems without dramatic changes in human behavior. We have the mega-machinery of the Internet and the media. Megamachines are infrastructures that have the capacity to dramatically redefine how a particular idea is perceived from a collective social standpoint. Mumford adds,

> Whether organized for labor or for war this new collective mechanism [industrialism] imposed general regimentation, coerced and punished, and it limited tangible rewards largely to the dominant minority which created and controlled the megamachine. Along with this, it reduced the idea of communal autonomy and personal initiative. (Mumford in Morrision, 1995, p. 33)

The limitation of individual autonomy and threat to collective democracy that Mumford describes is at the oppressive core of industrialism. The general regimentation associated with the megamachine does not attend to the aesthetic qualities of lived experience.

In an educational context, the industrial megamachine mentality has been imported into the classroom. Mary Doll identifies today's curriculum design as "linear, preset, mechanistic, atomistic, and detached" (in Lydon, 1992, p. 69). Indeed, we are steeped in fragmented learning environments where education is based on knowledge acquisition that is "mechanical, scientific, and atomized" (Lydon, 1992, p. 68). American education is anchored in the dogmatic principles of mechanism and "honors only one way of knowing" (Lydon, 1992, p. 69). This dogmatic adherence to honoring one way of knowing obfuscates our ability to forge alternatives. We are unable to forge alternatives to the mainstream, consumption-minded, machine-like operationality associated with industrial thinking. Industrial thinking is a rigid acceptance of one idea that prevents one from seeing from any other lens.

The myopic enterprise of mechanistic education is characterized by Peter Taubman (2009) as being built upon standards and accountability. One does not have to look far, within the realm of the industrial mind, to find the ideas of standards and accountability. Standards and accountability are part of the unsustainable industrial mind. David Orr (1994) notes that the "industrial mind-set" is laden with the "assumptions convenient to industrialization" (p. 178). Orr adds that at the top of the list of assumptions convenient to industrialization is the notion that "economy ought to be the central institution of modern life" (p. 178). This is illustrated by our compulsion towards making money over building community, paycheck over happiness, and consumption over fellowship.

Because of an overemphasis on industrial thinking, human values are being consumed by the juggernaut of capitalism. Due to the perfusion of mechanism and industrialism, people are beginning to think more robotically. Plant roots are being replaced with electrical wires and circuit breakers. Subsequently we are pledging allegiance to predictability and manageability. I submit that we need to stop chopping down the wildflowers and cultivate organic patches of natural educational discovery and exploration. Emerson once stated that wildflowers are God's laughter...we need to recapture the humor that is central to living on this world and embrace a more aesthetically situated mode of educational discourse.[11] The overemphasis on industry gives way to a mechanistic worldview.

---

[11] Pinar et al. (2004) posit that the "educational possibility for curriculum theory is to help you reflect more profoundly, and not without humor on occasion, on your individual, specific situation" (p. 9). In other words, it is important to embrace a sense of humor as we pursue a more integrated eco-curriculum for sustainability.

Industrialism, Efficiency, and Mechanism

An epidemic of mechanistic thinking is hijacking our schools. Students are being treated like drones in a series of replicated drudgery. This epidemic of mechanistic thinking has started to compromise the integrity of meaningful relationships. Ecological relationships are being compromised because students are taught to see only the bottom line of the dollar sign. Communal relationships are eroding due to an emphasis on individualism and competition. Individualism occurs when we think and act as if the only thing that matters is our personal advancement. Relationships are being put aside and replaced with mechanistic structures that fragment. The danger of viewing the world as a giant machine is catalyzed by an overemphasis on efficiency.

Industrialism invokes a mechanical way of interacting with and seeing the world. According to Morrison, "The triumph of industrialism is to make individuals not just servants of the machine, but part of the machine" (1995, p. 30). Pinar notes that the argument that individuals are becoming a part of the machine is a "critique [of industrialism that] was made a century ago" (PC, November 2009). The fact that this critique still exists is a call to action, a summons for us as curriculum theorists to respond to the mechanistic over-emphasis characterized by modern day education. The residue of industrial thinking has not been cleared from the curriculum that guides today's educational institutions.

Industrialism is a crippling force that wears heavily on the human spirit. Under the influence of industrialism people lose sight of their own unique passions and particularities. Industrialism advances anonymity over autonomy and monotony over variety. In a mechanistic worldview, there is an emphasis on utilizing mechanical terms and analogies to explain how the natural world works. This is a reductionary mindset which equates life with automation. When life is seen as automatic, it is viewed more as a cog in a machine—subsequently we see the living world as a series of replaceable parts. When there is a diminishment in the value of life, all living beings are viewed as resources. But, we are not drones in a colony of conformity—what is happening? The focus on people as resources makes us treat others like things, without reverence or respect. We must stop objectifying other humans and non-humans on this planet. Yet we hold strong to a mentality of breaking down life into repairable components.

Morrison (1995) suggests that "The machine has many components. It has a biological component of people, domesticated animals and plants, and those still-wild beings defined as 'resources' to be 'harvested'" (p. 32).

What happens when we treat wild beings as resources to be harvested? Perhaps it is this colonial attitude that maintains an entrenched commitment to the mainstream form of "prosperity." Morrison notes that there also are informational components and material components to the mechanistic worldview. He states that "[the industrial worldview] material component includes the planet itself—the machine classifies all material existence as inputs to satisfy its appetites or to serve as a dump for its wastes" (p. 32). In Morrison's conception of mechanistic thinking, every living being and non-living thing on this planet can be co-opted for personal well-being and success. What are the implications of this? Within the mechanistic viewpoint, it is believed that every living thing can be explained in a mechanical form of language. This thinking is tied to efficiency.

When applied to the natural world, organic thinking takes a backseat to the stopwatch of efficiency thinking. Like mechanistic thinking, the efficiency-based paradigm is predicated on the idea that the natural world is controllable and predictable. According to Wals (2007) this worldview is a primary contributor to today's patterns of unsustainability. He says, "A deeply embedded mechanistic worldview lies behind the global mega-crisis while efforts to realize a sustainable world are themselves hampered by our inability to remove residues of mechanism from our sustainability proposals" (p. 23). Mechanism is viewed as the most efficacious worldview and is thus handed down from one generation to the next.

Mechanism and Management

The pervasion of mechanistic discourse into Western lifestyle has also led to a managerialist mentality. Steen (2008) notes that "[m]echanism refers to understanding through compartmentalization and using an empirical or objectivist approach to make sense of isolated information" (p. 230). Making sense of isolated information is one of mechanism's hallmarks. How does this fragmentary approach impact our discourse? It advances agendas steeped in consumerism, management, and control. Vandana Shiva (2008) states that "[m]ost of the discussions and negotiations [surrounding the environment] have been restricted to the commercial, consumption-oriented energy paradigm rooted in a reductive, mechanistic worldview and consumerist culture" (p. 4). Mechanism pervades our curriculum and our research. According to Selby (2008), the "mechanistic worldview has dominated western culture for three hundred years" (p. 71). It has pervaded our discourse for so long we struggle to see beyond it.

Wals (2007) adds that "we are straitjacketed by our failure to see, let alone address, mechanism within our thought processes" (p. 23). There is an illusion of order and management-based predictability embedded within the mechanistic worldview.

Shiva (2008) points out that "[playing with nature] as if she were a LEGO set cannot be the appropriate response at a time when human intervention in Earth's living systems is threatening our very survival. The mechanical mind cannot solve the problems of the mechanical age" (p. 33). This is an important point that Shiva makes, as we cannot solve our current set of problems with an outdated mode of thinking. If we continue to address our problems in the same way, we will continue to get what we have already gotten.

The mechanistic worldview hijacks ecological thinking and perpetuates a fear of the unpredictable. It has led to a new form of management.

Understanding the Social Efficiency Movement

> Replicating the ideology of the industrial model of production, modern education...trains teachers to optimize and maximize student "output"; this, in turn, requires maximizing "time on task" so that students—as production units—can learn in the most efficient and productive manner.
>
> Clark in *Sustainable Living and Learning: The Connection Among Paradigms, Educational Theories, and Praxis*

One of the most prevalent areas of focus for modern education is efficiency. By understanding the Westernized focus on efficiency we are better able to comprehend its impact on the environment. What are the implications of promoting efficiency for efficiency's sake? I posit that these implications are far-reaching. In the context of education there is an overreliance on efficiency mindedness that has grown with industrialism and mechanistic thinking. Throughout the twentieth century, a variety of forces affected change within the American educational landscape. One of the greatest forces was that of the industrial revolution. A shift to models of production based on high efficiency pervaded the economic landscape. This idea of increasing efficiency caught on quickly. Subsequently, the emphasis on efficiency was transferred to schools (Spring, 1986; Franklin, 1999; Slattery, 1995). These educational changes profoundly impacted the human-Earth relationship and precipitated more environmental degradation (W. Berry, 1989). In this section, I explore the implications of social efficiency in terms of advancing intellectual curiosity, evoking a common sense of decency, and promoting ecological sustainability.

Industrial thinking has taken the place of more organically derived thinking models. Experts have been consulted to work on the task of identifying and eliminating "wasted time" in the educational system. The elimination of wasted time equates to removing the bends and curves in a wild river. Efficiency is a straightening of educational experience with the goal of accelerating learning and measuring it more effectively. This emphasis on speed and measurement is part of the carbon copy curriculum. A rigid adherence to what has already been established and an allegiance to pre-existing modes of thinking have led to the overemphasis on efficiency and productivity.

Within the social efficiency framework, the impetus of schooling is structured around improving student productivity and meeting the need for efficiency. Understanding the history and the ideas associated with social efficiency helps us to understand unsustainability within an educational framework. Accordingly, I argue that the Tylerian Rationale is unsustainable from the perspective of advancing scholarship and ecological revitalization. In this section, I explore the origins of the social efficiency movement and unpack its impact in relation to ecological sustainability. Also, I present an argument that social efficiency is an aspect of what I refer to as a carbon copy curriculum.

Social efficiency is founded on the notion that there should be no wasted time in the educational context. Casas (2003) notes that social efficiency was put into action with the belief that "exact measurement and precise standards" were hallmarks of efficiency (p. 2). Unfortunately, from the perspective of efficiency it is usually considered a waste of time to undergo an experience such as watching a sunset, creating art, or exploring nature. I agree with Mahatma Gandhi on his thought that "[t]here is more to life than increasing its speed" (in Dean, 1995, p. 98). I believe that optimal education takes time. To promote sustainability, teachers should cultivate an educational atmosphere that encourages inquiry and exploration. Education needs to be contextualized and related to a student's life. In contrast, an overemphasis on "exact measurement" neglects the nuances associated with experiential learning (Dewey, 1938). In this sense, the current modality of social efficiency is not a sustainable form of schooling. Supporters believe that social efficiency "promotes social stability in the face of the increasing demands for social change" and contributes to the maintenance of an orderly and predictable world (p. 2).

The primary focus within the social efficiency paradigm is that of building a "product" that is ready to be delivered to the working world. Within this framework, the student, upon graduation, is considered to be the product. Cubberley observes that, "Our schools are, in a sense, factories in which the raw products (children) are to be shaped and fashioned into products to meet the various demands of life" (in W. Doll, 1993, p. 47). Education becomes a de-humanizing enterprise when it focuses solely on creating a product. This product-orientation is another feature of the carbon copy curriculum. It is a factory model that is unfortunately most common within modern day education. Pinar (2009b) observes that "Almost 50 years now into school deform—the conversion of academic institutions into businesses obsessed with 'outputs,' [results in] teachers [being] downgraded to bureaucrats managing 'learning'" (p. ix). He continues, saying that learning itself has become "reduced to test taking" (p. ix). The reduction of learning to a mere test score and of academic institutions into businesses focused solely on output is not equipping students to adequately face the ecological crisis. We are failing to foster intellectual curiosity and environmental awareness. This failure is attributed to the irrelevant and irreverent forms of education that we see today. It is simply reproducing the dominant paradigm of student as a passive recipient of knowledge and as an active consumer of the marketplace.

The carbon copy curriculum is characterized by the tendency to duplicate existing models of industrially grounded education that perpetuates our heavy consumption habits. In this sense, a carbon copy curriculum not only replicates outdated and inadequate educational models, but also magnifies our carbon footprint and undermines the delicate, life sustaining balance provided by our biosphere. Our carbon footprint continues to propagate in an educational climate that is married to a conventional conception of wealth. This is material wealth, the kind that can be measured through bank accounts, number of vehicles, and in the square footage of one's living quarters. From an educational context, when material wealth is given greatest value, we fall into what Orr (2009) refers to as the "carbon trap" (p. x).

The carbon trap is a problem linked to the "ignorance of our impact on the biogeochemical cycles of Earth" (Orr, 2009, p. x). We are generally unaware of how anthropogenic consumption, production, and waste are destroying the planet. This lack of awareness is a result of the carbon copy curriculum. Our educational systems contribute to the human-centered thinking that is ravishing the planet. This contribution is associated with perpetuating a business-as-usual educational approach. Orr adds that "[h]uman actions have set in motion a radical disruption of the biophysical systems of the planet that will undermine the human prospect, perhaps for centuries" (p. 17). We have severed the human-

Earth relationship and we struggle to understand the consequences of this disconnect. It is a phenomenon linked to the arrogant irreverence and ecologically desensitized attitude handed down from previous generations. Earth's capacity to absorb the gradually rising carbon footprint is diminishing (Lynas, 2008). We are like the proverbial frog in a pot of water. A frog sitting in a pot of room temperature water that is gradually being heated up does not recognize the subtle increase in temperature. When the pot reaches boiling point, it is too late and the frog will get cooked. As humans on a planet that is gradually being warmed, we are unaware of the slow but deadly increase in temperatures and ecological disequilibrium. It is time to leap to action, but first we should work to free ourselves and dismantle the trap.

The carbon trap is a trap that at one point, when our population was less and we relied on wind and sunlight to meet our energy needs, "posed no serious problems" (Orr, 2009, p. x). However, now, with a world population of well of over 6.5 billion people (and growing), we have far exceeded the sustainable level of carbon emissions. In the United States and throughout the world, a majority of carbon emissions comes from generating electricity. Over half of the energy produced in the U.S. is generated from burning coal (Environmental Protection Agency, 1997).

Lynas (2008) explains that the coal burned to create electricity "is a larger contributor to greenhouse gas emissions than oil" (p. 293). Every time we flip a light switch or turn up our thermostats we contribute to the carbon problem. There is a direct link between burning coal and carbon pollution. Orr (2009) points out that we are living "carbon-intensive lives" with consumption habits that well exceed any of our previous generations' (p. x). Yet, there is still hope in the midst of this carbon crisis. It will take a great deal of innovative, imaginative, determined, and forward-thinking leadership to reverse this anthropogenic juggernaut, but I believe that we have the capacity to overcome and transform our carbon heavy consumption habits. As Capra (1996) once suggested, after several breakdowns we are likely to have a breakthrough. In this sense we have experienced a number of biospheric breakdowns. As articulated by the National Science and Technology Council, these breakdowns include: rising sea levels (up to 20 feet), hotter temperatures (especially in northern latitudes), more drought, compromised marine ecosystems (due to higher water temperatures), and a major loss in biological diversity (National Science & Technology Council in Orr, 2009, p. 18). Calamitous events, environmental hazards, and breakdowns like these urge us forward towards educational transformation. We are well situated for some breakthroughs. We have to be attentive to the current of creative energy that pulses from the ecological jeopardy that we face. A carbon copy curriculum does not provide room for a breakthrough; instead, it is weighted down by uniformity and conformity.

The social efficiency model that I describe in this chapter is a great example of the carbon copy curriculum. Instead of helping a student to actualize his or her potentialities, the social efficiency approach is oriented towards making the student fit a pre-existing mold and preparing him or her for the work world. It is this reliance on what has already been created that is unsustainable. Students are not being equipped to think critically about how their participation in carbon intensive lifestyles affects the living world. We subdue the vision and dreams of the next generation by stuffing irrelevant and fragmentary information into their heads. Today's educational model is built upon the premise that a fat bank account is the ultimate goal of our life journey. Accordingly, in this model, students are strongly encouraged to view material wealth as the highest good attainable.

Why does homogenous curriculum have so much of an appeal? It is much easier to "manage" when every student is doing the same thing. The problem is that we continue to educate in a way that is noncontextualized. We draw from standardized curriculum. Our content and pedagogy is typically produced and fabricated in faraway places that are disassociated with the beauty of our unique bioregions. Thus, the topomorphology of our curriculum is not diverse. That is, curriculum is predominately amorphous or "a-topographic." If there is a particular shape to a standardized curriculum it is only able to be adequately grounded in one region. This is unfortunate because when curriculum is myopic it is not sustainable. I believe that this curricular myopia exists because it would take too much time, work, and resources to create a different text for every bioregion. This, I argue, is the job of a good teacher. I propose that teachers need to be experts at situating their pedagogy and curriculum into their particular bioregion.

Management and Activity Analysis

Franklin Bobbitt explored activity analysis, which is a "procedure by which life's activities were analyzed in minute detail" (Schubert et al., 2002, p. 22). These methods complement Taylor's efficiency studies by enhancing the use of classroom time. Yet the downside to these analyses is less student-teacher time. This method is a reflection of the power wielded within the "scientific and technological approach" which determines the content and methods within schools. The time management approach enhances classroom efficiency via the emphasis upon "observable [and] practical consequences" (Schubert et al., 2002, p. 23). This managerial and scientific curriculum approach became situated at the forefront of curriculum and pedagogy. Social efficiency experts pushed for a curriculum that was viewed as an "assembly line by which *economically and socially useful citizens* would be produced" (emphasis added, Schubert et al., 2002, p. 95). This assembly line approach exemplifies Taylorism. Joel Spring notes that "Taylor believed that the basic problems of American industry stemmed from unsystematic organization and control of work. He argued that scientific study could determine the proper method for doing every job" (Spring, 1986, p. 231). Taylor's allegiance to scientific study generated an inadequate positivistic and instrumentalist education model.

Essentially, Taylor and Bobbitt's notion of scientific management held that the utilization of a controlled and planned work environment would result in a more "streamlined schooling process" (Spring, 1986, p. 231). It is an allegiance to micro and macro management that is grounded in utility. Unfortunately there was a movement to "transfer his ideas regarding the management of factories to the management of schools" (Casas, 2003, p. 5). Subsequently, social utility "became the sole value by which the curriculum would be judged" (Kliebard in Pinar et al., 2004, pp. 95–96). It is dangerous to dogmatically subscribe to a single, one-size-fits-all educational approach.

By evaluating curriculum effectiveness on the narrow-minded measurement of social utility, we miss the consideration of the environment, future generations, and our limited natural resource base. Education for social utility is not a sustainable form of education. It emphasizes corporate interests over the interests of the student. Education that is solely committed to *preparing one for adulthood* neglects the innate curiosity associated with childhood and stifles the creative capacity of the learner. Accordingly, social efficiency does not encourage a student to investigate and explore his or her own passions. It is what makes schooling such a grueling and tedious process grounded in extrinsic motivation, and ultimately it makes the quest of learning *official knowledge* unsustainable.

Today's teachers are moving further from the eco-contextualization process as they are inundated with messages of uniformity and threatened by tracking and surveillance. These messages come in the form of state- and nationally mandated "standards." It is getting much harder to educate in a way that honors our place. We struggle against the anonymous topography of uniform curriculum. In this sense, we move even further from being transformative educators and closer to "experience pirates" who steal the possibility for students to encounter their lived experiences and the curriculum associated with a "hands on" and "minds on" modality. Students who are exposed to uniform and boring curriculum feel lost in the crowd. Students are unable to learn in an optimal way because they feel anxious[12] and disconnected (Pool, 1997; Caine et al., 2004; Goleman, 2003, 1995).

The movement towards "saving time" has contributed to what has been referred to as the *quickening*. The quickening is a movement towards speeding up our lives in a way that gets things done faster (Price, 2009). However, it is argued that this frenetic pace of life is not sustainable (Price, 2009). Taylor's work provided "methodological guidance" for the social-efficiency movement through his theory of scientific management (Pinar et al., 2004, p. 95). His theory was "predicated upon economic practice, more specifically the structure of the workplace" (p. 95). The ripples of Taylor's social efficiency are far-reaching. His actions reduced education to a mechanically conceived enterprise emphasizing control and reproduction which is grounded in a factory worker modality.

From Craftsmen to Factory Workers

Taylor's work was influential in shifting labor from a nineteenth-century focus on craft guilds to a factory model. Professional labor became more of a science than an art. The craft guild emphasis required a "master craftsman who taught apprentices his knowledge of the total production process" (Pinar et al., 2004, p. 95). No longer were craftsmen needed, so they were replaced by the industrial craftiness of pre-made molds and jigs. This craftsmanship emphasis was replaced by a large factory emphasis. In the factory model, labor became "specialized and routinized" (p. 95). The social efficiency doctrine deemphasized the notion of craftsmanship and replaced it with the "importance of specialization and expertise in the new large-scale organizations" (Spring, 1986, p. 199). Craftsmanship is described by art historian Beth Carver (2004) as the ability to craft an item that is either functional or decorative.

---

12 For a more in-depth discussion about the impact of educational environments that compromise a student's ability to learn, see the conversation about "downshifting" in Pool (1997), "orchestrated immersion" in Caine, Caine, McClintic, and Klimek (2004), and emotional hijacking in Goleman (1995, 2003).

The products of craftsmen were made with quality and beauty. The craftsmen were also referred to artisans, who were skilled manual workers who craft items such as furniture, tools, household items, clothing, food products, etc. (Knox, n.d). In the early 1900s factory production had taken the beauty and unique craftsmanship away from items that were mass produced (Spring, 1986). The shift from craftsmanship to specialization suggested that efficiency was enhanced when each person is trained to focus on a "single individual task" (Spring, 1986, p. 200). For educators, specialization meant education of the student for a particular occupation. Education that is designed to sort students into pre-determined occupations is a nightmare. It is as if students are puppets controlled by the needs of industry. No longer is a democratic education favored in specialized training. The focus shifts to getting students skilled in doing a particular job. What does this do to their passion, wonder, curiosity, and souls? How can a student recover his sense of self in an anonymous setting grounded in a mind-numbing, reproductive, educational agenda?

Control and Speed

We compromise ecological health when we operate from a paradigm of control and speed. We also compromise psychological, physical, and spiritual health. The way that we may compromise ecological well-being—through an overemphasis on order and predictability—is addressed by the craftsman Richard Sennett. Sennett suggests that in today's efficiency-minded society we are obsessed with speed. He states, "When people are forced to do things quickly it becomes a type of triage. In the process of working very fast, we don't have the time for reflection and being self-critical. We tend to go into autopilot and mistakes increase" (in Ramljak, 2010, n.p.). An example of an ecological mistake that we can make because of our frenetic lifestyle is to overlook the environmental impact of our incessant drive for material consumption. We fail to notice the ramifications of staying inside all day every day. By overlooking the ecological consequences of what we do, we cut ourselves off from the natural world, unable to see the effects of our consumption patterns.

We are speeding up the natural rhythms that drive our biosphere. We are not only speeding up but also heating up the planet. Also, we are overcrowding the planet. The human population is well beyond Earth's carrying capacity. It has been estimated that if everyone in the world lived as Americans do, we would need four Earths (Wackernagel & Rees, 1996). We lack sensitivity, awareness, and attentiveness to this because we are enamored in a culture of speed. We see myopically through the lens of efficiency and are no longer in tune with how our actions are impacting bioregional and biospheric health. From an educational perspective, we simply march forward wearing our blinders.

Through exploring social efficiency, industrialism, and mechanistic thinking we begin to have a clearer picture of the unsustainable elements that compose a "carbon copy" education. It is this tendency to rely on outdated forms of curriculum and pedagogy that illustrates the inadequacy of today's carbon copy curriculum to address the ecological crisis. As Orr laments, the "carbon trap has sprung" (Orr, 2009). We must realize the level of impact that our outdated educational model has in generating even more habits of consumption. The response to this crisis must begin with understanding.

Analysis of the Social Efficiency Movement

Perhaps social efficiency is an effort to build a monoculture of thought (Shiva, 1993). Several notable writers and activists have countered the notion of the social efficiency doctrine (Counts, 1930; Orr, 1994; Sterling, 2001; Dewey, 1902, 1916, 1938). These authors insist that it is crucial to look beyond the idea of efficiency and to recognize other valuable educational aims. Slattery (2009) notes that in the early 1970s there was a movement in the "field of curriculum studies [which] began to shift the focus of curriculum from scientific management and the Tylerian Rationale to a process of understanding curriculum as an interdisciplinary study of educational experience" (p. 17). The "reconceptualization" was an epochal shift in curriculum studies discourse and was led by Pinar (1978) and Madeleine Grumet. The movement precipitated a dramatic re-thinking of curriculum and pedagogy. From a standpoint of sustainability, this re-thinking of education gains significant traction. When we look at curriculum studies as an interdisciplinary field we start to change our perception about how we should teach. We realize that there is intrinsic value to lived experience, and we begin to serve the interest of the students and sometimes the biosphere. Ultimately, we need to consider how to convert to an eco-curriculum—a form of education that is holistic and eco-centric. Due to an overemphasis on production and meeting the needs of the industrial paradigm, the social efficiency paradigm is not sustainable.

Regarding the function of education, Bobbitt declares that it "is primarily for adult life, not for child life... [Education's] fundamental responsibility is to prepare [children] for the fifty years of adulthood, not for the twenty years of childhood and youth" (quoted in Kliebard, 1995, p. 104). Dewey counters this argument and states that education designed to prepare children for their adult lives is dangerous. He maintains that the principle of preparation alienates children's energies and separates youth from the potentiality of the present. I agree with Dewey in that we need to consider how we can reach children wherever they are in their life journey. This may include providing learning experiences that cultivate compassion for one another and build the student's capacity to work with others in a variety of future situations, not just for future work environments.

George Counts (1930) warns that the industrial educational model contributes to a homogenous social structure. He states that "industrialism has made possible...the fashioning of an entire people after a single pattern" (p. 122). He suggests that it is becoming more and more common for Americans to eat the same food, don the same clothes, "play the same games, see the same sights, discuss the same thoughts, and laugh at the same jokes" (p. 122). This uniformity in human experience is scary. It is a form of experiential eugenics that sets out to eliminate experiences that do not align with socialized conceptions of success, progress, and prosperity. Industrialism is like fast food because it fills our educational gaps with low nourishment and high fat. Industrialism creates a sense of fullness but is empty from a nutritional perspective. Educational industrialism is fast food that has identical tastes, appearance, and smells throughout the world. When we make education standardized, we liquidate subjectivity and strengthen homogeneity. Counts (1930) warns against an education that encourages anonymity over individuality.

The social efficiency movement promulgates education as transmission. Education as transmission means to "deliver" information in pristine condition to a student, who is told to memorize it and show that she kept it pristine by giving it back in the same format and structure. This transmission process is similar to the way that our radios pick up signals from a radio station—there is no direct connection to the listener/student, and the content is preset and not adapted to the particular learning situation, time, or place. This transmissive model is structured in a top-down fashion. At the top, experts develop and create the curricula and then pass it down to the teachers. This predetermined curriculum approach accommodates the "education towards adulthood" model. It does not meet students where they are; instead it serves a preparatory function.

Social efficiency is an *unsustainable* form of education founded on a top-down knowledge transmission model. Instead of facilitating the transformative thinking associated with sustainability education, social efficiency advances a pre-determined mechanistic educational approach with an emphasis on extrinsic motivation. In this case teachers are not allowed to modify the curriculum; alternatively teachers are forced to deposit this expert-derived information into their students. Later, students are expected to recite this information without modifying it. Paulo Freire (1970) refers to this *learning as transaction* process as the educational banking model. This model is considered efficient, based on its uniformity and measurability. The efficiency movement places the greatest value in transmission of information over the organic development of student knowledge.

Although Bobbitt once maintained that social efficiency was a good approach to education, he later switched his view. Near the end of his career, Bobbitt surprisingly stated that education should not be designed to merely "prepare [children] for life at some future time"; instead he contended that it is quite the opposite; "it purposes to hold high the current living....Life cannot be 'prepared for.' It can only be lived" (quoted in Kliebard, 1995, p. 157). This notion of "living" over "preparation" is vital to an eco-curriculum. It is our experientially derived knowledge that is most potent in the landscape of our lived experience. It is refreshing to see Bobbitt's transformation into a more humanistic conception of education. Counts (1930) extended Bobbitt's refute of the social efficiency movement. He stated that it is "efficiency without purpose, an efficiency of motion" (quoted in Kliebard, 1995, p. 162). Counts critiqued the scientific curriculum-making effort associated with the social efficiency model. He believed that the curriculum experts would "reflect dominant interests in American culture" and that this would lead to the status quo being preserved (Kliebard, 1995, p. 162). Counts warned that the "inevitable consequence is that the school will become an instrument for the perpetuation of the existing social order rather than a creative force in society" (in Kliebard, 1995, p. 162). Counts also expressed a strong disapproval of the movement towards standardized testing, referring to it as "an archaic program of instruction" (in Kliebard, 1995, p. 158).

Counts (1978) proposed a counter narrative to the predominant mode of scientific curriculum making. He postulated that schools have the capacity to transform society instead of simply replicating and controlling it. This transformation would involve a complicated, but feasible, process of democratizing the educational conversation (Aubrey, 1984). Counts noted that the rapidly changing world needed schools oriented towards transformation instead of replication. He urged educators to participate "actively in the task of reconstituting the democratic tradition and of thus working positively toward a new society" (Counts, 2009).

Counts recognized the peril that was perpetuated through nondemocratic education and argued that changes had to be made. Counts believed that "not merely more education, but a certain kind of education" is the "foundation of all hope in meeting the danger today" (Cottrell, 1964, p. 238). He is referring to a kind of education that challenges the "development of the totalitarian mind" (p. 238). Ultimately, according to Counts, it will take a "positive education for freedom...to 'prepare for this test of popular liberty'...[this kind of education] 'should be the active purpose of American education'" (Counts in Cottrell, 1964, p. 238). I would like to add ecology to Counts' conception of the active purpose of American education. We need a transformative shift in thinking that embraces the principles of sustainability. How can Counts contribute to this shift in thinking? It is in his progressive vision of democratic transformation. He calls for "a certain kind of education"—an education that gives us a hope in meeting the dangers and challenges of today's ecological crisis. When we pull from Counts, we can draw inspiration and guidance in our effort to infuse sustainability into the integrality of educational experience.

Counts' observation of the interrelatedness between the political and the pedagogical is important. He argues that they are inextricable. From a standpoint of cultivating a more sustainable world, his argument is even more salient. It is important to note that the institution of education is just one element of generating sustainability. But as Counts points out, educational institutions can help challenge the dogmatism affiliated with totalitarian thinking.

In Dewey's book entitled *The Way Out of Educational Confusion* (1931) he discusses the social efficiency model. He suggests that the traditional classroom model situates students "at the end of a pipeline receiving material conducted from a distant reservoir of learning" (p. 34). This is a clever way to describe the anonymous "origins" of the curriculum that is imposed on children within the modern education model. Visually, the notion of being at the end of a pipeline resonates with our dependency on oil. From a consumerist perspective, we rarely know what resources were used to make the products that we purchase. We are conditioned to passively purchase items despite their eco-footprints. In many cases, we purchase items that deplete our supplies of nonrenewable resources. One example is our dependence on foreign oil to fuel the transport of the products we purchase. Without oil shipped from a distant land, today's economic system would crumble.

Carbon copy curriculum perpetuates the dependence on fossil fuels. We are disconnected from the source of our fossil fuels, and we are disconnected from the origin of the "official knowledge" that is taught in formal educational environments. Accordingly, we develop a stronger dependence on external knowledge and diminish our ability to learn through direct experience. We become even more reliant on others for our well-being and our interests disappear in the fragmented curriculum. Dewey insists that specialization and subject fragmentation lead to mis-educative experiences. He defines mis-educative experiences as those that inhibit intellectual growth and curiosity. Dewey (1931) believes that the active scholar does not isolate himself in one field. Instead, he claims that each experience is potential "grist for the [intellectual] mill" and that it is essential to not limit the "supply of grain to any one fenced off field" (p. 34). Dewey encourages us to expand our epistemological traditions and embrace a more holistic educational framework. The reconceptualization also plays an important part of expanding our epistemological traditions.

The reconceptualization of curriculum studies forged an interdisciplinary approach to understanding curriculum. It moved beyond the social efficiency educational paradigm and the entrenched focus of skill and drill while opening up alternative pathways for educational practitioners and theorists. Triche (2002) observes that the reconceptualization leads to a dramatic paradigm change where

> [C]urriculum theorists have the responsibility to inform everyone engaging in education that the practices associated with efficiently implementing bureaucratically determined educational objectives and activities are not the only possible curriculum practices. (p. 32)

As curriculum theorists, we have a unique opportunity to cross disciplinary boundaries to respond in pragmatic ways to the ecological crisis. We are in a position to forge alternative educational paradigms and possibilities. No longer are we to be married to the narrow-minded thinking associated with the carbon copy curriculum. We are at a turning point in the curriculum meta-narrative in which we can begin to embrace a more ecological form of theory and practice. It is an eco-curriculum in which sustainability is a "common democratic project" (Carlson, 1998) infused into educational praxis. It is the job of the reconceptualists to enable education to move beyond the "educational nightmare" (Pinar, 2004) that characterizes today's efficiency-based educational approaches.

It is important that we avoid the "miseducation" that happens in a mechanistic and managerial educational framework. Students begin to hate going to school when they are inundated with pre-determined curriculum and pedagogy. As Mathew Fox (2006) states,

> The problem and crisis that education lays before us is this: "miseducation" is as possible as good education. Miseducation is education that fails to educe, to lead out of individuals their best and noblest capacities—our capacities for joy and wonder; awe and sharing; biophilia, justice, and compassion. (p. 27)

When education fails to "educe" it no longer draws out the highest possibilities from the student and the teacher. Education that fails to *educe* has a lifeless and robotic quality that facilitates the extrinsic monotony experienced by the factory worker. Thus, factory-based, social efficiency-oriented education is not sustainable from an ecological perspective and from the perspective of advancing wonder, joy, curiosity, and compassion.

Implications of Social Efficiency Pertaining to Sustainability

From the standpoint of sustainability, there are a number of problems within the social efficiency framework. First of all, the focus on preparing children for their adult life reduces the significance of their developmental continuity. In a social efficiency model, students are not encouraged to have their own experiences. Instead, efficiency-based education is based on promulgating a pre-determined set of knowledge measured solely by written tests. It is an outcome-oriented measurement not a process-based assessment. Students are not given the space to develop in an experiential way; they are instead told how to develop within the confines of a plasticized, culturally acceptable manner.

Social activist Jane Addams argued for the importance of experience stating that "education was as broad as experience itself...education was experience" (Pinar, 2009b, p. 71). Within the social efficiency-infused carbon copy curriculum model students are expected to learn by the memorization and conformity that characterize Western education. They are missing out on cultivating their unique set of strengths and interests.

In the carbon copy curriculum, students are taught in fragmented and specialized ways. This specialization does not encourage the growth of critical thinking skills and it prevents students from seeing the interconnectivity between nature and man. Orr (2004) says "It is logical that the drive for standardization and uniformity might someday impose a grid-like pattern to the ecology of our minds until we are permitted to have no thoughts without right angles" (p. 84). It is the thoughts that are built solely upon "right angles" that compromise our ability to think in ways that are innovative. William Ayers urges that we "see people as whole...not as flattened out pieces of data." Instead, we must see students as "three dimensional people" (Ayers, 2009). In order to see students as whole humans, we must get rid of the social efficiency paradigm and its tendency to convert students into numbers. Social efficiency approaches prevent educators from positing relevant, sustainable, and progressive pedagogical frameworks for social transformation.

Wendell Berry (1989, p. 137) discusses the urgent need for a shift in business as usual. He indicates that we have no choice but to act upon the current environmental crisis in a collective fashion. We are called to collaborate with others in order to avert Earth's destruction. It is critical that we gather in solidarity with all nations to build an even stronger response to the anthropogenic environmental degradation which characterizes business as usual. We must not forget that ecological integrity is central to human well-being. When ecological systems are thrown out of balance because of threats such as climate change, there is what I call an "ecological boomerang." Ecological boomerangs are environmental responses that "come back" to humanity due to some form of anthropogenic threat to the environment.

The implications of adopting a social-efficiency oriented approach to curriculum and pedagogy are far-reaching. Not only do corporate and industrial interests overtake the interests of the student, but pre-existing structures of hegemonic power are reproduced. The reproduction of existing social structures perpetuates environmental degradation (Orr, 1994). Thus, it is important that educational theorists and practitioners understand the impact of the social efficiency paradigm from the perspective of sustainability and social solidarity. A further exploration of sustainability and sustainability education is found in the next chapter.

Unsustainable Education

Instead of working towards sustainability, contemporary education is "linked in policy and practice to the narrative of economic globalization" (Gruenewald & Smith, 2008, p. xiv). Schools today are turning towards the global marketplace for guidance. Ecologist Tom Wessels (2006) refers to this economically derived measurement of success as the myth of progress. Wessels predicts that "at some point economic expansion will outstrip both the availability of resources and the ability of Earth to absorb the waste products generated by this growth" (p. xix). This overconsumption is predicted to lead to an "ecological overshoot" (Meadows, 1972) in which humans exhaust all natural resources while attempting to achieve the myth of progress.

The juggernaut of globalization "powers" educational discourse and aligns education with meeting economically derived commercial interests. Gray-Donald and Selby (2008) explain that "a range of critics of the mechanistic worldview have argued that its omnipresence lies at the roots of the global ecological crisis and parallel and connected crises in the social, economic, cultural and personal spheres within human society" (p. 3). The impact of the mechanistic worldview is staggering. From the perspective of globalization, mechanization serves as the lynchpin for its propagation. Stephen Sterling (2004a) adds that from a curricular perspective "the purposes or objectives of...education largely fails to take into account sustainability, while undesirable side-effects include widespread ecological illiteracy and its consequences" (p. 53). Today's corporate interests are placed above making the planet more sustainable and subsequently trump the interests of promoting humanity, thus curriculum is geared towards the reproduction of a monoculture of consumerism.

Dewey (1933) refers to this drive for consumerism as the *acquisitive society*. According to Dewey "personal acquisition" has "taken possession of the minds of educators to the extent" that it controls "the whole educational system" (Dewey, 1933). Schubert (2006) explains that Dewey's conceptualization of the acquisitive society involves an "attitude of acquisition—the capitalistic ethos," an ethos that "penetrates our being in ways we scarcely realize" (p. 82). Dewey's conception of the acquisitive society recognizes that we tend to "transform everything we do into things that we accumulate" (Schubert, PC, 2009). He adds that in this framework "education is not seen as edification" or pursuing one's interests. It is instead, he suggests, reified "test scores and GPA" (PC, 2009). When education is most concerned with the things that one acquires it overlooks the impact that these acquisitions have on the biosphere. By overlooking the impact that our actions have on Earth, acquisitive society's myopia is advancing environmental degradation. From the context of higher education and sustainability, Orr (1994) suggests that it is those with PhDs who are contributing the most to the ecological crisis. More of the same type of education simply reproduces the errors (in thought and action) of prior generations. The generational duplication of the acquisitive society is what advances the ecological crisis that we face.

Peter Taubman (2009) adds that the "transformation that has proceeded under the twin banners of 'standards' and 'accountability' has over the last decade profoundly affected all aspects of teaching, schooling, and teacher education in the United States," and now it "threatens public education itself" (p. 12). It is this type of education that has "moved at remarkable speed" (p. 12). The acceleration of standards and accountability leave many children behind. The feverish need for speed forces us to overlook the importance of developing epistemological diversity. That is, an ecologically conceived worldview that enables us to think and act within the "pattern that connects" (Bateson, 1972). The pattern that connects is the series of relationships that compromise our eco-sphere. This pattern includes the way that we view and respond to the eco-crisis. Accordingly, our overemphasis on speed, in the educational arena, has led to an even greater separation between humans and nature. Students become more comfortable being indoors than they are outside. They lose touch with the enchantment of nature from the perspective of eco-destruction; "[t]oday, our schools are further behind than they were 25 years ago—even though we've doubled education spending over the last several decades" (Michael Bloomberg, NYC mayor, in Taubman, 2009, p. 30).

Mihelcic (2008) writes that "Issues such as population growth, climate change & variability, rising consumption, loss of biodiversity, and freshwater depletion [and associated water scarcity] are clearly recognized as major environmental challenges" (p. 1). These issues point to "one fundamental aspect of sustainability, that is, the economic and social well-being of every citizen and Nation is dependent on the health of the environment" (Mihelcic, 2008, p. 1). When we are disconnected from the natural world we are uprooted. This uprootedness and lack of connection is closely tied to the large ecological footprint that each human has in modern society. When uprooted, we lose the ability to comprehend our sizeable eco-footprint. Thus, we forget that Earth is the number one source of our sustenance. We lose touch with our ability to relate to place. John Daniel (2007) adds that "[o]ur rootlessness—our refusal to accept the discipline of living as responsive and responsible members of neighborhoods, communities, landscapes, and ecosystems—is perhaps our most serious and widespread disease" (p. 160). Resultantly, we continue to destroy our natural world by narrowly adhering to an anthropocentric viewpoint. Accordingly, Derrick Jensen (2008) asserts that "We are in the midst of an apocalypse" and adds that "this culture is killing the planet" (p. 9). Attempting to subvert this ecological crisis and potentially apocalyptic trajectory is not an easy task. Orr laments that "[t]he overwhelming fact is that virtually all important ecological indicators are in decline" (2003, p. 348). The increasing levels of anthropogenic-based environmental indicators urge us to educate for sustainability.

Moving Forward

By exploring the topics of efficiency, mechanism, management, and industrialism, we have a better grasp of what a carbon copy curriculum is. Once we are able to identify the influence of a carbon copy curriculum we can move from awareness to action. We need to move forward in a way that is mindful and informed. The process of transcending the carbon copy curriculum is what undergirds the rest of this book.

In the next chapter, I dive into the topic of sustainability and explore its history, various definitions, and its possibilities within the arena of education. As a culture, we have just scratched the surface of the potential for a type of education that can advance sustainability. It is necessary that we investigate the interdisciplinary and far-reaching concept of sustainability while situating it within the context of our environmental crisis.

CHAPTER 4

The Scholarship of Sustainability

> Will we move further from a society rooted in principles of social justice, real democracy, and ecological sanity?
>
> Why Now?, *Smart Meme: Changing the Story*

> Can the United States and the American people, pioneer sustainable patterns of consumption and lifestyle, (and) can you educate for that?
>
> Brown in *The Ecopedagogy Movement: From Global Ecological Crisis to Cosmological, Technological, and Organizational Transformation in Education*

SYNONYMOUS WITH "environmentally friendly" and "green," the idea of sustainability has extended into popular culture and international dialogue. It is a concept and process that has recently become a part of the vernacular of the Western world. But what is it about sustainability that makes it such an important topic? The looming ecological crisis is a call to action. Attempting to live sustainably is a way to answer that call. Education is an enterprise that can encourage ecologically responsible living. We not only need to educate students in a way that will foster an ethic of stewardship, but we also need to educate in a way that will sustain a student's interest in learning. When we encourage students to embrace their curiosities and passions we empower them to foster a critical inquisitiveness and a passion for engaging in continual learning. Sustainability education is a learning that happens both within and beyond the classroom.

In this chapter I seek to help the reader to better understand the concept of sustainability and the sustainability movement. I intend to articulate what I refer to as the scholarship of sustainability while recognizing that sustainability is a multilayered concept. Accordingly, I employ an ecologically grounded perspective to make the term more accessible to the reader. I initiate the discussion by exploring the history of sustainability, sustainability education, and other related sustainability initiatives. Also, I discuss the concept of curriculum as ecological text, and then I outline the value of understanding sustainability.

Etymologically, the word sustainability means to support, hold, or bear the weight of something (sustainability, n.d.). How can we promote the kind of ecological integrity that can support, hold, or bear the weight of a rapidly expanding human population? At this juncture in human history, moving towards sustainability is not an easy process. The physicist and ecofeminist Vandana Shiva notes that the term sustainability invokes a notion of resilience which means to enable something "to last out, give strength to, endure without giving way" (Shiva in Smith & Williams, 1999, p. 1). In order to survive, we must be able to bear the weight of the choices that we, as humans, make collectively and individually. Ecological sustainability pushes us to transcend the mechanical worldview and the scientific management that typifies American education today.

Interestingly, sustainability "has been traditionally used as synonymous with words such as long-term, durable, sound, or systematic, among others" (Filho, 2000, p. 9). I have personally been interested in the concepts of sustainability for several years. I did not call it "sustainability" when I was in high school, but I was interested in promoting environmentally friendly lifestyles. This interest was sparked after I worked, lived, and played in a wilderness area for five weeks during the summer of my junior year (in high school). That summer, spent in the Ouachita Mountains of western Arkansas, was a turning point for me. I got to learn about the environment by getting my hands dirty in an environmental restoration project. I learned about the extraordinary capacity for change that a small group of dedicated people can precipitate. More particularly, I learned that the classroom of the great outdoors has more knowledge available in it than a library of books. I learned that there is power in community and that there were other like-minded teens who wanted to change the world one water bar[1] at a time. My time at this program ignited my interest in outdoor education and environmental conservation. When I think back through my educational experiences, it was my time with the Student Conservation Association that put me on the path of sustainability and outdoor education. As I explore sustainability, I am continually intrigued by the intricate landscape that it represents.

There is an urgent need for a shift in our collective worldview. Our ecological crisis is getting more complex every day. Without a well orchestrated political, educational, and social response to this crisis, it is likely that we will experience an ecological apocalypse. A number of educational theorists believe that we are not going to thrive or even survive beyond the twenty-first century because of the damage we are

---

1   A water bar is a structure created by trail crews at carefully selected points on a trail to divert water out of the walking path (Phillips, n.d.). Water bars help prevent rapid erosion of soil, thereby keeping the tread of the trail intact for future use.

inflicting upon Earth (Van Kannel-Ray, 2006; Bowers, 2003; Hutchison, 1998; Orr, 1994). I am committed to playing a part in the necessary transformation towards ecological revitalization from an educational standpoint. I feel that there is much hope in this time of potential biospheric collapse. This is why I have chosen to take the initiative to formulate a theoretical response to our planetary emergency.

For the purposes of this book, I would like the reader to consider that perhaps the primary question pertaining to sustainability should not be *who am I to contribute to the project of building a more habitable planet?*...but rather it should be *who am I NOT to contribute to the sustainability project?* Paul Hawken (2007) posits that the sustainability movement is the largest movement that has ever taken place on this planet. He estimates that there are "30,000 sustainability groups in the United States and tens of thousands of groups worldwide" (in Edwards, 2005, p. 6). The movement keeps expanding and provides a progressive counter-narrative to the industrial mindedness perpetuated in today's educational system. The number of people involved in the sustainability movement serves as an indicator to its urgency. In this book my major goal is to help forge a dramatic shift in education through the vehicle of curriculum studies and the sustainability movement.

Human decisions can have an impact on virtually all living species. Gorbachev states that we "desperately need to recognize that we are the guests not the masters of nature and adopt a new paradigm for development, based on the costs and benefits to all people, and bound by the limits of nature herself rather than the limits of technology and consumerism" (Gorbachev, n.d., n.p.). To live sustainably, the human vote must be considered as just *one* of the many votes cast from the millions of species that compose this planet. Thus, living sustainably involves looking at the world ecologically. Ecology, the study of relationships, encourages us to look for the connections that exist between phenomena.

Viewing the world ecologically enables us to reduce the impact that we have on Earth. When we understand the environmental impact of our choices and actions we are better able to respond to the sustainability crisis, thereby reducing our ecological footprint. In this chapter, I explore the body of literature that comprises the field of sustainability. This exploration will include a discussion on the intersection between sustainability and education. Additionally, I will look at the history of the sustainability movement and attempt to unpack it and position it within the context of education and curriculum studies.

John Seed (1988) observes that to "survive our current environmental pressures; we must consciously remember our evolutionary and ecological inheritance" (p. 38). What does it mean to remember our ecological inheritance? It suggests that we must begin to understand the challenges passed down from previous generations that threaten ecological vitality. We have inherited an Earth that is resilient, dynamic, alive, and enchanted. To remember our ecological inheritance involves comprehending the ways that we can live in harmony within our places. Seed urges us to move beyond our human-centered thinking and "learn to 'think like a mountain'" (p. 38). His invocation, on behalf of the biosphere, asks us to move away from the anthropocentric thinking that places human interests above all other life forms. The implication of Seed's statement is that humans should think *ecocentrically*,[2] instead of thinking anthropocentrically. Seed is suggesting that we shift from the Westernized perception of Earth as a machine into a view that embraces the value of virtually all life. Philosopher Julie Sessions states that "ecocentric thought recognizes all 'beings' as having worth" (in Jones, 2001, p. xxix). In the next chapter, I will tell how we can embrace a more ecological worldview. I look at this from the perspective of a bioregional, watershed-oriented education model. It begins within the places that we inhabit.

If we are to abide by Seed's advice and live ecologically sustainable lives, we must think ecocentrically in order to think like a mountain. As I discuss in Chapters 5 and 6, thinking like a mountain involves localizing and ecologizing (Morin in Gadotti, 2008). To ecologize is to recognize the significance of the relationships that sustain us. This ecologically oriented shift in perception involves stepping outside of ourselves and honoring the relationships that sustain us. Thinking like a mountain involves a move into planetary citizenship. In Chapter 5, I argue that planetary citizenship must begin at home. It starts when we value the ecological vitality of our own backyards. When I discuss "planetary citizenship," I am suggesting a place-based, integrative relationship with our surrounding bioregion.

Cultivating planetary citizenship is fundamental to sustainability. Gary Snyder suggests that a planetary citizen considers the collective opinion of the "village council of all beings" (Snyder, 1995, p. 75). A village council of all living beings is a group that makes their decisions based on how it will affect every living being on Earth. To think sustainably we must recognize that Earth is "made up of many communities of diverse beings in which the species all play different but essential roles." It can be seen as a "village model of the world" (p. 76). The idea of

---

[2] To think ecocentrically is to move beyond human-centered thought—prompting a holistic consideration of the entire living Earth community.

promoting diversity is central to advancing sustainability, for it is only through healthy plurality of thought that we are able to transcend the entrenched mechanistic worldview that is partially culpable for the ecological instability that we face today.

Incorporating a diversity of opinions into our thinking is paramount to advancing a village model of all living things. Snyder (1995) invites us to "[i]magine a village that includes its trees and birds, its sheep, goats, cows, and yaks, and the wild animals of the high pastures as members of the community" (pp. 79–80). He is advocating for an attentive approach to harmonious collaboration, a form of co-existence that embodies ecological vitality. It is a mode of citizenship that values the integrated wholeness of our biosphere. It is a challenging endeavor to cultivate this advanced form of ecologically centered discourse, but it is worth it. Ultimately, it is a struggle to nourish a passion and love for life. As Blake once said, "life delights in life" (in Wilson, 1964, p. 41). A village council model recognizes the value of human and non-human life, the interconnectivity of all Earth systems, and the interdependency of all living beings.

History of Sustainability

Sustainability is a term that was virtually unheard of until the early 1980s (Lovins, 2008, PC). Environmentalism is something that dates back a little bit further. Regardless of the terminology, exploring the history of the ecological movement helps us to gain a better understanding of what is happening in education today. There are a number of initiatives that currently exist that have risen from the historical landscape pertaining to ecological sustainability. Green issues revolve around protecting and conserving our Earth—air, land, people, animals, and water. Efforts to conserve energy and protect our water (EPA, 2008a) and air (EPA, 2008b) have been hot topics since the 1960s. In terms of exploring the importance of greening education, it is important that we embrace a conservation ethic that is eco-centric. Eco-centric thinking is a form of thinking that is Earth centered. Living sustainably is a mindset.

Orr posits that the "ecological crisis is a crisis of mind, which makes it a challenge for those institutions which purport to improve minds...it is, in other words, an educational crisis" (in NCSE, 2003, p. 10). Clearly, education plays a significant role in averting the ecological crisis and teaching toward sustainability. In the 1960s the deteriorating condition of the planet's ecological health reached a critical point. From the perspective of stream ecology, a number of species were being killed by the overuse or misuse of insecticides.

In the 1950s and early 1960s one insecticide in particular, DDT, was compromising the integrity of eggshells for birds such as the eagle (Carson, 1962). DDT was getting washed into our streams from streets, fields, and parking lots. The chemical began to dramatically reduce the biodiversity of these fragile eco-systems. In response to the devastating misuse of these chemicals, Rachel Carson (1962) wrote a book entitled *Silent Spring* in which she argues that if the rates of chemical use continue to expand, spring would be a quiet time because virtually all life would have become extinct. Carson's book paved the way for the modern environmental movement. Accordingly, this was the decade that awareness about environmental degradation arrived at a tipping point. People began to realize that if dramatic changes were not made, we could destroy life as we know it. At this time, environmental groups started to form. With the uprising of groups, activism began to become more widespread.

In 1970, the first Earth Day was held. It took place on April 22, 1970, and it was a culminating event for a growing public concern about the ecological crises. According to the Nelson Institute for Environmental Studies "Earth Day was the product of local grassroots action to increase environmental awareness," as it "focused the nation's political agenda on urgent environmental issues" (NIES, 2010, n.p.). It was a turning point for environmental activism and awareness. In response to the overuse of Earth's resources and the subsequent environmental degradation, Dennis Meadows (1972) wrote a landmark book entitled *The Limits to Growth*. This book focuses on "five major trends of global concern" including: "accelerating industrialization, rapid population growth, wide-spread malnutrition, depletion of non-renewable resources, and a deteriorating environment" (p. 21). The primary argument of the book is that we as humans are beginning to exceed Earth's carrying capacity and subsequently we must reduce our footprint. This notion of exceeding Earth's carrying capacity is important. Before this book, the notion that there was a limit to growth was generally not recognized. Industry was booming and machines were zooming. Levels of deforestation were on the rise along with automobile production and general resource consumption. Something needed to be done about it. Meadows (1972) spelled out the major environmental problems and proposed solutions to the rapid levels of environmental deterioration.

Understanding the concept of carrying capacity is central to understanding sustainability. Carrying capacity is the amount of natural resources available on Earth to sustain human life. In a more scientific description it is stated that

> Carrying capacity refers to the upper limit to population or community size (e.g., biomass) imposed through environmental resistance. In nature this resistance is related to the availability of renewable (e.g., food) and nonrenewable (e.g., space) resources as they impact biomass through reproduction, growth, and survival. (Mihelcic, 2008, n.p.)

Therefore, carrying capacity comes down to ensuring enough food and space for this generation and future generations. If we are not mindful of Earth's carrying capacity, we may destroy it. If we draw more resources than Earth can regenerate, we destroy the ecological balance that sustains us. According to Meadows et al., (2004), "the carrying capacity is a limit. Any population that grows past its carrying capacity, overshooting the limit, will not long sustain itself" (p. 137). In response to the increased awareness generated from Carson and Meadows et al., there was action taken. At the international level, the United Nations Conference on the Human Environment (held in Stockholm in 1972) "initiated a growing international interest in the role of education in fostering a sustainable future" (NCSE, 2003, p. 13). The next section examines a range of initiatives central to the sustainability movement within an educational context.

Sustainability Initiatives

In terms of exploring the various environmental initiatives that have taken place, we begin with the *Stockholm Declaration* of 1972 and take a brief tour of the initiatives that led up to the more recent United Nations Decade of Education for Sustainable Development. This section is by no means intended to be a comprehensive historical exploration of the sustainability movement; instead it is an attempt to illustrate its wide range and scope while deepening the reader's understanding on the topic. This section will serve as a historical framework that contributes to the preceding chapters surrounding sustainability, education, and curriculum studies.

The Stockholm Declaration of 1972 was the "first declaration to make reference to sustainability in...education" (Wright, 2002, p. 203). Although the focus of this conference was centered primarily on environmental law it made a number of important contributions to the landscape of education related sustainability discourse. For example, the declaration initiated discourse on the "interdependency between humanity and the environment" (p. 203). Prior to the Stockholm Declaration, formal considerations of human and environmental interdependency were largely overlooked. Working to protect our environment for future generations was not a part of educational discourse in the early 1970s. This was, according to Wright, "one of the first documents to discuss inter- and intra-generational equity amongst humans" (p. 203). There was, however, a clear emphasis on advancing human well-being over environmental well-being. The document indicates that nations must "improve the *human* environment for present and future generations...a goal to be pursued together with, and in harmony with, the established and fundamental goals of peace and world-wide economic and social development" (emphasis mine, UNESCO, 1972, p. 1; also in Wright, 2002, p. 204). Despite its human-centered focus, the document makes a profound contribution to the sustainability movement. The Stockholm Declaration enabled us to recognize the significance of protecting the ecological relationships that sustain us. It was a watershed moment to put environmental issues at the forefront of international discussion.

There were 24 principles delivered by the Stockholm Declaration. The goal was to achieve environmental sustainability "stressing bilateral and multilateral arrangements" (Wright, 2002, p. 204). So, instead of focusing on fragmented and isolated efforts to green our discourse, the Stockholm Declaration led the way to systemic ecological thinking. It was a "green" light, if you will, for the environmental movement as we know it. Among the listed principles is the emphasis on education, principle 19, which emphasized and stated "the need for environmental education from grade school to adulthood" (p. 204). The notion that environmental education should be a central feature to curriculum and pedagogy was revolutionary at the time. It encouraged the advancement of a whole new dimension to educational discourse, theory, and practice. Principle 19 indicates that education can "broaden the basis for enlightened opinions and responsible conduct by individuals, enterprises and communities in protecting and improving the environment in its full human dimension" (UNESCO in Wright, 2002, p. 204). The Stockholm Declaration was a powerful first step for education and sustainability.

Another turning point in the sustainability movement occurred with the World Commission on Environment and Development's (WCED, 1987) publication of *Our Common Future*. This document, (informally referred to as the *Brundtland Report*), states "that the time has come for a marriage of economy and ecology, so that governments and their people can take responsibility not just for environmental damage, but for the policies that cause the damage" (back cover). In this document, the WCED states, "The earth is one but the world is not. We all depend on one biosphere for sustaining our lives. Yet each community, each country, strives for survival and prosperity with little regard for its impact on others" (in Lydon, 1992, p. 56). Accordingly, *Our Common Future* calls for a collective effort towards generating sustainable development which, as previously discussed, is a kind of development that "meets the needs of today's generation without compromising the ability of future generations to meet their needs" (p. 43). Even today, this is the most commonly used definition of sustainability.

A few years after the publication of *Our Common Future* the inaugural UN Conference on Environment and Development (referred to as the *Earth Summit*) took place in Rio de Janeiro, Brazil, in 1992. At the *Earth Summit*,

> An attempt to make a systematic statement about the interrelationship between humanity and the Earth was conceived of and demanded—a document that would formulate the environmental concerns of education once and for all in both ethical and ecological (as opposed to technocratic and instrumentalist) terms. (Kahn, 2010, p. 12)

This document is referred to as *Agenda 21*. *Agenda 21* served as a detailed "green print" for building a sustainable future. Chapter 36 of *Agenda 21* stated, "[regarding] Education, public awareness and training...education is critical for promoting sustainable development and improving the capacity of the people to address environment and development issues" (in NCSE, 2003, p. 14; and in Thompson, 2008, p. 37). The possibility for education to transform the citizenry into environmental stewards is profound. Thompson (2008) adds that education "is a massive priority having a huge potential to liberate" (p. 37). She continues by discussing the potential evolution of environmental education:

> I see it as the next step in environmental education to move towards sustainability for all—starting in our communities in solidarity with others around the world, as environmental equity issues are both local and global. This evolution of education involves environmental justice, environmental health, and traditional ecological knowledge. (p. 58)

Composed of communal solidarity and environmental equity—sustainability for all is a powerful concept. When we strive for ecological mutuality and participatory democracy we are working towards sustainability. It is time that we return to the traditional ecological knowledge embodied in indigenous cultures—the kind of knowledge that enables us to cultivate a deeper association with the life force that is found in all living beings. Aligned with Thompson's call for an evolution in environmental education, the Agenda 21 document served as a catalyst for further dialogue surrounding education for sustainability.

A United States based sustainability initiative was founded in 1993. The President's Council on Sustainable Development (PCSD), established during Clinton's presidency, maintains that, "Today, educators face a compelling responsibility to serve society by fostering the transformations needed to set us on the path to sustainable development" (PCSD, n.d.). The urgency of this responsibility comes at a pivotal time in the educational and political landscape. "The time has come to ensure that the concepts of education for sustainability—in the broadest sense—are discussed and woven into a framework upon which current and future educational policy is based" (PCSD, n.d.). Educating for sustainable development is at the forefront of the PCSD's agenda. Ultimately, sustainability within virtually any context refers to the act or process of maintaining the integrity of a social, ecological, or economic system while honoring the needs of both present and future generations.

Jaime Cloud, director of the *Cloud Institute*, posits that efforts aimed at developing a more Earth friendly and socially equitable world are found throughout many programs around the world (Cloud Institute for Sustainability Education, n.d.). According to Cloud, forging a collective framework for building the capacity of existing organizations while orchestrating alliances is critical. These alliances will assist in the reduction of humanity's ecological footprint and subsequently give way to a more integrated, robust, and less pervasive global community of Earth-minded citizens. The shared responsibility of transformative and sustainable educational efforts calls for the systematic development of alliances within all types of learning institutions. The sustainability movement is situated at the forefront of programs such as the National Council for Science and the Environment.

The National Council for Science and the Environment (NCSE) released a report that articulated a vision for teaching towards a sustainable and secure future (Blockstein & Greene, 2003). In this report, several aspects of education for a sustainable future are examined, including its historical foundations and the implications for teaching in a more just and humane directionality. Here, many possibilities are listed for sustainability in education. One is that "Sustainability can be used as an integrating force in education to improve and facilitate academic and community relationships" (Blockstein & Greene, 2003, p. 11). The NCSE report identifies Environmental Education as a foundational component to education for sustainability (EFS). Particularly, the notion of interdependence is discussed within the context of EFS. Mark Van Doren (1965) observes that "The student who can begin early in life to think of things as connected, even if he revises his view with every succeeding year, has begun the life of learning" (p. 115). To see the world as an interconnected tapestry of life that is dependent on balance involves a new method for viewing and interacting with the world. Accordingly, "EFS calls for integrated decision making based on integrated information to enable individuals...[and groups] to incorporate environmental considerations and goals into social, economic—and even security—decisions" (p. 10). One of the most notable EFS initiatives is that of the Earth Charter.

The Earth Charter

At the 1992 Earth Summit an unsuccessful attempt was made to generate a document called the Earth Charter. The Earth Charter was a project spearheaded by the United Nations World Commission on Environment and Development. It was an effort to unite leaders to help guide an internationally driven transition into sustainable development (Kahn, 2010). After the 1992 Earth Summit, more environmentally focused international conferences were initiated. These international conferences started to generate greater interest in applying sustainability within educational contexts throughout the U.S. and the rest of the world. This international movement included a "commitment to sustainability in the teaching, research, outreach, and operations of schools and universities" (NCSE, 2003, p. 13). The international effort embodied by the Earth Charter was advanced at the turn of the century.

The final text of the Earth Charter was approved in 2000 (Corcoran, 2004, p. 109). The Earth Charter sets out to create a collaborative global effort aimed at generating a more sustainable presence through a global alliance of stakeholders. It states:

> We stand at a critical moment in Earth's history, a time when humanity must choose its future. As the world becomes increasingly interdependent and fragile, the future at once holds great peril and great promise. To move forward we must recognize that in the midst of a magnificent diversity of cultures and life forms we are one human family and one Earth community with a common destiny. We must join together to bring forth a sustainable global society founded on respect for nature, universal human rights, economic justice, and a culture of peace. Towards this end, it is imperative that we, the peoples of Earth, declare our responsibility to one another, to the greater community of life, and to future generations. (Earth Charter website; also in Hutchison, 1998, n.p.)

The dynamic tension between a potential environmental collapse and an ecological overhaul that leads to environmental revitalization demands action. The Earth Charter is oriented towards mobilizing a worldwide effort towards sustainability. According to Hessel (2002) the Earth Charter is a "holistic, layered document that articulates the inspirational vision, basic values, and essential principles needed in a global ethic for Earth community" (p. 598). This effort demands well-orchestrated and transformative leadership initiatives which enable communities to restore their cultural heritage and reclaim their connection to the natural world (Gruenewald, 2003).

Peter Blaze Corcoran (2004) argues that the "Charter deserves educators' attention as an integrated vision of social justice, peace, and ecological sustainability" (p. 108). He believes that the Earth Charter "can help transform our conception of what is foundational to include solutions to the deepening anthropogenic ecological crisis" (p. 108). He urges educators to use the momentum generated from the Earth Charter to "deeply engage [with] the problems of our time" (p. 108). He highlights sub-principles 4a and 4b from the Earth Charter:

> 4. Secure Earth's bounty and beauty for present and future generations.
>
>   a. Recognize that the freedom of action of each generation is qualified by the needs of future generations.
>
>   b. Transmit to future generations, values, traditions, and institutions that support the long-term flourishing of Earth's human and ecological communities. (The Earth Charter principle 4, sub-principles 4a, 4b in Corcoran, 2004, p. 108)

The implications of these sub-principles are far-reaching. To situate intergenerational thinking within the context of virtually every decision is powerful. Even more powerful is the notion of transmitting the "values, traditions and institutions that support the long-term flourishing" of Earth's human and non-human communities. Working towards the long-term flourishing of this planet is an eloquent description of sustainability. Interestingly, there are similarities between the Earth Charter and John Dewey's conceptualization of education.

Jickling makes a link between principle 4b and John Dewey's work. Dewey wrote in his book *A Common Faith*,

> We who now live are parts of a humanity that extends into the remote past, a humanity that has interacted with nature. The things in civilization we most prize are not of ourselves. They exist by grace of the doings and sufferings of the continuous human community in which we are a link. Ours is the respon-

sibility of conserving, transmitting, rectifying and expanding the heritage of values we have received that those who come after us may receive it more solid and secure, more widely accessible and more generously shared than we have received. (1934, pp. 57–58; also quoted in Corcoran, 2004, p. 108)

Dewey's writing is as relevant now as it was in his time. Unfortunately, current modes of educational discourse compromise the continuous human community "in which we are a link." As Counts (1978) suggests, schooling is not the remedy to our ecological and social problems. Instead, Counts hints that it is a *particular kind* of schooling that can advance sustainability. Counts (1978) states that "Teachers must abandon much of their easy optimism, subject the concept of education to the most rigorous scrutiny, and be prepared" for the challenges that are inherent to affecting social transformation (p. 2). The Earth Charter is transforming the sustainability initiative as we know it. The democratic process that unfolded into the Earth Charter is telling of its potential impact.

Corcoran (2004) tells us that "[t]o the best of our knowledge, the Earth Charter Initiative has involved the most open and participatory consultation process ever conducted in connection with the drafting of an international document" (p. 109). He notes that "tens of thousands of individuals and hundreds of organizations from all regions of the world, different cultures, and diverse sectors of society have participated" (p. 109). This widespread participatory process is encouraging and insightful for those interested in advancing the Scholarship of Sustainability. Ruud Lubbers, the United Nations High Commissioner on Refugees and Earth Charter Commissioner, observed, "The Earth Charter offers a way forward by adopting this integrated approach. It links the various stakeholders who have an impact on our future. It is fundamentally about universal responsibility and interdependence" (Earth Charter Commission in Corcoran, 2004, p. 111). Indeed, the Earth Charter offers a "way forward" and guides us into a collaborative effort which will enable us to achieve a more ecologically sustainable world. Even more helpful to practitioners is *The Earth Charter Briefing Book* (2000).

> The Earth Charter is a valuable resource...Discussion of the Earth Charter in classrooms, conferences, and workshops can heighten awareness of the basic challenges and choices that face humanity. It can help people learn to think globally and holistically. It can focus attention on fundamental ethical issues and that interconnectedness. It can serve as a catalyst for cross cultural and interfaith dialogue on shared values and global ethics. It can be used to generate in individuals and communities the kind of internal reflection that leads to a change in attitudes, values, and behavior. (Earth Charter International Secretariat, 2000; also in Corcoran, 2004, p. 111)

Cultivating an "internal reflection" that catalyzes transformation is central to an education that is formulated around the Earth Charter. It is an education that equips students with the ability to think holistically and understand that the challenges which face our biosphere are inextricable from the challenges that face humanity.

In *A Voice for Earth: American Writers Respond to the Earth Charter,* a number of authors discuss the Earth Charter (Corcoran, Wohlpart, & Hollingshead, 2008). This collection of essays offers a salient analysis of the significance of the Earth Charter. From ecological integrity to social solidarity, a number of important themes are discussed. The significance of living in a more sustainable way is explored. Important connections are made in this text which link human and ecological wellness. Accordingly, in the foreword, Homero Aridjis (2008) recognizes the urgency of fighting for "the safekeeping and survival of thousands of animal and plant species" (p. xi). Aridjis maintains that the survival of these species "is an integral part of the struggle for the safekeeping and survival of the human race" (p. xi). Aridjis suggests that honoring the association between human well-being and ecological health is paramount. He argues that "An environmentally degraded planet degrades humankind because our physical and spiritual welfare depends on the health of our natural environment" (Aridjis, p. xi). Aridjis urges us to recognize that virtually everything we do to the natural environment we are doing to ourselves. Understanding the interconnectivity inherent to environmental health is fundamental to the advancement of a sustainability ethic.

The myopia of embracing short-term economic wellness jeopardizes the long-term survivability of the planet. It is this notion of intergenerational and interspecies-based thinking that Aridjis (2008) suggests is at the core of living more sustainably. He implores us to honor all life in an equitable way, stating that the "excessive enrichment of a small number of individuals or groups impoverishes us all" (p. xii). It is our role, as planetary citizens to ensure that we take on a role of stewardship. This is a stewardship that honors the integrity of the biosphere. Accordingly, it is important that we realize that

> Earth must not become a silent, sterile desert, the dark garden of our worst imaginings. It is up to humans, who are rational animals with a moral conscience, to defend the right of other creatures, and of plants—and not to be their executioners. (p. xii)

Instead of being *executioners* of our biosphere, we are called to be *stewards* that propound a meaningful and symbiotic relationship with the earth. Aridjis captures the essence of the Earth Charter stating it "provides us with an ethical framework for recognizing the Rights of Nature that will allow us to live a sustainable existence" (p. xii). He adds that, ultimately, the "unique contribution of the Earth Charter is to demonstrate the interconnectedness of human rights and the Rights of Nature" (p. xii).

Terry Tempest Williams speaks about the commitment that is embodied by the Earth Charter. Williams (2008b) notes that there is a visceral propensity within all of us, urging us to become better Earth stewards. She states we "know in our bones that the world is broken....Governments and corporations around the world are fostering the old patterns that promote and profit from a consumptive model of growth" (p. xiv). The consumptive model of growth exploits our natural world. The Earth Charter recognizes the perilous human impact on Earth and calls for a reordering of priorities. Williams states that the Earth Charter "is a visionary document that creates a template for ecological consciousness around the world, rooted in local actions. It asks us to embrace the planet while taking care of our own backyards" (p. xiii). The implications of the Earth Charter are further explored by Georgia-based nature writer and eco-warrior Janisse Ray.

Ray (2008) observes that the Earth Charter is a critical document that profoundly contributes to the sustainability movement.

> The Earth Charter, a brilliant and far-reaching document, puts into words a remarkable vision, "an ethical foundation for the emerging world community." Powerfully succinct, the charter contains only four major tenets: Respect and Care for the Community of Life; Ecological Integrity; Social and Economic Justice; and Democracy, Nonviolence, and Peace. (Ray, 2008, p. 119)

The simplicity of the document adds to its salience. Not only does the Earth Charter advocate for a comprehensive restructuring of the human-Earth relationship, it calls for the application of a form of ecological democracy that supports Michael Ben-Eli's definition of sustainability. That is, the Earth Charter inculcates an effort to foster the type of "interaction between a population and the carrying capacity of an environment such that the population develops to express its full potential without adversely and irreversibly affecting the carrying capacity of the environment upon which it depends" (Ben-Eli, n.d.). To enable all living beings to operate at its fullest expression is a powerful concept. Ray notes that the "Charter calls to 'guarantee human rights and fundamental freedoms and provide everyone an opportunity to realize his or her full potential'" (in Ray, 2008 p. 122). Self-realization is a crucial concept in sustainability...as Terry Tempest Williams suggests, it involves compassion and care.

> ...care is the true essence of human beings and to the cosmological and biological fact that the universe and life itself would not exist without care....Boff suggests that care can provide a foundation for a new way of being in this time of crisis that can lead us from the path of self-destruction toward a path of "universal co-responsibility." (Williams, 2008, p. xxvi)

This notion of care brings us to the idea of "universal co-responsibility." When we show an eco-centric concern for all life, we are better positioned to instantiate the kind of sustainability that is described in the Earth Charter.

Decade of Education for Sustainable Development

International efforts pertaining to sustainability and education were mobilized in the inception of the United Nations Decade of Education for Sustainable Development (DESD). The DESD serves as a momentous response to the modes of education that are ecologically degrading. Momentum towards a more comprehensive and cohesive approach towards sustainability education culminated at the 2002 World Summit on Sustainable Development. Here it was recommended that the United Nations General Assembly declare a Decade of Education for Sustainable Development to begin in 2005 (Blockstein & Greene, 2003). This decision helped to "bring renewed global attention to the issue [of sustainability]...the General Assembly approved the Decade in October of 2002" (Blockstein & Greene, 2003, p. 13). The United Nations decision to declare 2005–2014 the Decade of Education for Sustainable Development demonstrates recognition of the urgency associated with living in a more socio-ecologically harmonious way (Bergea et al., 2006). Educational institutions around the world are called to action through this declaration with a request for the fundamental retooling of curriculum and pedagogy towards sustainability. This effort was adopted at the UN General Assembly (December 20, 2002) through the *Draft Resolution on the United Nations Decade of Education for Sustainable Development*. The primary goal of this resolution is to "integrate the principles, values, and practices of sustainable development into all aspects of education and learning" (UNESCO, n.d., n.p.). To this end, the "educational effort will encourage changes in behavior that will create a more sustainable future in terms of environmental integrity, economic viability, and a just society for present and future generations" (UNESCO, n.d., n.p.). Efforts towards building a more sustainable and just global community have taken many different shapes.

Historically speaking, the DESD was ratified because of work that took place from "1987 to 1992, [when] the concept of sustainable development matured as committees discussed, negotiated, and wrote the 40 chapters of *Agenda 21*" (Decade of Education for Sustainable Development [DESD], n.d.).

The text of the DESD reveals its broad commitment to environmental vitality, social justice, and economic solidarity. According to UNESCO, "This educational effort will encourage changes in behavior that will create a more sustainable future in terms of environmental integrity, economic viability, and a just society for present and future generations" (UNESCO, 2005, p. 6). The DESD views sustainability as a critical priority within educational and curricular discourse at all levels. The DESD has the potentiality to better situate our next generation with skills that are necessary to promote sustainability. The DESD is situated to equip us with the tools to avert the "disastrous anthropogenic environmental crises, failing political systems, religious intolerance, and unsustainable and inequitable economic development" (Corcoran & Wals, 2004, p. 3). Mitigating human generated environmental degradation is a complicated process—but it is a way in which the DESD assists us. The complexities affiliated with investigating, understanding, and responding to the environmental issues that we face warrant close attention and mindful action. The required ecologically based inquiry, comprehension, and response integral to advancing sustainability is more likely to happen in the midst of the DESD. The DESD provides a platform of intentionality that provokes ecological awareness through integrated intellectual exploration of ecology and democracy. Ultimately, the DESD decreases the "scope and range of the negative impacts of [publicly] educated people on the natural systems that sustain Earth" (Corcoran & Wals, 2004, p. 3).

As previously discussed, with the DESD, considerations are made for promoting ecological vitality, social solidarity, and economic integrity. The DESD mobilizes a cadre of schools, communities, and governments in a collaborative effort to transform education into a more sustainable enterprise aimed at increasing the well-being for present and future generations. This effort aims to foster both human and non-human coexistence. The mere fact that the UNDESD is in place helps us understand the overwhelming consensus amongst many stakeholders that education can help to transform unsustainable behaviors into sustainable action. In order to make the transformation from unsustainable behaviors to sustainable action it is important to build upon what has already been done. This way we don't have to "reinvent the wheel."

Curriculum as Ecological Text

The notion of sustainability offers hope within the staggering immensity of the planetary challenges we face. What I call an eco-curriculum for sustainability serves as a point of departure for advancing an ecologically derived educational system. An eco-curriculum for sustainability is an ecological response to the overwhelming influence of mechanism and efficiency. An eco-curriculum for sustainability emerges from an ecological framework that recognizes the importance of the human-Earth relationship in both contexts of education and survivability. By recognizing the capacity for transmuting the current, predominantly mechanistic worldview into an ecologically derived worldview, an eco-curriculum for sustainability has great transformative potential.

The ecological orientation of my book follows in the tradition of Gregory Bateson's (1979) notion of the "pattern which connects" (p. 11). Bateson posited that we need to cultivate a greater awareness and understanding of that which brings us together. He indicates that if we break the pattern that connects we will "necessarily destroy all quality" (in Steier & Jorgenson, n.d., p. 6). If we do not celebrate and facilitate ecological knowledge, we might compromise the integrity of the very systems that sustain us. Bateson asks, "What pattern connects the crab to the lobster and the orchid to the primrose and all four of them to me? And me to you?" (in Steier & Jorgenson, n.d., p. 6). He encourages us to reflect upon the patterns that define us and the patterns by which we live. In Bateson's tradition, I embrace an ecological approach in attempting to understand sustainability. I refer to this as ecological text.

Ecological text is the text represented by the places that we inhabit. It is grounded in educational experiences that facilitate inter-relational knowledge of our local bioregion. This book is an attempt to instantiate awareness and appreciation of the possibilities for integrating sustainability and curriculum studies. Viewing curriculum as ecological text provokes the use of an "ecological world view" (Sterling, 2001; Capra, 1982) as a theoretical framework. Stephen Sterling (2001) states that "Ecological thinking entails a shift from relationships based on separation, control and manipulation towards those based on participation, empowerment and self-organization" (p. 49). This is the transformative essence associated with thinking ecologically. It is a move towards participation which emboldens a collective and individual trajectory towards living more harmoniously with each other, Earth, and all of its inhabitants. This movement takes into account life in this generation and the well-being of future generations. I posit that we need to be more aware about how the education system teaches students to think in terms of participating in the human-Earth relationship.

Sustainability is oriented towards the elimination of ecological exploitation as well as the advancement of healing and vitality (Good, 1998, p. 82; Clifford & Friesen, 1994). From an educational perspective, there is a great deal of opportunity for ecological restoration. After all, it is education that enables us to valorize the importance of being connected to our bioregion. When we become aware of the role that we can play in revitalizing a natural area, we can get excited to get out there and get our hands dirty in conservation projects. Robin Good (1998) postulates that sustainability education needs to be formulated in a way that "heal[s] those aspects of the modern paradigm which have been individually, societally, and biotically damaging" (p. 82). Furthermore, in this context, "all students [need to] become healers of the ecological and social damage" (p. 82). This is a powerful statement. When I think of all students becoming healers, I am inspired. I envision a cadre of eco-socially minded stewards leaving the classroom to restore green spaces, build a bioswale, canoe a river, pick up any trash that is seen, and much more. Eco-socially minded stewards will embrace the solar economy (see Weisman, 2008) and shift towards utilizing renewable modes of energy. These stewards are able to "think small" and begin within their own places to make the changes necessary for sustainability. Accordingly, sustainability education is committed to identifying and responding to the ecological and social unease associated with the mechanistic paradigm. This notion of healing lies in the restorative propensity inherent to natural and social processes.

Healing is the process or effort of making something whole again. Jardine et al. (2004) postulate "that an orientation toward integrity and wholeness has something to do with health, healing, and the mending of relations, and, therefore, that pursuing curriculum integration in our classrooms has something to do with 'choosing to be healers'" (p. 324; Clifford & Friesen, 1994). To "choose to be a healer" is, in my opinion, critical to the project of eco-revitalization. I believe that we need more people to choose to be healers. We need to celebrate the healing capacity that exists in virtually all life. Our life force helps us to seek healing.

Working towards wholeness and healing is central to the conversation surrounding sustainability and education. This conversation is thus grounded in exposing and mending the unease attributed to contemporary curriculum and pedagogy. By unease I am referring to the effect of the Cartesian rift between mind and body. People are uneasy because they feel disconnected at many levels. We are disconnected from ourselves, from nature, and from one another—this disconnectivity is dangerous. Accordingly, healing the unease promulgated in traditional education enables all to get back on a more sustainable pathway. It addresses the onslaught of frenetic thought promulgated in a culture of factory-minded efficiency. Healing, from an educational perspective, involves embracing plurality and ultimately advancing a more robust form of inquiry grounded in sustainability.

Achieving sustainability is both a logically grounded and an intuitive concept. It is noted that the "concept of sustainability can be overwhelming because of the comprehensive nature of the word, but the root meaning is actually a simple concept that is nearly intuitive to most people" (Center for Ecoliteracy, n.d.). However, the implementation of sustainability in education involves a *complicated conversation* (Pinar, 2004) that entails understanding the human impact on the land and how to reduce this impact. Understanding and reducing one's impact is a fundamental process grounded in education (Environmental Protection Agency, 2007). There are epistemological, ethical, and ecological implications associated with a turn towards sustainability. The conceptual landscape that comprises sustainability is a contested terrain. Accordingly, sustainability takes on many shapes and is consequently, from a linear perspective, an indefinite term (Orr in Edwards, 2005, p. xiv). In its simplest form, a sustainable world "will be able to continue indefinitely into the future" (Center for Sustainability, n.d.). To create a more sustainable system of education requires a multi-level systemic shift in perspective. It is a transformation that can lead to a paradigm shift in pedagogical theory and practice.

The complexity of the term sustainability is revealed through the range of definitions associated with it. There are over 300 definitions that span many disciplines (Dobson, 1996). Within the scope of education, several thinkers, activists, and practitioners tackle the topic of sustainability as it relates to education (Sterling, 2001; Orr, 1994; Bowers, 2006). Various themes emerge from the discourse associated with sustainability including; bio-diversity, unity in diversity, intergenerational equality, ecological literacy, and biomimicry. It is beyond the scope of this book to provide a complete description of every major author and writing related to sustainability. Instead, this chapter is dedicated to promoting a greater, although somewhat abbreviated, understanding of the dynamic and organic concept of sustainability. One of the central themes in this chapter is identifying and explicating the overlap between education and sustainability.

Understanding Sustainability

People respond differently to the concept of sustainability. The diversity of thinking related to sustainability is "influenced by one's training, one's working experience and one's political and economic setting" (Filho, 2000, p. 10). The word sustainability is commonly found in scientific and social dialogue. In fact, "Sustainability is today one of the most widely used words in the scientific field as a whole" (Filho, 2000, p. 9). For the purposes of this book it is important to sharpen the focus and use a theoretical framework that embraces environmental sustainability. Accordingly, an ecological and an educational lens will be utilized to further explore sustainability. I seek to uncover and understand, through ecological, curricular, and pedagogical lenses, the through-lines that exist pertaining to education and sustainability.

Davison (2001) posits that the process of trying to understand sustainability begins with asking good questions. He states that "[t]he ideal of sustainability gives rise to an *agenda of good questions*, practical questions that bear directly on our forms of life, drawing out and giving practical substance to our disquiet and to our hopes" (emphasis mine, p. 13). I am intrigued by the idea of an agenda of good questions. It is, I believe, central to all educational discourse to advance good questions. The practical and theoretical aspects of sustainability are hard to comprehend and are also debatable, but Davison encourages everyone to keep inquiring. He tells us that "Responses to the questions are essential; they demand of us not categorical certainty but the capacity to articulate what we feel to be most worthy of being sustained in our lives" (p. 13). It is only through opening ourselves to the questions and the resulting dialogue surrounding sustainability that we can formulate answers. Everyone has something to contribute to this discussion. As Gadotti states, "Each person is equally responsible for Earth's community as a whole, even if, individually, we have different roles and responsibilities" (2008, p. 16). Sustainability is not just in the hands of the powerful; it is in everyone's hands. Education has the capacity to move our world towards ecological sustainability.

I argue that living sustainably involves a mindful and intentional commitment to living within the means of the planet. This involves reducing one's negative impact on Earth and on others in both the human and non-human spheres. More importantly, I argue that ecological sustainability is characterized by "living simply so that others can simply live" (Prakash, 1995, p. 332). It is a cultivation of a spirit of ecological stewardship informed by biospheric health and social solidarity. Ecological sustainability advances a form of solidarity that enables all of those involved to participate in the restorative conversation. In this sense, I believe that sustainability education needs to be grounded in Dewey's conceptualization of the "democratic ideal." The democratic ideal is oriented towards advancing "individual liberty and social equality" and "emerges out of the faith in the individual to define and develop her particular capacities in harmony with the needs and demands of others as they define and develop their own powers" (Hewitt, 2007, p. 111). Furthermore, the democratic ideal addresses "the individual's conscious tendencies to grow in a way that is considerate, sympathetic, and enriching towards those who share in the consequences of his or her actions" (p. 111). To put it succinctly, Hewitt's conceptualization of Dewey's democratic ideal embraces compassion. Compassion implies empathy and the desire to enrich other people's lives. When we are compassionate we have faith in other people's abilities to define and develop their particular capacities while not compromising the needs and demands of others.

From an environmental perspective, what I call the *ecological democratic ideal* (EDI) is a commitment to grow in ways that honor virtually *all life*, both human and non-human. To build upon Hewitt's (2007) notion of democracy, I posit that the EDI values working toward ecological vitality, addressing the student's conscious tendencies to practice sustainability in a way that is understanding, sensitive, and enriching to every living being that is affected by the consequences of her actions. Embracing the EDI involves an attunement to the particular problems that face our ecological (planet), economic (profit), and social (people) well-being.

This focus on planet, profit, and people is referred to as the triple bottom line because it moves beyond the standard, dollar-driven bottom line and considers the vitality of all three of these as true sustainability. Integrating these three elements is central to advancing EDI's derived discourse. The EDI works to recognize and celebrate the integrality of the triple bottom line within the framework of advancing a more participatory form of sustainability. The EDI, according to Hewitt (2007), enhances "a standard of judgment...[referring] to the degree to which happiness and harmony are brought about in actual effect of acting upon his or her idea of the good" (p. 111). In other words, the EDI considers all living beings' happiness in the context of living well on this planet—it is not just surviving; it is thriving. The EDI is not a prescriptive answer to all social and ecological problems, though. According to Hewitt, the EDI "poses rather than solves the constant problem of achieving the right balance between individual freedom and social equality—justice, in a word" (p. 111). Hewitt suggests that ultimately the democratic ideal leads to a broader conceptualization of the common good. The EDI therefore cultivates a conceptualization that has significant and broad ecological applicability.

In the spirit of Dewey, this book is committed to advancing democracy in the context of an ecological democratic ideal. What are some other ways that we can understand the anatomy of sustainability? To understand sustainability we need to explore the body of literature that exists.

The journey towards understanding sustainability is a circuitous road. I am interested in the ecologist Michael Ben-Eli's approach to the topic. As mentioned earlier, he defines sustainability as

> [A] balanced interaction between a population and the carrying capacity of an environment such that the population develops to express its full potential without adversely and irreversibly affecting the carrying capacity of the environment upon which it depends. (n.d.)

The implications of Ben-Eli's conceptualization of sustainability are far-reaching. His argument that sustainability relies on enabling a population to "express its full potential" adds important substance to the sustainability conversation. His argument suggests that sustainability operates on the moral framework of ecological democracy (see Shiva, 2005).

When we strive to cultivate the conditions that contribute to the expression of a population's full potential, I argue that we are working towards justice. Within Ben-Eli's conceptualization of the term, working towards sustainability is "just," because we are advancing equity and fairness for a particular population. In the context of advancing fairness and equity, justice is deepened by working to not "irreversibly affect" the carrying capacity of an environment. Justice demands a type of thinking that is integrated, divergent, and contextualized. It mirrors Dewey's democratic ideal in that it "emerges out of the faith in the individual to define and develop her particular capacities in harmony with the needs and demands of others as they define and develop their own powers" (Hewitt, 2007, p. 111). To develop one's capacities in a way that is harmonious with the needs and demands of others is sustainable. However, one aspect that Ben-Eli leaves out in his definition is that of intergenerational equity. I would add "without irreversibly affecting *the resource base for future generations*" to deepen the attentiveness to our successors. In my formulation of the notion of ecological democracy we need to struggle to advance individual liberty, *ecological equality*, and *intergenerational equity*.

Several thinkers have addressed the topic of ecology within the scope of education. Accordingly, the multidisciplinary scholarship of curriculum studies in the realm of ecology is far-reaching. Authors who address this topic add a critical perspective to educational discourse (Jardine et al., 2006; Bowers, 2001a; Orr, 1992, 2003; N. Gough, 1989, 2006; Morris, 2002; Fien, 1993; Lydon, 1992; Marsden, 1971; A. Gough, 1993; Bowers & Flinders 1990; Gough & Robottom, 1993; Prakash, 1994). These authors weigh in on the important discussion of integrating ecology and education. Recognizing the value of education, E.F. Schumacher (1973) posits that education is our greatest resource. Che Guevara (1994) shares this sentiment, noting that education builds the capacity to respond to the situations posed by life.

I agree with Schumacher's and Guevara's stance that education is one of the most important institutions that enable a culture to deal with a situation and to ultimately meet the culture's difficulties. I agree with them because it is through education that we foster critical consciousness, the type of consciousness that enables students to think deeply and relevantly. Once a person is able to see how his or her living and consumption habits are affecting the surrounding environment, he or she is more likely to adopt an attitude of ecological frugality. When we see the "patterns that connect" (Bateson, 1972), we are better situated to advance lives of more in-depth stewardship. Education is capable of building the capacity to respond to our ecological crisis. Morris (2002) observes that many scholars are grappling "with rethinking education ecologically" (p. 571). To rethink education ecologically involves a major shift in the predominant "student as consumer" paradigm. Instead of promulgating the prevailing consumer-focused orientation of education, an ecological perspective emboldens a more sustainable discourse.

An eco-curriculum for sustainability fosters eco-literacy. By teaching today's youth to be able to "read their [environmental] world" we are enabling them to "read the [ecological] word" (Freire & Macedo, 1987). The process of being able to read the ecological world involves developing a framework of understanding that advances stewardship. When students understand the complex relationships that exist within the natural world and how they fit into and affect these relationships, they are better able to recognize the role that humans play in fostering healthy ecosystems. Thus, an eco-curriculum for sustainability encourages a coalition between all living species and an alliance between present and future generations. This flies in the face of the more dominant anthropocentric paradigm. Ernest Partridge characterizes anthropocentric thinking as "the view that humanity's needs and interests are of supreme and exclusive value and importance in nature" (Partridge, n.d.). Instead of promoting anthropocentric thinking, an eco-curriculum for sustainability precipitates a reconceptualization of how humans perceive and interact with Earth.

The Threat of Collapse

Without a diverse and healthy community, ecosystems can easily "collapse" (Diamond, 2005). In order to prevent a human level collapse, humans must participate in community-making. Participating in community-making allows us to embrace the full potentiality of the ecological movement. Without forging a strong sense of community and sense of place, it is likely that we will experience large-scale eco-social collapse. It is individual mindedness that is partially culpable for our ecological situation. When people focus on meeting their own needs and completely disregard the needs of others they can become blinded by solipsism. If this is the case, it is likely that they are oblivious to the impact that their choices have on others, both human and non-human. A solipsistic society is likely to experience a dramatic collapse.

Diamond (2005) notes that a collapse refers to "a drastic decrease in human population size and/or political/economic/social complexity, over a considerable area, for an extended time" (p. 3). If we do not work towards building a greater sense of community and creating a more ecologically sound human-Earth relationship we may encounter major problems that compromise the habitability of our biosphere. One of the most effective ways to forge a harmonious eco-social relationship is to recognize the intrinsic value of all life. In this book, I explore notions of sustainability that are grounded in a "village council of all beings" (Snyder, 1995; Seed, 1988). This village council of all living beings honors the importance of all life on Earth; it is a way of connecting the dots towards advancing ecological vitality. When we advance eco-vitality we also encourage eco-reconceptualization.

Ecological Literacy

An eco-reconceptualization leads to what Orr (2005) and Fritjof Capra (2005) refer to as eco-literacy. In essence, eco-literacy deals with advancing our ability to understand our relationship with the natural world and to build our knowledge about how we affect it. The prefix "eco" comes from the Greek word "oikos" which means "home." Gary Snyder refers to our biosphere as our "earth home." This notion of home gives a whole new meaning to *homework*. In this sense, homework is what we do when we "listen to the land" (Jensen, 1995) and work to serve its interests. Eco-literacy explores the interrelationships and interdependence that exist and develop fluidly on our "earth home." Orr (1992) posits that eco-literacy involves the capacity to "observe nature with insight" which is characterized by understanding the natural systems that make life on Earth possible (p. 86).

Observing nature with insight is a central tenet to eco-literacy. When we understand the interdependence of the living world we begin to recognize our role in advancing sustainability. We start to realize that we can find the "whole" in the pieces. Orr (2005) states that an ecologically literate person would "have at least a basic comprehension of ecology, human ecology, and the concepts of sustainability, as well as the wherewithal to solve problems" (p. xi). Facilitating the wherewithal to solve problems advances stewardship and ecological ingenuity. Stone and Barlow (2005) maintain that developing ecological literacy is a fundamental component to building sustainable communities because it enables a student to think critically and contextually. Accordingly, a student who develops ecological literacy is able to not only recognize the particular environmental problems of the place in which he dwells, but is also able to formulate practical action steps to mitigate the problems in question. Ecological literacy is described as understanding how to partner with natural systems to encourage a "mutual benefit [between all living beings]" (Stone & Barlow, 2005, back cover). Partnering with the environment is an important aspect of sustainability. It is this partnership that espouses a mutually beneficial relationship between humans and nature.

Education for Sustainability

> A sustainable society is one that can persist over generations, one that is far-seeing enough, flexible enough, and wise enough not to undermine either its physical or social systems of support.
>
> Meadows in *Ecological Sustainability and Integrity*

It is clear that education is currently reproducing a non-sustainable mode of inquiry leading to what Pinar (2004) refers to as the "nightmare" of education that we see today. Jensen (2006) points out that "our schools are filled with bored children preparing for bored lives" (p. 95). Sustainability education aims to convert the school learning environment from a sterile environment of drudgery to something more dynamic and meaningful. Corcoran and Wals (2004) maintain that "Sustainability is not just another issue to be added to an overcrowded curriculum, but a gateway to a different view of curriculum, of pedagogy, of organizational change, of policy and particularly of ethos" (p. 5). It is a gateway that mobilizes a more respectful and ecological way to interact with the biosphere. Schooling that embraces a more sustainable framework has the capacity to transform modern day education into a more robust and enduring enterprise.

Education for sustainability[3] involves a radical de-emphasis on monetary gain as well as a focus on the non-commoditized features of life that include place-making, community building, aesthetic inquiry, and Earth-based stewardship. Janice Crede (2009) indicates that education for sustainability "involves teaching and learning about our environment and its ability or inability to sustain us based on our human actions" (p. 27). This involves a move away from conventional education steeped in mechanism. In this way, sustainability education leads to a restoration of ecological equilibrium in a curriculum that is currently "crowded and corroded by consumption and capitalism" (Williams, 2001, p. 6). It is a shift from the unsustainable education approach that characterizes modern day curriculum and pedagogy.

Terril Shorb (2009) tells us that "Education for sustainability assumes some kind of template for topics pertinent to bringing sustainability into wide practice" (p. 11). It is an education model "based on paths to learning and practice that effectively sustain the community of all beings" (Shorb, 2009, p. 14). Within the context of education for sustainability, a reconfiguration in pedagogy and theory that centers on improving the quality of "our lives and the lives of our children while restoring the gift of natural systems upon which our lives depend" is required (Santone, 2007, n.p.). Teaching towards self-actualization and increasing the wellness and solidarity of humankind provides the possibility for a more healthy and balanced way of living. I argue that we can revitalize today's unsustainable economic and social structure in an equitable and effective way through educating for sustainability.

Susan Santone offers that sustainability education promotes justice by seeking out ways to "democratize institutions, eliminate the exploitation of people and the environment, and achieve a more equitable distribution of resources and power" (in Chabot & Wavle, 2005, p. 62).

---

3   Education for sustainability is also referred to as education for sustainable development, education for sustainable living, education for eco-literacy, and sustainability education (this last term being most prevalently used in this book)

Although these goals are idealistic, I believe that they are also achievable. Indeed, it is beautiful to think of schools in this way—steeped in democracy, committed to eliminating exploitation, and working towards equality. Accordingly, sustainability education has a far-reaching range of duties. It is a form of education that works towards democracy and preventing environmental degradation. Additionally, sustainability education "equips students to become informed, caring, and effective citizens" (Santone in Chabot and Wavle, 2005, p. 62). I think the importance of being a caring citizen should be a priority. We must care before we seek out knowledge and work towards environmental restoration. In this sense, sustainability education invokes a form of compassion that is extended to all living beings. The Trappist monk Thomas Merton says, "The whole idea of compassion...is based on a keen awareness of the interdependence of all these living beings, which are all part of one another and all involved in one another" (in Fox, 1979, p. 24). Compassion involves recognition of the inherent interdependence between all the living beings in the biosphere. It is compassion that leads to the attentiveness and recognition of how we affect others, both human and non-human. Compassion is engendered by sustainability and sustainability education. I argue that we cannot live sustainably if we are not compassionate.

As the theologian and educator Mathew Fox (2006) states, "Compassion means justice. Another very current word for justice—and therefore compassion—is sustainability" (p. 123). To enhance social, ecological, and intergenerational equity we need to cultivate compassion within students and within ourselves as educators and curriculum theorists. Fox adds that "compassion is the living out of our interdependence" (p. 122). Compassion is not the "living out" of our isolation as propounded in a managerial and mechanistic curriculum. It is the understanding of our cosmological responsibility to be responsive to and caring towards the visible and invisible life that surrounds us. Fox (2006) summarizes the importance of compassion stating that a mindful education "would grow our capacity for creativity, as well as our...love of the earth, and our capacity for compassion" (p. 28).

Dewey (1989) states that "inquiry is the controlled or directed transformation of an indeterminate situation into one that is so determinate in its constituent distinctions and relations as to convert the elements of the original situation into a unified whole" (p. 394). The notion of pursuing a unified whole is pertinent to the current discussion on sustainability. In sustainability education there is an emphasis on ecological and social reconciliation through critical inquiry. In the context of environmental health, the disorienting dilemma that instigates the inquiry subsumed by sustainability education is the need to address the fact that human behavior is contributing to the destruction of our biosphere. Thus, the primary emphasis in the inquiry associated with sustainability education is grounded in restoring a more harmonious human-Earth relationship (T. Berry, 2006). In *Dream of the Earth*, the late Thomas Berry (1990) calls this momentum towards a more ecologically derived mode of human discourse the *Ecozoic* movement.

Thomas Berry acknowledges that there is currently a "crisis of human-earth relations" and adds that the "present story is inadequate to meet the survival demands of [the] present situation" (in Lydon, 1992, p. 55). He refers to the unsustainable trajectory that humanity is on, being in the midst of the Cenozoic era. The Cenozoic era "places all our faith in the capacity of technology to pull us out of the current crisis without changing our polluting and consumption-oriented lifestyles" (Gadotti, 2008, p. 34). In *The New Story* (1978), Berry notes: "A structure of knowledge can be established with its human significance from the physics of the universe...to an understanding of the entire range of human endeavor...to all those studies whereby [humanity] fulfills [its] role in the earth process" (in Lydon, p. 74). Berry urges that humanity's role on Earth is to operate within a "mutually beneficial human-nature" relationship. To this end, Berry's notion of the "Ecozoic path...is founded on a new healthy relationship with the planet, recognizing that we are part of the natural world and live in harmony with the universe, and which is [informed] by [responding to] present ecological concerns" in a pragmatic fashion (Gadotti, 2008, p. 34). This touches on the essence of sustainability education—to equip students with the tools for ecological reconnection.

Developing a healthy relationship with the planet involves encountering the primordial silence of the wilderness, experiencing a sunset over a large body of water, and celebrating the diversity that is inherent to healthy ecosystems. The reality of this is that one does not have to go into designated wilderness areas in order to commune with nature in a way that fosters biophilia. On the contrary, biophilia can be cultivated in small urban green spaces. In some cases it can happen through spending time on an outdoor patio simply planting flowers. Gardening has the potential to help a person young or old connect to Earth. Nurturing a healthy relationship with the planet is one way to mobilize an Ecozoic approach. It is the Ecozoic path that must guide sustainability education. To further understand sustainability education we turn to Stephen Sterling.

Sterling (2001) states that sustainability education is "A changed educational paradigm, one that addresses and indicates positive directions" (p. 22). This transformation "takes us into the depth of things" requiring a "change of educational culture which both develops and embodies the theory and practice of sustainability in a way which is critically aware" (Sterling, 2001, p. 22). To work towards critical awareness, I believe sustainability education needs to be grounded in building a student's capacity to identify and comprehend the ecological maladies that face us. Sustainability education takes us into the depth of things by revealing the complexities and simplicities involved in drawing out ecological vitality. It is a freeing of the ancient processes that advance a form of human wisdom grounded in an ecocentric framework. Accordingly, sustainability education is informed by eco-vitality, a process dedicated to advancing the critical thinking capacity of students, staff, faculty, and all stakeholders in the educational process.

Sterling states that "Ecologically sustainable development depends on sustainability education and learning—which in turn manifests and sustains sustainable development: they are neither separate nor the same" (Sterling, 2001, p. 22). Here Sterling makes a distinction between *education for sustainable development* and *sustainability education.* It is beyond the scope of this book to explore the semantics of the various terms related to sustainability. Instead, in this book, I embrace the notion that overall, these terms are analogous in the context of working towards a more sustainable form of curriculum and pedagogy grounded in (but not limited to) advancing ecological and social well-being. Thus, I argue that curriculum studies for sustainability must strive to embrace what Corcoran refers to as "a radical plurality of views" (PC, October 2009). What does it mean to embrace a radical plurality of all views? It means that we must initiate and engage in a form of participatory ecology. That is, we must strive to look at environmental health from the perspective of others, including minorities and marginalized people.

Sustainability education is situated within the sustainability movement and is ultimately geared towards advancing ecological justice and democracy. Sterling et al. (1992) explain that:

> We believe that education for sustainability is a process which is relevant to all people and that, like sustainable development itself, it is a process rather than a fixed goal. It may precede—and it will always accompany—the building of relationships between individuals, groups and their environment. All people, we believe, are capable of being educators and learners in the pursuit of sustainability. (p. 2; in Fien, 1993, p. 14)

As Sterling et al. indicate, recognizing sustainability education as process-focused and not outcome-focused is fundamental to pursuing sustainability. Process, in this sense, is just as important as the "product" that comes from an educational experience. That is, instead of overemphasizing outcome, assessment, and pre-determined standardization, sustainability education honors the education that emerges from direct experience. It is of key importance that sustainability is not seen as a "fixed goal." Instead, we must turn towards a more dynamic conception of sustainability, one that embraces the ever-changing landscape of the environmental restoration project. To this end, we need to acknowledge the inherent value of relationship, working towards connection of individuals, groups, and the communities in which we are situated. Sterling et al. (in Fien, 1993) argue that education for sustainability is a process which

> Enables people to understand the interdependence of all life on this planet, and the repercussions that their actions and decisions may have both now and in the future on resources, on the global community as well as their local one, and on the total environment. (p. 14)

Thus, education for sustainability is afforded an intergenerational responsibility and a globally relevant understanding of how we impact planetary health with our choices as individuals and as groups. Sustainability education "[i]ncreases people's awareness of the economic, political, social, cultural, technological, and environmental forces which foster or impede sustainable development" (p. 14). This aspect deals with the far-ranging implications of becoming ecologically literate in many spheres.

Sterling et al. (in Fien, 1993) expand upon the notion of increasing awareness in the realm of sustainability education. They state that we must strive to

> [Develop] people's awareness...enabling them to be effectively involved in sustainable development at local, national and international levels, and helping them to work towards a more equitable and sustainable future. In particular, it enables people to integrate environmental and economic decision-making. (p. 14)

The idea of sustainability as an integrating context is highlighted in this notion of understanding the interface between environmental and economic decision-making. It is a big project to develop people's awareness and to equip them to be a part of the sustainability movement. However, I believe that it is well within our grasp both pedagogically and politically. But, how do we cultivate the "pedagogical will" for sustainability in teachers, administrators, and other educational stakeholders? How do we foster awareness in a time of economic and ecological emergency? As I discuss in the next chapter, we must start in our own backyards. When we understand the way in which our choices affect the health of our own neighborhood, we are more likely to investigate ways that we can help keep other neighborhoods in good shape from an ecological perspective.

Sterling et al. argue that sustainability education "Affirms the validity of the different approaches contributed by environmental education...and [espouses] the need for the further development and integration of the concepts of sustainability" (p. 14). This affirmation explores "these and other related cross-disciplinary educational approaches, as well as in established disciplines" (in Fien, 1993, p. 14). Sterling's affirmation of the environmental education approaches integrated with sustainability is significant. The transdisciplinarity of sustainability is exemplified by its broad appeal and potential application. Next I will explore Aldo Leopold's land ethic as I formulate a discussion surrounding the development of an ecological worldview.

The Land Ethic

A major contributor to the sustainability movement is Aldo Leopold. Leopold is a leader in advancing ecologically centered thinking. C.A. Bowers (1995) notes that Leopold provides a moral framework for judging whether human behavior meets the "hard test that must be met by all ecologically sustainable cultures" (p. 5). Accordingly, Leopold argues that "A thing is right when it tends to preserve the integrity, stability, and beauty of the biotic community. It is wrong when it tends otherwise" (Leopold, 1989, pp. 224–225; also in Nicol, 2002, p. 208; also in Bowers, 1995, p. 5). Leopold's notion of preserving the integrity, stability, and beauty of the biotic community is integral to the notion of sustainability. His land ethic is an excellent way to evaluate our progress towards sustainability. When something works against the integrity of the biotic community we must find a way to mitigate its impact. Leopold advocated for a "state of harmony between men and land" (Leopold in Callicott, 2001, p. 177). He believed that we must forge a balance between human needs and ecological needs. If ecological integrity is compromised, so is the support system for humans. They are inextricable from each other.

Leopold was "especially interested in promoting land health as the conservation norm for the extensively modified" landscapes of our industrial-centered culture (Callicott, 2001, p. 177). If industry were to follow Leopold's conception of land health, we would not build Wal-Marts on wetlands or shopping malls over wilderness areas. Leopold's philosophical presupposition is referred to as the "land ethic." Kenneth Goodpaster explains that, "In short, a land ethic changes the role of Homo sapiens from conqueror of the land-community to plain member and citizen of it" (in Callicott, 1989, p. 83). This is an epochal shift in thinking that encourages a mutually beneficial human-Earth relationship. The land ethic facilitates a holistic transformation of thinking. No longer are human needs placed over the needs of the biosphere. Callicott states that, "as 'The Land Ethic' develops, the focus of moral concern shifts gradually away from plants, animals, soils and waters severally to the biotic community collectively" (p. 83). So, instead of viewing nature as a series of fragmented and isolated parts, it is viewed as an integrated whole. The overall biotic community becomes the primary indicator of health. It strives for an all embracing conceptualization of ecological integrity that involves a dramatic shift from mechanistic thinking. Accordingly, in the land ethic, there is an implied "'biotic rights' of species" (p. 84). To better understand the land ethic, it is important to use ecological thought.

Callicott (1989) points out that "Ecological thought, historically, has tended to be holistic in outlook" (p. 87). It is the holistic quality of ecology that promotes transdisciplinary inquiry. In this sense, ecology relates well to curriculum studies, which is defined as the "interdisciplinary field committed to the study of educational experience" (Pinar, 2004, p. 20). Both ecology and curriculum studies strive to create a better living condition for all. Generically, ecology is defined as "the study of the relationships of organisms to one another and to the elemental environment" (Callicott, 1989, p. 87). Leopold further articulates his conception of a land ethic:

> It is at least not impossible to regard the earth's parts—soil, mountains, rivers, atmosphere, etc.—as organs or part of organs of a coordinated whole, each part with a definite function. And if [only] we could see this whole as a whole...we should respect it collectively not only as a useful servant but as a living being. (Leopold in Callicott, 1989, p. 88)

Thus, the notion of a land ethic embraces seeing the "whole as a whole" where each entity, human and non-human, plays an important role in sustaining life. In Leopold's view, the *sonum bonum*[4] of ecological whole-

---

4   Sonum bonum comes from the Latin denoting supreme good.

ness is wilderness. Leopold states that wilderness provides "the most perfect norm of ecosystem health" (Callicott, 2001, p. 177).

Wilderness is where we can see an ecosystem at work. An ecosystem that is virtually unaltered by human development is a beautiful sight. I have traveled through several wilderness areas throughout the United States and continue to be awestruck at each visit. What strikes me as the most incredible element of a wilderness area is its unique landscape and feel. There is a palpable sacredness that pervades the wilderness. Environmentalist Sigurd Olson (1998) refers to this as our "racial memory" (p. 10). David Backes tells us that racial memory is spawned from "the idea that humans have a biological attachment to nature that arises from our long evolutionary heritage" (in Olson, 2001, p. xxxii). Olson believes that our "instincts *demand* that we seek contact with nature" (p. 185). I agree with Olson, as it seems that we as humans do have an intrinsic need to encounter wilderness. Olson (1998) states that "We all have a pronounced streak of the primitive set deep in us—an instinctive longing that compels us to leave the confines of civilization," a longing that drives us to "bury ourselves periodically in the most inaccessible spots we can penetrate" (p. 5). As a wilderness enthusiast, I am passionate about finding and exploring the most inaccessible spots that I can penetrate. These places provide refuge from the industrial world, allowing me to return to a silence that opens up personal regenerative space. The value of encountering wilderness is seemingly infinite. But unfortunately, the ecological and physical space of wilderness is limited.

Robin Good (1998) comments that "nature is finite and of a limited carrying capacity" (pp. 68–69). We need to be mindful of the capacity of this planet to prevent the liquidation of all its resources. Good adds that abiding "by nature's limits means maintaining the integrity of nature's processes, cycles, and rhythms so that she can renew and regenerate herself" (p. 69). Maintaining the integrity of nature's processes is a central tenet to living sustainably. If we work in opposition to the integrity of nature's processes, we might lose valuable resources. When we live sustainably we value the ephemeral quality of wildness. Therefore, enabling nature to undergo regeneration is critical to ecological sustainability. Good adds that

> Abiding by nature's limits means maintaining the integrity of nature's processes, cycles, and rhythms so that she can renew and regenerate herself. It is this renewal ability, arising from within a cyclical pattern of time, that allows for the nourishment, sustenance, and perpetuation of all life forms. Thus in adhering to a biotic code, humans protect and preserve nature's re-

generative ability and thereby preserve their own regenerative ability. (Good, 1998, p. 69)

Leopold honors the intrinsic value of the life-support systems that make up the biotic community. As a result, Leopold's land ethic encourages the development of our ecological awareness. He urges us to think more holistically and to take precautions if we ever do "mess with nature." Interestingly, he states that "the first rule of intelligent tinkering is to keep all the parts" (Leopold in Kimmins, 1999, p. 9). This notion of intelligent tinkering is precautionary and recognizes that there may be utility in the parts of nature that we think are "useless." Precautionary thinking enables an ecological awareness characterized by a more mindful and intentional restoration effort that advances the agenda of environmental stability. Through Leopold's efforts, a framework has been laid to advance environmental philosophy. In *A Sand County Almanac* Leopold adds that humans belong to a "community that includes all life forms: plants, animals, and human beings" (in Corcoran, Wohlpart, & Hollingshead, 2008, p. xv). There are significant epistemological implications that are associated with belonging to a community of all life forms.

Participating in an eco-curriculum involves looking from a broader worldview. Instead of making decisions based solely on the good of human advancement, an emphasis is placed on the *parliament of all beings* (Benyus, 1998). When we make decisions based on the parliament of all beings, we line up with Leopold's land ethic by placing the emphasis on the integrity of the biotic community. What about education and the land ethic—what does one have to do with the other? Milbrath (1989) argues that we need to work towards an education that is oriented towards helping people to "think integratively, to expand their frame of reference to include the biosphere as a total system and to think in long time frames" (p. 99). In essence, Milbrath's philosophy lines up with Leopold's—both argue that we need to think holistically. Leopold expounds on holistic thinking, sharing that

> The science of relationships is ecology, but what we call it matters nothing. The question is, does the citizen know that he is a cog in an ecological mechanism? That if he will work with that mechanism, his mental wealth and physical wealth can expand indefinitely? But that if he refuses to work with it, it will ultimately grind him to dust? If education does not teach us these things, then what is education for? (Leopold in Gookin, 1999, 5-2)

Education must help us to advance the integrity, stability, and beauty of the biotic community—by enabling us to realize that we are a cog in the ecological mechanism.[5] Leopold's contribution to the field of sustainability extends beyond eco-centric thinking. He argues for fostering a greater relationship with the land by suggesting that we "sing our love for the land and our obligation to it" (in Jensen, 2008, p. 202). Thus, in order to further advance the sustainability movement, we should work towards advancing a narrative of radical love for Earth.[6] By radical love I am referring to a kind of love that transcends traditional conceptions of the human-Earth relationships—a kind of love that enables us to embrace a deeper connection to the biosphere while advancing Leopold's notion of the land ethic. When more people understand the value of maintaining the "integrity, stability, and beauty of the biotic community" it is likely that there will be greater effort aimed at promoting sustainability. Several authors apply Leopold's land ethic to their own work (Orr, 1991; Bowers, 1995; Jensen, 2006). Building on Leopold's conception of a land ethic is the ecological worldview.

Ecological Worldview

When we try to pick out anything by itself, we find it hitched to everything else in the universe.

John Muir in *Ecological resistance movements: The global emergence of radical and popular environmentalism*

It is necessary now to ecologize everything.

Edgar Morin in *Education for sustainability: A critical contribution*

---

5 The ecological mechanism that Leopold refers to here is not derived from the mechanistic worldview; instead it is his way of articulating our role on this planet, from an organic perspective.

6 In *Pedagogy of Indignation* (printed posthumously) Paulo Freire (2004) advises, "It is urgent that we assume the duty of fighting for the fundamental ethical principles, like...the life of birds, the life of rivers and forests." He continues, "I do not believe in love between men and women, between human beings, if we are not able to love the world" (p. 46). These thoughts by Freire about love and the environment, serve as a conceptual foundation to the eco-pedagogy movement (Kahn, 2008). This notion of love for all life—human and non-human—is central to the theme of sustainability. See Susan Edgerton's (1996) discussion on the "eco-erosic," where she argues "love of the land and of the earth. Love of one's neighbors and intimates (local) and love of humankind (global) cannot be separated from one another, or from love of land and earth, under penalty of hatred" (p. 70; also in Martusewicz, 2001, p. 117).

to the Decade of Education for Sustainable Development

Morin's call to "*ecologize* everything" is a response to the overwhelming pressure of today's environmental crisis. To *ecologize* is to understand the inherent interconnectivity between systems and subsystems. It is an effort to advance sustainability within a more holistic framework than today's mechanistic approach. An ecological worldview honors the dynamic interdependence between all living beings. The conception of an ecological worldview that I discuss here is anchored in systems theory as articulated by Capra (1982, 1996) and Gregory Bateson (1972). It is built upon the presupposition that virtually everything is connected (Cobb, 1988). Instead of seeing the world through a fragmentary mechanistic lens, an ecological worldview recognizes the significance of both human and non-human well-being. Accordingly, it involves a major epistemological and metaphysical reconceptualization.

As Sterling (2004b) indicates, the ecological worldview operates under the assumption that "we know that everything can't be known (therefore appreciation is vital)" and that "we know our knowing, being participative is inevitably limited" and lastly that "we know that we 'don't know'" (p. 169). Thus, an ecological worldview is in opposition to the mechanistic worldview's assumptions that "we believe that in principle everything can be known (and...controlled)" and "we think we know—through observation and measurement" and lastly that "we don't know that we 'don't know'" (Sterling, 2004b, p. 169). An ecological framework recognizes that mechanism is a "limited conceptual model" (p. 163). In other words, an ecological worldview transcends mechanism by embracing an integrated paradigm honoring the interdependence between all life. David Jardine (2000) observes that "ecology concerns not what we can do but what is proper, what is properly responsive to the place in which we find ourselves, those actions which have propriety, those which are 'fitting,' and which issue up out of a place as a considerate response to that place (i.e., a response that somehow acts in accordance with the sustainability of that response)" (p. 30). Doing what is "properly responsive to the place" where we live is a powerful concept. It is both pragmatic and practical—it gives traction to the sustainability argument.

Thomas Merton (1968) suggests that the ecological worldview recognizes that the "Cartesian consciousness remains...imprisoned in itself" (p. 23). He intimates that the imprisonment associated with Cartesian thinking emboldens a "need to break out of itself and to meet 'the other' in 'encounter,' 'openness,' 'fellowship,' 'communion'" (Merton, 1968, p. 23). To fellowship with others is an idea that resonates with my theoretical work pertaining to sustainability. I believe that as scholars, we are obligated to *fellowship* in an intergenerational context. We must commune with our predecessors by reading their work and building on existing conversations. We must also fellowship with future generations by creating more theoretical space in which they can formulate carefully constructed responses to contemporary ecological issues. In the context of advancing ecological sustainability, we must meet the *other*, and we must recognize that this *other* is an entity that reflects the integrity of the universe. The "other" is what adds to the conceptual and environmental diversity necessary for living in a sustainable way.

There is an experiential atonement associated with seeing the world ecologically. Phenomenologically speaking, this atonement is similar to the *unitive experience* described in Gerald May's (1987) work. May states that a *unitive experience* is always "characterized by being-at-one" (p. 59). Instead of cultivating greater separation from nature, an ecological worldview encourages unitive reconnection with the earth. Sterling (2001) posits that "[e]cological thinking entails a shift of emphasis from relationships based on separation, control and manipulation towards those based on participation, empowerment and self-organization" (p. 49). Thus, there is a fundamental shift in perception associated with the ecological worldview. It involves an organically derived, participatory, and cosmological reconnection.

Stephen Sterling (2004a) adds that a shift in education towards a more systemic perception is essential. He believes that radical changes need to take place and suggests that

> A change of...educational paradigm [is necessary]—because sustainability indicates a change of cultural paradigm which is both emergent and imperative. Many commentators maintain the fundamental issue at stake is a "crisis of perception" which most of us are part of, and that a change of cultural worldview based on some form of systems thinking is both necessary and emerging, if still fragile. (p. 51)

Systems-oriented thinking calls for a more participatory process of integrated educational research. As Sterling indicates, the move towards sustainability invokes a cultural paradigm that is emergent and imperative. A cultural paradigm committed to equipping our youth with the ability to comprehend that the way they view the world is central to how they will treat it.

Porritt (1990) articulates the urgency in which we must incorporate education into the effort to move humanity towards a more sustainable worldview.

> Whatever the nature of the changes required, education is of paramount importance. The well-being of all future generations depends on the skill and effectiveness with which we inform and inspire the knowledge base and values of those currently in our schools and colleges. The challenge is daunting, in as much as each and every delay in bringing about the necessary transformation will cost us dear in the future. (Porritt, 1990, p. 1; also quoted in Fien, 1993, p. 11)

Fundamental to advocating for the well-being of all future generations is the cultivation of an ecological worldview in an educational context. In this book I embrace an ecological worldview that emphasizes relationships while cultivating an ethic of environmental stewardship.

Buckminster Fuller poses the question "how do we see and think in terms of wholes?" (in Fox, 2006, p. 105). He suggests that we must think more expansively than contractively and subsequently seek out the right balance for our life journey. In the realm of thinking and education, thinking holistically favors divergent thought over convergent thought. In contrast, the traditional, mechanically derived education model emphasizes convergent thinking. A convergent thinking model limits learning to fragmented areas of specialization and thus emphasizes a unilateral epistemology locked in a limited way of understanding the world. Convergent thinking is described as a form of thinking that emphasizes a single correct answer and thus needs very little creative thinking to solve (convergent thinking, n.d.). Alternatively, divergent thinking is discursive in nature and pluralistically derived. It is thus a form of thinking that "moves away in diverging directions so as to involve a variety of aspects and which sometimes lead to novel ideas and solutions" (divergent thinking, n.d.). Thus, divergent thinking enables one to produce a number of solutions to a given problem. In this sense, ecological thinking is primarily divergent in that it is grounded in an organic epistemological tradition. This organically derived notion of ecological thinking is significant from the context of sustainability and education.

Answering the S.O.S.

The vast and diverse terrain of scholarship that is subsumed by sustainability studies provides much intellectual possibility. But, first and foremost we must work to "save our ship" through an informed scholarship of sustainability. By embracing the themes of eco-literacy, curriculum as ecological text, and the land ethic—we can answer the S.O.S. of Earth and position environmental intelligence at the top of our educational priorities.

To best answer the S.O.S., I posit that we need to bring our education back home. We must recognize the educational possibilities of our surrounding eco-systems and the nuances of our cultural heritage. The value of developing a greater sense of community is embedded in our need to feel connected. In the next chapter I argue that a sense of place must undergird our educational transition to sustainability.

CHAPTER 5

Place and Education: Bringing It All Back Home

Places are profoundly pedagogical.

David Gruenewald, "Foundations of Place: A Multidisciplinary Framework for Place-Conscious Education"

Everybody needs beauty as well as bread, places to play in and pray in, where nature may heal and give strength to body and soul.

John Muir, *Nature Writings*

KANSAS. WISCONSIN. Vermont. Oregon. Georgia. Wyoming. All states in which I have lived. So far in my life journey I have resided in 14 different states. I continue to be intrigued by the uniqueness embodied by each of these places. It is the particularities of these localities that set them apart from each other both culturally and ecologically. I loved the green mountains of Vermont and the beauty of Crater Lake in Oregon. When I first moved to northern Wisconsin, I noticed that the mailboxes were on swivels and that the fire hydrants had red flags sticking up out of them, three feet into the air. I was not sure why. When winter rolled around and the first big snow dropped over two feet, I discovered the significance of these seemingly random accoutrements. In the event of a fire, when the hydrants are under deep snow, these flags enable firefighters to find their water source. At times, the snow banks were over ten feet tall! The mailbox swivels were set up so that snow plows would not break the mailbox by shoving roadside snow into them. As an outsider, a "newbie," I was surprised and awed by the volume of snow precipitated in the winter storms, but natives did not even flinch, as it was part of northern living.

Grocery stores can serve as an effective indicator of cultural particularity. During my first Wisconsin grocery store visit, I heard a voice over the intercom asking all "beggars" to come to the front. I thought to myself, hmmm, I might qualify, and then went up to the front. I found out that they were calling for all of the "baggers" not beggars. It was a long "a" sound that would take some time to get use to. I am nourished by the novelty of exploring new places. The places in which we live serve as the backdrop, and sometimes as the foreground, for our educational experiences.

As a curriculum theorist and an experiential educator, place is a central component to my teaching philosophy. I continue to be astounded by the possibilities of grounding curriculum and pedagogy in the local.[1] I posit that when education becomes more local it becomes more authentic. By turning the educational lens towards the social and ecological communities in which we inhabit, education becomes more experiential. Students get a sense of authenticity while participating in place-based education[2] because the curriculum is contextualized within their home region. Students are better able to relate to curriculum that incorporates their back yard—because it is something with which they are familiar and something about which they care. Also, by going out into the community, students cultivate understanding through direct experience. In the experiential education model, these carefully chosen experiences are succeeded by opportunities for guided reflection, processing and integration of the learning, and transference. Transference occurs when one is able to apply the learning that emerges from a particular experience to different situations. Thus, the experiential cycle is grounded in enhancing one's judgment (Dewey, 1916, 1938).

In this chapter, I explore the importance of developing a sense of place. I adopt Sanger's (1997) definition—he states, "A sense of place refers to an experientially based intimacy with the natural processes, community, and history of one's place" (n.p.). In essence, a sense of place is grounded in encountering one's bioregion and getting to know its cultural, ecological, and historical nuances. I am interested in the possibilities of building place consciousness in a globalized world that is rapidly being colonized and thereby losing its ecological and cultural commons. What are the "commons" and how does their destruction affect us? C.A. Bowers says that the commons are represented by Earth's natural systems, such as water, air, forests, soil, rivers, etc. and by diverse cultural systems (intergenerational knowledges, arts, crafts, ceremonies, medicinal practices) that are shared without cost (in Mueller, 2008, p. 155). The commons exemplify diversity both ecologically and culturally. Mueller adds that "they may represent the last great envi-

---

[1] Joe Kincheloe and William Pinar (1991) introduced the concept of place to curriculum studies in 1991 emphasizing "its historical, cultural, and political (not geophysical) elements" (PC, Pinar, 2010).

[2] Please note that I use the term place-based, local, and bioregional education interchangeably throughout this chapter.

ronmental places and traditions that have not been transformed into market commodities" (2008, p. 155). The commons are the places and cultures that have retained originality—they are historical places because they tell the story of how a cultural or natural landscape has been shaped through time.

Tom Wessels (2005) insists that our surrounding ecological landscape is much more than mere scenery to be observed or terrain to be trekked. We can learn volumes from the natural history of our place. Wessels notes that, "etched into the land is the history of how we have inhabited it, the storms and fires that have shaped it, and its response to these and other changes" (Wessels, 2005, book jacket). There is wisdom hidden in our surrounding landscape. We can learn so much from getting to know the place in which we live. When we study our home ground, we participate in a process that Jensen (1995) refers to as "listening to the land." When we listen to the land, we can start to piece together its story—it involves attunement to the specificities of our place. Working to protect our ecological commons involves educating the next generation in a way that will enable them to read their landscape. We need to create educational situations that familiarize students with the tools for informed stewardship. As an outdoor explorer, and a person who likes to work directly with the land, I have developed an informed stewardship. Gardening and composting are interests of mine. It is through nature exploration, gardening, composting and simply playing outside that I have familiarized myself with my home ground.

In this chapter I also explore the potentiality of a bioregional eco-curriculum to generate a more fecund and grounded sense of place. One component of an eco-curriculum is that of exploring the world through ecological text. Ecological text is not the text traditionally found in a textbook—although it is academic and scholarly. Instead, ecological text is a place-based experiential phenomenon. Ecological text deepens our intellectual attentiveness to our environmental situation—including social, ecological, and personal connectedness to the land. Ecological text is composed of the natural and social relationships that surround us. It is a form of text that we find in a natural landscape, the cultural terrain of our surrounding community, or in the topography of the wilderness. Ecological text includes the texture and nuances of the social and cultural landscapes that make up the places that we encounter. When we learn from ecological text, we draw understanding from the particularities of the places in which we live. Ecological text is the sinew that holds our experiences together, as it involves learning from the relationships that sustain us. In Kathleen Abowitz's (2000) words, ecological text strengthens the "bonds of experience" helping us to "construct the shifting structures of consensus on which shared life is continuously built" (p. 900). Ecological text helps to hold our experiences together because it is grounded in the relationships that make up our lived experiences. Accordingly, when education is steeped in experience, it is likely that the learner is surrounded by ecological text. This is because ecological text is not merely limited to being in the natural world—it includes learning in a social context about the relationships that are subsumed within one's immediate community.

The opportunities that enable us to develop a more fecund sense of place make up ecological text. In other words, ecological text is both formal and informal. We do not have to be inside a school to gain awareness and wisdom from the relationships that sustain us. As Dewey (1916) once suggested, education is life, not preparation for some distant and irrelevant task. This is the case with ecological text—the separation between school and the community becomes more pervious (Dewey, 1938, 1990). Accordingly, in this chapter, I also explore the opportunities that pertain to a place-based educational approach. I argue that once a person gets to know her place, she is more likely to want to protect it. Also, when a person explores her surroundings, she will probably develop a greater appreciation for the aesthetic dimensions of her educational and lived experiences (Greene, 2001). Learning from place is a process of appreciating beauty, which can build our aesthetic attunement. My discussion about place-based education differs from what has been done (in the field of curriculum studies) by emphasizing the possibilities of a watershed-oriented model of bioregional education. Also, I draw from a few of my personal and professional experiences that have emerged from the field.

A bioregion is a slice from our biosphere that is composed of several ecosystems, typically falling within the same boundaries as a watershed. Bioregions are places in which we can study and begin to develop a deeper appreciation for the relationships that sustain us. They are the areas that sustain us, because they are the areas in which we live. Ecologist Robert Thayer (2003) explains that a bioregion "is literally and etymologically a 'life-place'—a unique region definable by natural (rather than political) boundaries" (p. 3). I am interested in the power of getting to know our life-place. With the focus on technology, efficiency, and speed that characterize today's pace of globalization, our life-place is easily taken for granted and overlooked. When we recognize the significant role played by the places in which we dwell, we are better equipped to live in a way that is mindful and attentive to our bioregion.

When I was in middle school, my favorite class was life science because we got outside and explored the natural world firsthand. In my life science class, we went on field trips to nearby wildlife management areas and hiked through the woods. I loved these field excursions because it did not feel like we were in school. Also, I got to learn cool things about the forests and wetlands of southeastern Kansas. This is the essence of place-based education—to study and to celebrate the idiosyncrasies of the exceptional places that we inhabit. I am particularly interested in how watersheds delineate bioregions.

A watershed is an area of land that drains into a common body of water. Rivers, lakes, and streams serve as "vital expression[s]" of a watershed (Project WILD, 1992, p. 146). I have been fascinated by the concept of watersheds since I moved to southeast Georgia, and the Ogeechee River basin, over four years ago. This interest surfaced from times swimming in, paddling in, and hiking along the Ogeechee River. The mysteries of the untamed river, its black water, the Cyprus trees with their "knobby knees," and the riparian corridor which provides refuge for a diversity of wildlife intrigues me. I am enthralled by how the deep, slow-moving water of the Ogeechee River leaches out the tannins from decaying vegetation and how this contributes to the water's tea-like appearance.

My work at a local botanical garden has helped grow my appreciation for understanding and exploring bioregions. There, I learned about the uniqueness of a longleaf pine ecosystem and had the opportunity to teach children and adults about some of its wonders. The longleaf pine ecosystem is endemic to the southeastern United States. At one point, the entire Ogeechee watershed was made up predominately of longleaf pine forests. Before European colonization, the longleaf pine wilderness covered about 90 million acres in the southeastern United States (Carolina Sandhills National Wildlife Refuge, 2009). Now, after urbanization and fire suppression, there are only about 3 million acres of longleaf pine forests left in the world—all situated in the southeastern United States. Ecologically, these are magnificent forests—they are composed of rich biodiversity.

The longleaf pine tree is able to live up to 500 years, and it does not reach maturity until 150 years (Carolina Sandhills National Wildlife Refuge, 2009). I am enthralled by the longleaf pine tree's beauty and its lifecycle. The tree starts in the "grass stage" as a small clump of long pine needles growing from the soil. The grass stage kicks off the tree's 500 year growth journey. Understanding the timescale of a longleaf pine tree's life is an interesting imaginary excursion. That is approximately

7.5 times as long as the average human lifespan. If we think about the longleaf pine's lifecycle from the scale of a human lifecycle, it helps us put things into perspective. The longleaf pine stays in grass stage for eight years—it is basically a "baby" until then. During these first eight years the tree grows a deep taproot (six to ten feet long), and then—almost magically—it shoots up as high as six feet in one growing season. The rapid growth stage is referred to as the "rocket stage." While in rocket stage, long pine needles grow out of the tree trunk and all of the branches, which makes it look like "my cousin It" from the Addams family.

When I first saw the tree in its rocket stage, I was surprised by its unique appearance. I had never seen anything like it in any of the other forests that I hiked. The openness of the pine stands and the abundance of wildlife make longleaf pine forests feel like wilderness. I learned a lot about these forests when I was charged with the task of teaching youth and college students about longleaf pine ecology. The longleaf pine habitat is characterized by a wide-open canopy, sandy soil, wiregrass tufts, and very tall, straight trees. The trees are so straight they look as if God shot very long arrows into Earth from the heavens. Longleaf pine habitat is ideal for gopher tortoises, indigo snakes, and red cockaded woodpeckers. These forests are also as rich in nutrients as they are in biodiversity.

At one point, the ecosystem of the longleaf pine was home to the most species-rich communities reported in North America (Kirkman, 2004). The sandy soil of southern Georgia creates a prime environment for longleaf pine and wiregrass ecosystems. The open and gently rolling terrain of the southeastern coastal plains—along with porosity of the soil—makes it an ideal place for longleaf pine trees to grow. Kirkman (2004) notes that wiregrass "once carpeted the forest floor of the state's...coastal plain" (n.p.). Wiregrass grows in clumps and is a tasty treat for gopher tortoises. The gopher tortoise is one of the keystone species of the longleaf pine ecosystem. A keystone species is a species that plays an integral role in maintaining the health and vitality of organisms (plant and/or animal) in an ecosystem. If a keystone species is removed from a system, the system will encounter a dramatic shift.

> A keystone species is analogous to the role of a keystone in an arch. While the keystone is under the least pressure of any of the stones in an arch, the arch still collapses without it. Similarly, an ecosystem may experience a dramatic shift if a keystone species is removed. (Keystone species, 2010, n.p.)

The gopher tortoise burrows deep into the ground (about 10–15 feet) and they tunnel another 50 feet horizontally. These tortoises are neat animals and play an important role in their habitat. The profusion of wiregrass in pre-colonization years offered an expansive range for wild game and livestock. For the purposes of this chapter, a full discussion on the longleaf pine and wiregrass ecosystem is not warranted. The point is that there is an abundance of natural history that can be accessed in virtually any bioregion. I am not the only one blessed to live among abundant beauty. You also are likely to find abundant beauty in your backyard.

Understanding the natural history of our places is an important aspect of bioregionalism. Everyone lives in a watershed. Whatever watershed you live in, it is also a bioregion. Accordingly, your watershed is your life place. Watersheds are composed of several smaller streams, rivers, and lakes that eventually make their way to an ocean. The interconnectedness we see within a watershed basin mirrors the interconnectedness of humans to their bioregions. When humans dump chemicals into their watershed it aversely impacts human and non-human life throughout the entire watershed. However, the impact doesn't simply stop at the boundary of the watershed—it is carried into other watersheds that are downstream. Lohan (2008) notes that "we all live downstream" (p. 8). Recognizing our fundamental aquatic-based interconnectivity enables us to think at a larger scale. We are connected to each other by our reliance on water, and this is manifested in how we participate in its use. Sterling and Vintinner tell us that "All life on Earth is linked through water as it cycles at different scales across the planet, from wetlands to rain clouds to rivers to oceans" (in Lohan, 2008, p. 15). The hydrological cycle describes the continuous movement of water on, above, and below the surface of Earth (Water cycle, 2010). Our role in the hydrological cycle is to help reduce surface water runoff, to minimize the amount of pollution that we add into our watershed, and to encourage others to conserve water. When we understand the water cycle we are likely to be better stewards of our most precious resource—water.

Inculcating mindfulness is a primary goal to bioregional education. One way to do so is to think about how you use water. Have you thought about your water footprint? Our water footprint is a measurement of the amount of water that we use to meet our needs. It can be measured collectively or individually. We generate a water footprint every single day. Lohan and Lohan (2008) share that our water footprint is affected by "[e]ach shower, each flush, each time we flip on the A/C or water the lawn" (Lohan & Lohan, 2008, p. 147). When you gain awareness of your average water footprint you are likely to be more mindful about your water use.

Bioregional nature immersion experiences enable students to develop environmental awareness and appreciation. To inculcate sustainability in an educational context for today's youth, it makes sense that we start in our own backyards. Ultimately, bioregionalism is a form of education that cultivates an ethic of stewardship. The places in which we live become educational clearinghouses. Environmental features, such as watersheds, become a significant area for integrated study. In this chapter I unpack place-based education, while exploring the benefits and possibilities for applying a watershed bioregional approach to education. I explore the significance for advancing sustainability in the educational context and propose strategies for infusing a watershed oriented eco-curriculum into a variety of settings.

Unpacking Place-based Education

Place is central to the narratives that make up our lives. In place-based education these narratives are infused into the learning process. Place-based education induces images of wholeness because it encourages a more ecologically oriented way of looking at things. By promoting the study of relationships and cultivating a connectedness with one's surroundings, place-based education becomes a robust form of curriculum and pedagogy. When we develop a holistic understanding of our place, we feel as if we play an integral role in our specific ecosystem.

Place-based education is transdisciplinary and experiential. Everything humans experience is contextualized in the place where it happens (Casey, 1993). The existential importance of place is stated by Edward Casey (1997). He says,

> To be at all—to exist in any way—is to be somewhere, and to be somewhere is to be in some kind of place...We are surrounded by places. We walk over and through them. We live in places, relate to others in them, die in them. Nothing we do is unplaced. (p. ix)

Understanding the significance of the places that we encounter is crucial to meaningful education. We "are immersed [in place] and could not do without it" (Casey, 1997, p. ix). In some situations, place serves anonymously as a mere backdrop for lived experience. Other times, place is at the foreground of our learning.

Within place-based education, the environment becomes an "integrating context" by offering a platform in which various disciplines can be explored simultaneously (Chawla & Escalante, 2007). It weaves together the collective narratives that exist within the community and the environment by providing space for each student to construct and build upon their own story. Professor David Sobel says that place-based education emphasizes "hands-on, real-world learning experiences" which increase "academic achievement [and] help students develop stronger ties to their community" (in Gruenewald & Smith, 2008, p. 7). Place-based education utilizes the unique texture of the local "eco-social" landscape (which varies from region to region) to inform its curriculum and guide the pedagogy. Due to the variety of places in this world, it is virtually impossible to deliver a "one-size-fits-all" place-based model. Instead, this approach to learning demands a pragmatic and "creative interaction between learners and the possibilities and requirements of specific places" (Gruenewald & Smith, 2008, p. 4).

Understanding one's place is critical for understanding oneself. Wendell Berry writes that "if you don't know where you are, you don't know who you are" (in Ivanco & Kivirist, 2004, p. 58). Thus, according to Berry, a sense of self is closely tied with a sense of place. Mueller-Worster and Ebersole (2005) define a sense of place as the "ecological and social knowledge necessary for the development of one's ecological and social identity associated with a place" (p. 2). A sense of place is the recognition of our ecological address, our place in this biosphere. Thayer (2003) notes that the question "where are we?" is a "simple question with a deceptively complex answer" (p. 2). By learning from our place, we gain a deeper and more authentic understanding of the fundamental relationships that sustain us and the life forms with which we share our bioregion. We cultivate a sense of interconnectedness by interacting with our surrounding ecological and social communities.

Place-based education is a powerful tool that can advance the restoration of the human-Earth relationship. Educational philosophers David Gruenewald and Gregory Smith (2008) state that place-based education is "a movement to redefine schooling, and a theory about how we should ultimately view education" (p. 7). This movement is founded in an open dialogue that occurs between the learner, his surrounding community, and the subject matter. However, due to the multidisciplinary trajectory of a place-based model, a single definition is hard to articulate. Thus, in this section, I set out to unpack the significant themes that compose this educational orientation.

Place-based education weaves together the collective narratives that exist within the community and the environment and provides space for each student to construct and build upon his own story. It is an approach that enables teachers and students to situate mandated learning standards within a relevant, active, and experiential context. Sobel (2008) says that this approach to education emphasizes "hands-on, real-world learning experiences" which increase "academic achievement [and] help students develop stronger ties to their community" (in Gruenewald & Smith, p. 7). This learning process strengthens student appreciation for the natural world and instills a greater sense of civic engagement. When civically engaged, a student is likely to gain an affinity to be a better steward of the natural life surrounding her. E.O. Wilson calls this love of natural life *biophilia*. Biophilia is the innate tendency to "focus on life and lifelike processes" (in McLennan, 2004, p. 166).

Place-based education has made a dramatic difference in my life. As I discussed earlier, I began learning from the Spring River watershed of southeastern Kansas at a very early age. I enjoyed visually following the storm water to the gutter, and when I was old enough, I paddled on the water. There were three major floods in my town when I was a teenager. Each time that the local park flooded, my brother and I inflated a beat-up yellow raft that a friend gave us and went paddling in the park. The water covered the entire park like a lake. It was weird to float over the swing sets and merry-go-rounds that we had spent time on as children. One of the city parks had an underground concrete tunnel that routed storm water runoff from the park. One day, after a heavy rainfall (but not a flood), my brother and I took a float trip through the tunnel. It was pitch black in there and we were moving fast. Luckily neither of us fell out of the boat. What an adventure! We also loved playing, exploring, and studying Cow Creek.

My brother and I learned how to fish in Cow Creek. Although the creek was relatively polluted, it was fun to explore. I caught my first fish there. We also enjoyed paddling Cow Creek and hiking next to it until we reached a place where the vegetation grew too thick to continue. The time that we spent playing on and exploring the river cultivated an interest in both of us for studying the outdoors. We learned early in our life the value of learning from our surroundings—from our place—which is something that has stuck with me ever since.

As a graduate assistant for the Georgia Southern University Coastal Rivers Water Planning and Policy Center a few years ago, I was able to realize my passion for place-based education by starting a watershed-based outreach education program[3] here in the Ogeechee River Basin. My love for protecting my bioregion has grown from my experiences in the

---

3 This program was called Project RIPPLE (Riparian Investigation Promoting Place-based Limnology Education). Due to funding, the Center closed in 2008.

Ogeechee River bioregion (of southeastern Georgia) and from the time that I have spent in its longleaf forest. I have gained biophilia through these nature-based encounters, and I want to help others to experience it as well. Facilitating biophilia is at the very essence of a bioregional educational model—the cultivation of an affinity for the local ecological and social systems that enable us to thrive. Cultivating biophilia is an aesthetic process because it helps people to see the beauty of the places in which they dwell. I get excited when I think about the possibilities of infusing sustainability and bioregionalism in education. I envision a future generation that embraces the robust beauty of untrammeled natural systems as the ultimate goal for sustainability. I see a citizenry of thoughtful people and citizens who are committed to enhancing ecological well-being on behalf of themselves and others, non-humans and humans alike. These folks will labor on behalf of both present and future generations. This is why I have selected place-based education as a primary theme in my book—because I am passionate about connecting people with their place—and I believe it is the knowledge of place that can help us to live more environmentally friendly lives.

I argue that when one develops an affinity for stewardship, then she will likely take responsibility for protecting her bioregion. Any work that one does to protect a bioregion is a form of community service because we are helping the entire community. This is true because everything within a bioregion is somehow connected. Deeper interest in community service arises out of active and authentic encounters with one's natural or social community. These encounters can take the shape of field trips to public green spaces, river cleanups, museum visits, and conversations with local artists, writers, and other professionals. Through place-based education, students are equipped to become better social and ecological citizens invested in restoring and preserving the vitality of community relations and environmental quality.

In bioregional education the walls between the outside world and the classroom become more permeable. Hence, local organizations, businesses, citizens, and natural resources become more infused into the school curriculum (Gruenewald & Smith, 2008). This approach to learning demands a pragmatic and "creative interaction between learners and the possibilities and requirements of specific places" (Gruenewald & Smith, 2008, p. 4). Place-based education honors the unique eco-social heritage of each bioregion. It recognizes the significance of each learning context and draws from the nuances and particularities that shape each bioregion's identity.

Bioregional Poiesis

I am intrigued by the capacity of bioregional education to help one shift her frame of reference. When one explores her bioregion she is likely to view the natural world more holistically. When we see the possibilities of our place we can start to notice the poetry of our watershed. This is why I have coined the phrase "bioregional poiesis." Bioregional poiesis denotes a profound connectivity with place. It is a place-specific attentiveness and an eco-social relatedness that values the uniqueness of our surrounding landscape. It serves as an aesthetic-based recognition of our particular bioregion and its potentiality. Bioregional poiesis draws from the uniqueness of our surrounding ecological and social contexts.

I am intrigued by the *poiesis* that can emerge through formulating a sense of place. Poiesis is at the root of the word "poetry," and it means to make meaning and bring forth (Coupe, 2000, p. 89; Heidegger, 2001, p. 212). It follows that bioregional *poiesis* is central to the process of becoming and being. As an outdoor education instructor, I have experienced bioregional poiesis directly and indirectly. When I reflect on the times that I felt most connected to the natural world, I realize that these experiences fit my description of bioregional poiesis.

I remember the first time that I backpacked on Stockton Island located on Lake Superior. It was my freshman year at Northland College—where I completed my undergraduate work. I was a participant on a week-long backpacking outdoor orientation trip in late summer prior to starting classes my first semester at the new school. According to the college website, Northland's outdoor orientation trips give incoming students "the chance to get to know other new Northland students, start creating their unique relationship with the College, and make connections with student leaders all while experiencing the amazing north country environment" (Northland College, n.d., n.p.). For me, being from Kansas, I was astonished by the beauty of Lake Superior.

The ferry ride to Stockton Island was memorable. It was my first time on big open water. Lake Superior is the largest freshwater lake in the world. There was a dramatic difference between it and my hometown's Cow Creek. Cow Creek was just a trickle compared to the vastness of what the Ojibwea people refer to as Gitchee Gumee. Gitchee Gumee is Ojibwea for the "great one"—which refers to Lake Superior. The lake gave me a sense of awe—it was inspiring just to see it. But it was even more meaningful to take a trip to one of its islands. It was powerful to depart the mainland with a group that I barely knew, and to travel to a land that I had never seen. This rite of passage,[4] in a wilderness context, helped me to prepare for an academic journey that I could not fully anticipate.

The boat captain talked about the natural history of the Apostle Islands[5] through the loud speaker. He let us know that Stockton Island had the greatest density of bears per square mile than anywhere else in the world. The history of bears on the island is interesting. The captain told us that the process to relocate "problem" bears has been very hard. Problem bears are the ones that frequently return to and pillage campsites after discovering that easy food rewards await them. After being notified about a problem bear, the National Park Service finds the bear, tranquilizes it, and relocates it far into the mainland. The captain noted that it had been hard to relocate these bears because they recognize the island as their home. Even when they are relocated several miles away, across the lake, and deep into the mainland, they find their way back. These animals are loyal to their bioregion. It is as if the bears have some sort of natural homing mechanism that guides them back to the island. They swim for miles and miles to get back to their homeland.

From a distance, Stockton Island looked like a mere dot way out on the horizon. As we approached, though, the island began to slowly reveal its beauty. We backpacked as a newly formed expedition team along the shoreline of the island. Under the weight of the large pack, the hike seemed to take forever. Six miles later, we arrived at our campground. We had plenty of daylight left to set up camp, explore our campground, and to take a swim in Gitchee Gumee. On the first evening of this expedition I experienced bioregional poiesis.

As the sun was setting on "night one" of my first Stockton Island trip, I experienced the poiesis. At dusk, the group sat on the sandy beach in quiet reflection and relaxation. The sun shimmered off the surface of the lake and generated the classic reflective trail of light between it and the observer. The sound of the water gently lapping against the beach created a halcyon moment. As the sun was going down, the moon and the stars were coming up. I was impressed by how the lake served as a reflective canvas of the night sky. As the natural light dimmed, the stars got brighter. The shift from dusk to night was like the beginning of a

---

4 Read Medrick (1987) for an interesting and more in depth discussion about the transformative capacity associated with wilderness expeditions.
5 The Apostle Islands are composed of a series of 22 islands in Lake Superior situated near the Bayfield Peninsula in northern Wisconsin (Apostle Islands, n.d.).

movie in the theater—dimming lights and anticipation of the feature film—but in this case the celestial sphere was the key player. This was a moment of peace and deep connection to our selves, the land, and one another. I experienced a sense of nature-induced connectedness that rivaled anything that I had previously experienced. I was provided with a holistic shift in my perception.

Optimal Experience

A number of researchers have looked into what has been referred to as optimal experiences. These are experiences when we feel most alive, intensely connected to ourselves, the natural world, and our community. Time tends to disappear along with self-criticism. Maslow refers to these moments as "peak experiences." Csikszentmihalyi (1990) calls them "flow." Gerald May (1987) calls them "unitive experiences." Whatever we call it, it is a powerful moment of feeling alive. We are affected mentally, spiritually, physically, and emotionally when we encounter the sacred. In this sense, bioregional poiesis is a holistic phenomenon—an experiential atonement. I propose, in some cases, that bioregional poiesis is simply another way to explain a response to the sacred. When we find our special places in nature, we are better able to attain a bioregional poiesis. We are able to participate in deep introspection and tap into a level of clarity that is not accessible in moments of boredom or anxiety (Csikszentmihalyi, 1975). When we are bored, we become disengaged and may tune out anything that is going on around us. In contrast, anxiety can make us fearful and unable to think clearly. In the context of place-based education, it is important for a teacher to be sensitive to their students' skill level and to teach accordingly. We must have open channels of communication with our students so that we can know if they are bored or anxious.

Bioregional poiesis is a form of deep universal and local connectedness. Everyday worries about money, time, and success disappear when we achieve this level of connectedness. We tap into the "flow" of life.

Flow and Place-based Education

Psychologist Mihaly Csikszentmihalyi's[6] (1975, 1996, 1997a, 1997b) discovery and articulation of the flow theory is invaluable in the realm of understanding optimal experience. Flow is described as "a state of deep absorption in an activity that is intrinsically enjoyable, as when artists or athletes are focused on their play or performance" (Shernoff, Csikszentmihalyi, Schneider, & Shernoff, 2003, p. 160). While in flow, individuals "perceive their performance to be pleasurable and successful, and the activity is perceived as worth doing for its own sake, even if no further goal is reached" (p. 160). Flow, as its name implies, is characterized by a continuous movement from one moment to the next in which "there is little distinction between self and environment, between stimulus and response, or between past, present, and future" (Csikszentmihalyi, 1975, p. 36).

The types of activity that induce flow are widely varied and include (but are not limited to) hobbies, games, sports, rock climbing, surgery, and art. As the wide array of activities from which flow emerges indicates, flow can be induced in a number of ways. It follows that "[f]low describes the spontaneous, effortless experience you achieve when you have a match between a high level of challenge and the skills you need to meet the challenge" (Csikszentmihalyi in Scherer, 2002, p. 13). It is important to note that Csikszentmihalyi's conception of flow does not come from apathetic inertia or "passive pursuits", instead, flow requires action and activity (Sherman, 1991, p. 184). For flow to happen, it must be configured within the variables of concentration, interest, and enjoyment simultaneously (Shernoff et al., 2003). Thus there is an experiential triangulation that is associated with flow. This triangulation invokes deep concentration, autotelic interest, and spontaneous enjoyment. In this section, I argue that bioregional education can bring forth each component of the experiential triangulation associated with flow.

Concentration in a flow experience is characterized as a state of deep immersion in an activity (Csikszentmihalyi, 1990). In the educational arena, the ability to maintain intense focus is central to promoting optimal learning experiences. For example, researchers reported that "a sample of talented teenagers concentrated more than their average peers

---

6   Csikszentmihalyi's work on flow has intrigued me for years. His scholarship surrounding optimal experience serves as an excellent template for exploring happiness and what he refers to as positive psychology (see Seligman & Csikszentmihalyi, 2000).

during classroom and study activities, but comparatively less while watching television and engaging in social activities" (Shernoff et al., 2003, p. 161). The distinction between the focus during a challenging activity and a non-challenging activity illustrates the possibilities that are integral to high challenge and high skill endeavors. Csikszentmihalyi (1990) suggests that when a person is unable to attain a focused and intense level of concentration, a flow experience is virtually impossible. Concentration and interest typically overlap one another. It follows that an integral component of deep concentration is that of interest.

Authentic interest is a cornerstone to optimal experience and is paramount to promoting intrinsic motivation. In the educational context, learning something in which one is interested implies freedom and autonomy. The notion of freedom is suggested in Maxine Greene's (1995) book entitled *Releasing the Imagination*. Releasing the students to learn and pursue their own interests is liberating. Thus, when a student is free to explore her own interests, she is more likely to develop a deeper relationship with the topic. As Dewey (1916) proposed, interest is the "driving force" of what fuels inquiry (p. 152). Experiences exploring one's watershed help to release a person's interest in learning about nature. "Acting on intrinsic interest alone, individuals seize opportunities to learn, read, work with others, and gain feedback in a way that supports their curiosity and serves as a bridge to more complex tasks" (Shernoff et al., 2003, p. 161). Outdoor education and nature immersion are vehicles that can transport someone towards the participation in more complex tasks. In traditional classroom environments teachers can facilitate flow by integrating an experiential project-based approach within the scope of the surrounding community. The freedom that a student experiences in self-initiated inquiry leads to intrinsic motivation and fosters joy.

When an individual experiences joy in an activity, he or she is more likely to seek out that activity again. Teaching towards enjoyment is mindful and student centered. Thomas Aquinas referred to joy as "the human's noblest act" (in Fox, 2006, p. 28). When a person feels free to explore his own interests in nature or in place-based education, she is more receptive to joy. Her receptivity to joy increases because she realizes that she is liberated from the traditional—pre-determined—constraints typically found in the classroom. Csikszentmihalyi (1975) insists that "freedom is the essential criterion of an enjoyable act" (p. 25). Thus, a perception of freedom is sometimes a contributing factor to experiencing flow and joy. Intellectually demanding tasks can be satisfying and enjoyable. Learning about sustainability can "provide a feeling of creative accomplishment and satisfaction" (Shernoff et al., 2003, p. 161). The joy experienced in a flow activity—such as place-based education—encourages one to sequentially seek out his or her full potential or *funktionlust*. *Funktionlust* is "the pleasurable sensation that an organism experiences when it is functioning according to its physical and sensory potential" (Csikszentmihalyi, 1975, p. 24). Thus, when one is in the flow channel he or she is better situated to experience funktionlust. It follows that enjoyment is a primary ingredient to autotelic activities. "An autotelic person is one who is able to enjoy what he is doing regardless of whether he will get external rewards for it" (Csikszentmihalyi, 1975, p. 22). Bioregional poiesis can facilitate autotelic situations because students naturally want to learn more—for their own enrichment and not for an external reward.

Georgia Southern University professor Dan Rea (2000) indicates that the benefits of flow are what teachers should aim for:

> Flow is proposed as a form of optimal motivation because it exemplifies the optimal quality and utilization of sustained effort. When students' efforts are flowing, they are clearly focused, totally involved, and highly enjoyable. They become so absorbed in a task that time seems to fly by and their efforts seem effortless. (p. 192)

The notion of effortless but high quality performance is appealing, Caine and Caine refer to this effortlessness as "relaxed alertness" (in Scherer, 2002, p. 75). Students experiencing relaxed alertness are more likely to engage in classroom dialogue and take healthy risks. Thus, students experiencing flow and relaxed alertness are more motivated to learn and tend to have a good time doing it.

Caine and Caine propose some strategies to promote optimal experience; "To maximize learning, we need to establish an environment that allows for risk taking. In essence, we need to eliminate pervasive or continuous threat" (Caine & Caine in Scherer, 2002, p. 75). Removing threat and building up trust fosters that sense of safety that "welcomes appropriate risks" which is integral to a flow experience. Relaxed alertness is the optimal state of mind that encourages the expansion of knowledge. It is defined as a state of "low threat and high challenge" (Caine et al., 2004, pp. 10–11). Rea (2000) refers to the state of mind catalyzed by flow as a place of calmness. Rea's notion of calmness is analogous to relaxed alertness which "combines the moderate to high challenge that is built into intrinsic motivation with low threat and a pervasive sense of well-being" (Scherer, 2002, p. 132).

Exploring Our Life Place

Typically, when we experience bioregional poiesis we are situated in place. There is an alignment of events that allow us to feel the "wide awakeness" (Greene, 2001) associated with a bioregional poiesis. Bioregional poiesis enables us to expand our creative capacity and to restore our sense of purpose on this planet. I argue that there are four necessary components to attaining a bioregional poiesis. These are: slowing down, unplugging, reconnecting, and re-imagining. Each one of these components comes together in meaningful ways that inspire us and empower us to better face the situations posed by life.

When I was on the beach that first night of outdoor orientation at Stockton Island, I was able to step away from the "regular" world and "slow down." This slowing down occurred because I was not tempted to make a phone call, or to check my e-mail, and I had put away my watch so I would not be concerned about time. I had "unplugged" from the fast and furious world of television, voice mail, video games, and radio. We were surrounded by the wildness of Lake Superior and the pristine beauty of the island. This replaced the movie screen, billboards, the highway, and all that other "developed world" clutter. I "reconnected" by embracing a deeper sense of place than I have felt in a long time. This sense of place gave way to a deeper sense of self. I was able to reflect on my life journey in regards to how I ended up at Northland College. The combination of solitude and silence provided a safe place for introspection and reflection. I remember feeling carefree during that moment of bioregional poiesis. I was not concerned about the details of the next day. I was able to be fully present in that particular moment. Being fully present is a beautiful thing. It is a feeling of robust connectedness to that moment. Lastly, I was able to re-imagine. I "re-imagined" the possibilities for my academic studies, forging friendships, and exploring nature. It turned out that each one of these aspects became integral to my time as a student at Northland.

Bioregional poiesis is a form of place-making that resists globalizing forces, the marketplace, and mechanistic thinking. Offering a counter-hegemonic, place-specific project of restoration and revitalization, bioregional poiesis helps to formulate an eco-curriculum of the wild. An eco-curriculum of the wild is a call to seek an education that is not solely reliant on the reductionist Cartesian worldview but rather the pursuit of a wild education. A wild education is organic; it facilitates a return to our Earth home, a reconnection with ourselves, our surrounding bioregion, and a restoration of community. Wild is defined as "[a]cting or moving freely without restraint...unconfined, unrestricted" (Wild, n.d.). An eco-curriculum gone wild is an education no longer married to the factory model proposed by Ralph Tyler in the early 1900s. Instead it embraces the vibrant movement towards the aesthetic dimensions of lived experience. It is a form of education that is developed around the recognition of the inherent beauty found in nature and in life itself.

Serving as a counter-narrative to the Westernized commitment to the global marketplace, bioregional poiesis has multiple tasks. Denoting a place-specific attentiveness and an eco-social relatedness, bioregional poiesis values the uniqueness of our surrounding landscape. A bioregional poiesis sets out to decarbonize the tendencies of the previously discussed *carbon copy curriculum* and facilitates wholeness. To this end, it serves and protects the call of the wild. Place-based education addresses our fossil fuel dependency and our compulsion to consume. In short, place-based education cultivates inquisitive thinking over acquisitive thinking (Sargent, 1945/1976, p. 541). Instead of overemphasizing the acquisition of more stuff, a place-based model fosters a more adequate mode of being. It is a mode of being grounded in advancing democratic inquiry and ecological responsiveness. When we respond to the challenges that compromise the integrity and vitality of our ecosystems we are practicing bioregional stewardship. This is a stewardship that is grounded in a bottom up (not top down) model. Bioregional stewardship is grass roots and organic in that it is situational and localized. Adapting to the particular landscape in which it is being implemented, bioregional stewardship has abundant possibilities.

The possibilities tied to bioregional stewardship continue to grow with the looming ecological crisis. Some theorists believe that going local is our only way out of the ecological crisis (Esteva & Prakash, 1998). When we turn our focus from globalization to localization we advance a more realistic form of ecological relatedness. By focusing on the local, we get to see, firsthand, the interrelationships that make life on Earth possible. The permaculturist Brock Dolman urges us to honor the connections that make our life on this planet possible. He refers to these connections, at a local level, as our basins of relations. Dolman states that our home basins of relations are our lifeboat (in Prandoni, 2009, n.p.). He uses the term basins of relations synonymously with watersheds and notes that everybody lives in a watershed. I posit that it is our duty—as ecological citizens—to protect the watershed in which we live. The ideas that are embodied within the basins of relations concept gets to the very essence of the localization that serves as a thematic thread throughout my book. If we overlook the relations that sustain us, we will inevitably take them for granted. As Roszak once said, "how we treat things affects how we treat people" (in Unsoeld, 1974, n.p.). We must reverse the trend of being ecologically illiterate and cognitively asleep. This is at the essence of cultivating bioregional poiesis—to cultivate a deeper connection with our home ground.

Dolman states that the basins of relations "are about honoring and rekindling our relationship with all our relations on the planet" (in Parandoni, 2009, n.p.). Interestingly, Dolman adds that watersheds are the most "efficacious place" for revitalizing and restoring our Earth relations. I am personally drawn to a "basin of relations" model because it feels right. There is an intuitive and visceral quality to intentionally cultivating the relations that sustain us. If we think of our watershed as our lifeboat, there is salience to it. What better way to "rescue" ourselves and those around us than through participating in the sustainability at the bioregional level. It is only through cooperative action that we can be resilient at the human and ecological scale. I believe this is what Schumacher (1973) was referring to when he made the claim that small is beautiful. If we start at a small scale, we are more likely to make a difference at a larger scale. This is true because when we forge alliances at a small scale we are better able to respond to challenges (social, physical, ecological, or emotional) at a larger level. We need to think within the framework of our bioregion and become more attentive to the needs of our home ground.

Bioregional poiesis is a phenomenon that can contribute to the sustainability movement. It advances what Joanna Macy (1998) calls the "great turning" by encouraging a shift towards a life-sustaining civilization. Macy maintains that "[w]e want to strengthen our courage and commitment to take action to heal our world" (in Seed, 1988, p. 79). This commitment towards healing is a commitment to draw on the solidarity and strength of partnering with our unique bioregions. This transition would be an example of a move towards inquisitive thinking over acquisitive thinking. When there is a shift from acquisitive thinking to inquisitive thinking, education is better situated to respond to the ecological crisis. Bioregional poiesis nurtures pragmatic critical thinking that emboldens Aldo Leopold's land ethic. Leopold's land ethic and pragmatic critical thinking are aspects of an eco-curriculum which demonstrate a dedication to the sustainability movement. As I discussed in an earlier chapter, Western education is obfuscating our ability to appreciate, study, and explore ecological text. What I call the carbon copy curriculum is a form of education that insulates the learner from her locality and subsequently leaves her with a feeling of having no real affiliation with place. A bioregional poiesis enables us to move beyond a carbon copy conception of curriculum.

Place-Consciousness and Education

As humans we are relatively new to Earth. Our infancy as a species should perhaps prompt a more precautionary approach to ecological situations. It is important that we do not disregard the environmental utility of seemingly superfluous ecological features. If we destroy something in the natural world that we do not understand, the result could be the destruction of a series of other interrelated natural processes. As Leopold said, "[t]he first rule of intelligent tinkering is to save all the pieces" (in Guruswamy & McNeely, 1998, p. 258). Keeping all the pieces is crucial as we attempt the restoration and revitalization projects that are central to the sustainability movement. How can we ensure that we keep all of the pieces and maintain the integrity of the ecological processes of which we are not aware? It may start by simply treating nature with reverence and respect. It all boils down to ecological stewardship.

Within a context of stewardship, I resonate with Orr's (1992) argument that we need to become *inhabitants* not *residents* in the places where we live. To inhabit a place is to be a dweller in it, and being a dweller involves learning and appreciating the nuances of a place. It is a process that involves communing with our surroundings. Orr states that the "inhabitant dwells...in an intimate, organic and mutually nurturing relationship with a place" (p. 130). To truly inhabit a place means to live richly there. For me, to dwell means to formulate an acute sense of belongingness within a particular bioregion. It is communing with one's surrounding in a symbiotic yet authentic way. Orr points out that good "inhabitance is an art requiring detailed knowledge of a place, the capacity for observation, and a sense of care and rootedness" (p. 130). In contrast, Orr describes a resident as "a temporary occupant, putting down few roots and investing little" (p. 130). A resident is a superficial member of the natural and social community who knows and cares "little for the immediate locale beyond its ability to gratify" (Orr, 1992, p. 130). The resident views the world from a self-centered lens and focuses first and foremost on meeting his own needs.

The inhabitant is a person who knows how to live sustainably while drawing from ancestral and indigenous knowledge. An inhabitant's knowledge is grounded in wholeness. According to Orr (1992) "those who dwell can only be skeptical of those who talk about being global citizens before they have attended to the minute particulars of living well in their place" (p. 103). This statement is right on the mark. We must be careful about judging someone else's resident-based lifestyle before we adopt the mentality of a dweller.

The inhabitant is one who works to learn the rhythm and cadence of the land. He is attuned to the nuances of his place and knows how to live in a way that complements the life processes that make up his bioregion. An inhabitant is sensitive to the well-being of all living organisms in her place and strives to protect them. Ivan Illich notes that the inhabitant has an "intimate organic and mutually nourishing relationship with place" (in Orr, 2005, p. 92). Inhabitants are better stewards than are residents of their and others' places. Orr notes that inhabitants "make good neighbors and honest citizens" (p. 92). An inhabitant is able to use all of her senses to become better acquainted with her bioregion.

Using all of our senses has been advocated amongst educational theorists for quite some time. Jean-Jacques Rousseau (1712–1778), the Franco-Swiss philosopher and educator, heralded the importance of enlivening the educational value of sensory experience. Rousseau argues that "our first teachers are our feet, our hands, and our eyes. To substitute books for all these...is but to teach us to use the reasons of others" (in Bisson, 2009, pp. 112–113). In other words, according to Rousseau, we need to return to nature in order to deepen our capacity for learning. Instead of learning only through reading, Rousseau advocated that we embrace the integrality of learning through all our senses. Rousseau ascribed top value to the holistic and experiential learning available in the outdoors. It is this notion of exploring the natural world that typifies learning through ecological text. By learning through ecological text students are enabled to gain access to the vitality of direct experience. Nature immersion is an integral part to the eco-curriculum for sustainability that I am exploring in this book. I believe that interaction with the natural world has the capacity to cultivate what Freire and Macedo (1999) refer to as our "epistemological curiosity" (p. 50).

Fostering Epistemological Curiosity

To reorient educational discourse towards promoting environmental stewardship, it is essential to cultivate what Freire calls "epistemological curiosity" (Freire & Macedo, 1999, p. 50; Freire & Macedo, 1995). Freire explains that "epistemological curiosity is the readiness and eagerness of a conscious body that is open to the task of engaging an object of knowledge" (Freire & Macedo, 1999, p. 51). Engaging an object of knowledge is central to the inter-species inquiry process related to the sustainability movement. For it is only through promoting inter-species coexistence that we can gain the ecological vitality necessary to attain sustainability. Lydon (1992) explains the importance of taking ecological action. "According to the Worldwatch Institute...'human society is not only diminishing the future prospect of planet Earth but is also causing the deterioration of the earth's life systems'" (pp. 54–55). When we recognize the ecological emergency that we face, we are propelled towards taking action. According to Dewey (1916), the inquiry process is instigated by an indeterminate situation. In the human sphere, I believe that engaging an object of knowledge pertaining to advancing sustainability is our fundamental indeterminate situation. Thus, to facilitate the inquiry-based learning that characterizes an eco-curriculum for sustainability, it is imperative to build the eagerness and readiness to advance the sustainability associated with Freire's conceptualization of epistemological curiosity.

Epistemological curiosity fosters the critical consciousness implicit to understanding and responding to the evolving and complex issues that make up today's world. Therefore, epistemological curiosity can serve as an impetus for building student capacity for affecting ecological change. To precipitate this curiosity and advance human agency, it is crucial to encourage a participatory dialogue. Freire and Macedo (1999) indicate that dialogue is essential to epistemological curiosity. Freire states that "dialogue as a process of learning and knowing, presupposes curiosity" (p. 51). He observes that "life is curious, without [curiosity] life cannot survive" (p. 50). For it is curiosity that drives our inquiry, and it advances a climate of scholarly exploration that has the potential to be tied to what I refer to as the scholarship of sustainability. The scholarship of sustainability is the study of restoration and vitalization from an ecological lens. It is the curriculum that embraces both ecological and traditional texts to infuse sustainability into the transdisciplinary conversation that makes up bioregional poiesis.

Epistemological curiosity emboldens the potential for building critical eco-literacy in our complicated world. In the arena of sustainability, curiosity is a prerequisite for engaging in the critical reflection and action that characterize praxis. When students are curious about their bioregion, they are more likely to get out and explore the areas in which they live. Their explorations encourage them to protect the area they have learned to love. Thus, without epistemological curiosity, students are not likely to engage in the thought and action related to environmental sustainability. A lack of passion results in no epistemological curiosity, which can lead to apathy. Place-based education is one way to nurture the epistemological curiosity that can advance the interest in service which is inherent to lifelong stewardship.

Watershed Education as an Eco-curriculum of Place

I posit that outdoor education can help students develop an ethic of stewardship, a land ethic, and a sense of place. Outdoor education is essentially experiential education that is in, for, or about the outdoors. Within the context of sustainability, outdoor education's capacity to foster a healthier worldview is far-reaching. How do nature immersion experiences bring about a healthier human-Earth relationship? Educational experiences in the outdoor context[7] enable students to encounter the natural world firsthand—it allows them to explore ecological concepts in ways that are concrete, kinesthetic, and therefore memorable. In Orr's (1992) words, nature immersion helps us to re-inhabit our land. This is at the very essence of an eco-curriculum, to reacquaint the student with their place, their bioregion, and their community.

One way to implement an eco-curriculum of place is to build educational experiences around the theme of getting to know your watershed. As mentioned before, a watershed is an area of land that drains to a common body of water. When we are able to grasp the idea of a watershed—from a conceptual perspective—we are better able to understand the importance of living sustainably. This is true because when we recognize the inherent connectivity between all the living beings in a particular bioregion we will develop a sense of compassion. We reflect on how we all live "downstream," and how we are all affected by someone's actions "upstream." Thus, I argue that infusing the study of our surrounding watershed into the curriculum has universal applicability. Watershed-based education embraces the notion that we should honor a "worldwide but not uniform" (IAACS, n.d.) curriculum and pedagogical perspective. Education needs to be contextualized to fit our place, the place we inhabit. Sustainability education has a worldwide urgency, impact, and relevance, which emerge from the ecological crisis that we face. If we do not respond to environmental emergencies such as climate

---

7   For an interesting discussion on implementing an education that pivots on "Ecotexts" see Hartsfield (2009). He posits that frequent, direct, and intimate encounters with a transect of green space enables students to become more creative and inspired. Hartsfield notes that students who participate in the "Ecotext" assignment commonly say it is "one of the best 'academic' experiences" they've ever had, and that they are "going to continue these visits and make them a part of their lives" (p. 265).

change in a united manner, there will be nothing to stop the erosion of the biospheric health and integrity.

A person who gains familiarity with his watershed is more likely to see the world holistically. This holistic shift in perspective comes from the recognition that the river serves as an indicator of ecological health for an entire bioregion. When a chemical is spilled or if there is overgrazing in a bioregion, the toxins and the dirt will show up in the river. Understanding the interdependence and ecological inter-relationality of a watershed helps us to connect to a greater sense of community. J. Glenn Gray believes that the connected person is "one who has fully grasped the simple fact that his self is fully implicated in those beings around him, human and nonhuman, and who has learned to care deeply about them" (in Orr, 1992, p. 100). Recognizing that we are "fully implicated" in the living world is at the very essence of an ecologically minded person. By recognizing that, we no longer operate from the self-centered industrial mind that fragments and competes; we are instead operating from a framework that unites. Accordingly, there is a fundamental shift in our recognition of ecological urgency.

The Ogeechee and Me

When we gain more watershed-based ecological literacy we develop a sense of urgency. We begin to understand the vital need to protect our rivers. I have spent many afternoons canoeing on the local Ogeechee River. The alligators and the circuitous undulations that make up the river's path appeal to me. These features draw me back to the river. I enjoy getting out during the summer when life is abundant on the river. I commonly hear the sound of frogs, American toads, mocking birds and more. For me the Ogeechee River is a sacred place, a place that cultivates spiritual connectedness. It is a place of re-creation and recreation. Each time I canoe the river I learn something new about the river, the watershed, or even about myself.

One summer afternoon my wife and I were paddling the Ogeechee with our friend Steve. We were just coming around one of the river bends when we heard some scuffling and splashes downriver. When the cause of the noise came into clear view, we were surprised to see eight wild boars crossing the river, four adults and four babies. This was quite the sight to see! Before this trip, I was not even aware that wild boars lived in this part of Georgia. This is just one experience on the river, one part of one afternoon on the Ogeechee.

There is an abundance of learning that can be drawn from direct encounters with the natural world, especially on rivers. Our education is like a river, ever changing as it flows. A watershed-based education is one way to achieve a more sustainable curriculum and pedagogy. It nourishes the imagination, feeds the spirit, and draws out our creativity.

Lake Superior Connections

The Ojibwea Indians of northern Wisconsin refer to water as our lifeblood. When I lived in the Bad River Indian reservation in northern Wisconsin, I was given the opportunity to participate in a ceremonial Ojibwea sweat lodge right off the shore of Lake Superior. The Ojibwea consider Lake Superior to be sacred, which is why the lodge is located right on its shores. At the sweat lodge ceremony one of the themes was respecting nature. The group of participants that participated in the "sweat" included a couple of other students, but was made up predominantly of Ojibwea community members. The Ojibwea exhibit a great deal of respect for the natural Earth. After I entered the sweat lodge I was greeted by a pile of red hot rocks, the rocks onto which water would be poured to create the sauna effect. It was a powerful ceremony, but one of the most memorable themes for me was that of being reverent to Lake Superior. We were community members of the Lake Superior watershed basin, and during the ceremony this was made very clear. After the sweat was finished, we all ran to the lake and jumped in. It was very cold and invigorating. This ceremony was one of my earliest experiences of fully appreciating water, and it helped me develop a deeper reverence for the lake and for watersheds in general.

Rivers as Pathways

Chief Seattle, of the Duwamish tribe, said the "rivers are our brothers..." and they "quench our thirst." We rely on rivers for our sustenance. He adds that "The rivers carry our canoes and feed our children.... You must give to the rivers the kindness you would give your brothers" (in Abbey, 1982, p. 2). Chief Seattle's words call our attention to the liveliness and livelihood embodied by the river. Rivers serve as pathways[8] into place-consciousness. They offer aesthetic and spiritual renewal and simultaneously serve the utilitarian needs of giving us sustenance (water). When

---

8   As I found out when I lived in northern Wisconsin, rivers become nature's highways in winter because they freeze over and serve as a flat, open, and easy to navigate trails for humans and animals.

we educate for sustainability, we cultivate meaningful relationships with the ecological world. "Rivers are roads that move, and carry us where we wish to go," said Pascal (in Abbey, 1982, p. 3). Similarly, an eco-curriculum is a road that can move and carry us where we need to go. When educators embrace an experiential river-based eco-pedagogy, they are likely to inspire an ethic of aquatic stewardship amongst students. As Edward Abbey said, "fasten your life jackets" because we are getting ready for a journey of epic proportions. Annie Dillard (1982) says we should not wear our straw hats to church because churches should be places where momentous events occur. I think her belief can be applied to schools as well. To adapt her quote,

> It is madness to wear ladies' straw hats and velvet hats to [school]; we should all be wearing crash helmets. [Teachers] should issue life preservers and signal flares; they should lash us to our [seats]. For the sleeping God may wake, some day and take offense, or the waking God may draw us out to where we can never return. (p. 52)

In other words, education needs to be recognized as a process that embraces daring adventure. When we push ourselves into uncharted territory, we get to see how we adapt to uncertainty and novelty. In terms of wearing a crash helmet to school—instead of a straw hat—I think there is a lot of possibility for an education that is built around the theme of our home environment. We can find aspects of our own backyard that is uncharted. These are places that have been neglected or overlooked. Adventure can happen in familiar places—it just takes a bit of challenge to compel a person to pursue the next level.

Back to Nature

Jean-Jacques Rousseau's contemporary, Johann Heinrich Pestalozzi (1746–1827), shares Rousseau's sentiments for nature immersion. Pestalozzi believes that "children should be free to explore the world to find answers" (in Bisson, 2009, p. 113). Instead of being bound to the four walls of the indoor classroom, Pestalozzi encouraged learning in the great outdoors. L.B. Sharp, known as the "Father of Outdoor Education," also a student of John Dewey, says, "That which can best be learned inside the classroom should be learned there. That which can best be learned in the out-of-doors through direct experience, dealing with native materials and life situations, should there be learned" (Sharp in Carlson, 2009, p. 4). Pestolozzi agrees, telling educators to

> Lead your child out into nature, teach him on the hilltops and in the valleys. There he will listen better, and the sense of freedom will give him more strength to overcome difficulties. But in these hours of freedom let him be taught by nature rather than by you. Let him fully realize that she is the real teacher and that you, with your art, do nothing more than walk quietly at her side. (In Bisson, 2009, p. 113)

Letting nature serve as a teacher is something that enlivens a discourse between the student and the subject matter. Within a place-based curriculum the student gets to participate with the educational content, working in solidarity with natural processes to cultivate a deeper understanding of how the world works. There is irony in the fact that learning locally enables one to access a more universal viewpoint, a cosmological shift in perception. Students access this universal viewpoint when they start to realize that within nature you can find the "universe in a grain of sand" (Blake). In other words, when students realize that they can find the "whole" in the "part," they will begin to see more cosmologically. Mathew Fox (2006) believes that "when creativity and cosmology are part of education, meaningfulness returns" (p. 23). A shift to a more integrated educational cosmological consciousness is something that enables the student to become more than a product that is going through a factory-based educational assembly line.

Ecology and the Pedagogy of Particularity

In this section I discuss the value of place in cultivating a more ecological worldview. Getting to know our places enables us to participate in the pedagogy of particularity. Kimberly Whitney (2001) draws from Annie Dillard, stating that the "notion of 'place' is multivocal in its address of what could be called a veritable 'scandal of particularities'" (p. 12). She is hinting at the multifariousness of understanding place, for there are a number of layers that make up the subjectivity of one's conception of place. In the midst of exploring our places, the complexity and simplicity of nature begin to unfold. After we get to know a place intimately, it is no longer merely a dot on a map, it becomes something that we relate to at a visceral level. Hence place-based education is a form of learning that subsumes the veritable educational buffet that is embodied in our regionally derived lived experiences.

Embracing ecological text, from a pedagogical perspective, is at the crux of a place-based pedagogy. I resonate with Gruenewald, who states that "places are profoundly pedagogical"[9] (Gruenewald, 2003, p. 621). The ecological and the cultural elements of place are the features that interest me the most. Within the context of fostering a greater human-Earth relationship, place-based education helps people to get outside and explore nature. Living sustainably is the process of honoring the voice of the village council of all living beings. Indigenous people have lived sustainably for generations. Intimately connected to the land, indigenous people are aware of the fundamental interdependence between ecological vitality and human well-being. We can learn a lot from indigenous people,[10] as they show us that living in solidarity with the land is not only possible but that it can be done in comfort.

Understanding the relationships that sustain us is a unifying theme in this book. Nelson (2002) quotes a Native American elder who discusses the importance of being connected:

> The country knows. If you do wrong things to it, the whole country knows. It feels what's happening to it. I guess everything is connected together somehow, under the ground. (p. 5)

Recognizing the web of relations that sustains us is fundamental to living with the sensitivity of an indigenous person. How do we develop this attentiveness? It takes work and mindfulness. How can we apply native approaches to today's resource management? Keye writes that "Native peoples managed the North American landscape, cutting trees and using fire to perpetuate desirable forest conditions. There is no reason that we cannot equal or better this record of stewardship" (in Jensen & Draffan, 2003, p. 5). Perhaps "going native" takes less work than most people think. Working towards a more harmonious human-Earth relationship is at the essence of living like a native. Can we educate in a way that helps people to live closer to Earth? I argue that we can.

Living sustainably involves living compassionately. Nussbaum (1996) recognizes that compassion "is an emotion rooted, probably, in our biological heritage. But...it is not devoid of thought" (p. xi). Being compassionate involves being able to comprehend our own vulnerabilities. Compassion necessitates thought because we need to be able to recognize that bad things happen to people and that these bad things are sometimes beyond these people's control. Accordingly, compassion enables us to build a bridge between "our own self-interest and the reality of another

---

9   Similarly Mary Doll posits that "place is pedagogy demanding interrogation" (in Casemore, 2008, p. 103).
10 See Ng-A-Fook, 2007

person's good or ill" (Nussbaum, 1996, p. xi). By cultivating solidarity between self and others, compassion helps us to relate to other human and non-human life in our bioregions. By striving to understand the relations that sustain us, we can forge an alliance between those that compose our social and ecological habitats. We gain sustenance from interacting symbiotically with the natural world and with our human community.

Nussbaum (1996) posits that compassion "begins with the local" (p. xiii). This is a powerful statement, when we recognize the importance of starting with the local we can initiate a better educational response to the ecological crisis. Nussbaum continues:

> But if our moral natures and our emotional natures are to live in any sort of harmony we must find devices through which to extend our strong emotions and ability to imagine the situation of others to the world of human life as a whole. (p. xiii)

I would like to add an ecological component to Nussbaum's conception of compassion. I argue that we must strive to identify strategies that enable us to reach out and imagine the situation of others while extending this awareness to the world of *both* human and non-human life as a whole. When we embrace both human and non-human life, we transcend our anthropocentric tendencies and adopt an eco-centric mode of living. Eco-centric living is an integrated way of communing with the world. The health of the watershed becomes just as significant as the quality of food that one consumes. In an eco-centric mentality, high quality communal green space is valued just as much as one's own backyard. It is an extension of thought and feeling well beyond anthropocentric limitations.

Nussbaum's argument about compassion and education is significant to advancing sustainability. Nussbaum (1996) observes that "since compassion contains thought it can be educated" (p. xiii). Prior to reading Nussbaum I never gave much thought to the idea of actually trying to teach compassion. However, it makes sense to me that we can cultivate one's capacity to care more for others. From the standpoint of living in harmony with Earth, it follows that compassion must be integrated into an eco-curriculum for sustainability. How do we teach compassion? Teaching about compassion does not involve a uniform and standardized approach. Instead it is a process of cultivating one's attentiveness to others. It is not something that can be transmitted through indoctrination. Instead, compassion emerges through experiential encounters with the lived experience of human and non-human life. When we see the suffering that a forest undergoes after it is clear-cut, we are better able to think ecologically. Similarly, when we work in solidarity with homeless people we can begin an authentic form of compassion for the struggles associated with living on the street.

When we honor the voices of the parliament of all living beings, we recognize the criticality of embracing unity in diversity. For, as in ecological systems, in human thinking there is strength in diversity. Jack Campbell (2001) argues that "it is widely accepted that education is a crucial agency in developing a sustainable measure of unity in diversity" (p. 9). From a biological perspective, ecosystems depend on diversity in order to be resilient. When a bio-diverse ecosystem experiences a stressor such as a fire or extreme temperature change it is more likely than a monoculture-based ecosystem to recover in a way that is suitable for its native inhabitants. For example, if there is a disease that kills off all elm trees in a particular forest, a bio-diverse forest will easily bounce back because there are several other species of trees, besides elm. Similarly, from a human ecology perspective, it is important that diversity is cultivated in the realm of beliefs, individuality, and living habits. If we have a "monoculture of mind" (Shiva, 1993) in a particular community, it is possible that everyone will approach a given problem in the same way. It is the myopia associated with monoculture-based thinking that is most dangerous. Diverse thinking enables communities to forge alternative approaches to the most pressing problems. Corcoran suggests that promoting a radical plurality of thinking is central to advancing sustainability (PC, 2009). To facilitate diversity and plurality, within an educational context, I propose that we need to give students the opportunity to explore their bioregion.

When students explore their bioregions they are better equipped to identify the ecological threats in their locality. Learning about sustainability must begin with a contextualized comprehension of one's surrounding environment. By introducing students to their own "backyard," educators encourage the development of biophilia. This love of nature can cultivate an interest in protecting and conserving the biosphere. It may lead to a more robust ethic of stewardship.

Eco-humanization

I believe that there is a reflexive partnership between one's self and one's surrounding eco-scape. I refer to the process of utilizing nature immersion to become more fully human as eco-humanization. Eco-humanization is a call for deepening ecological understanding as a means to become more fully human. When we understand the ecology of life we are better able to understand ourselves in the context of what our role is on this planet. Eco-humanization is advanced when we develop a strong sense of place. A sense of place can allow one to unfold in a socially mindful and environmentally conscious framework that enables a person to further actualize her full potential. Eco-humanization weaves an ecologically oriented view of humanization into the realm of Curriculum Studies for Sustainability. In my conceptualization of eco-humanization, I am not referring to the shallow form of ecology that is tied to anthropocentric economic development—instead I am referring to an eco-centric frame of thinking that embraces the integrality of place-based nature immersion in deepening one's sense of self. It is similar to Freire's conception of humanization. Freire (1970) posits that, "Authentic liberation—the process of humanization—is not another deposit to be made in men" (p. 66). Thus according to Freire, the humanization is a freeing process. It encourages an attitude of stewardship. He says, "Liberation is a praxis: The action and reflection of men upon their world in order to [understand it]" (p. 66).

My notion of eco-humanization departs from Freire's in that I do not argue (as Freire does) that humans need to transform the natural world. Instead, I believe that we are transformed *by* the natural world. Also, I believe that our transformative encounters with the natural world will enable us to stand up to the colonizing forces of industrialization and globalization. Eco-humanization forestalls the generative dialogue that is inherent to advancing a more sustainable approach to teaching and living. It is through an eco-curriculum that we begin to learn our ecological address. Learning our ecological address requires that we begin to explore the particularities and nuances that make up our bioregion. This exploration can precipitate a more generative and appreciative form of stewardship.

Attunement

After spending time in a number of wilderness areas, I have developed a more refined and attuned-to-nature frame of reference. This frame of reference enables me to forge an even greater appreciation for the ecological area in which I reside. My experiences in nature have given me a framework that helps me to recognize the nature-based beauty in whatever environment that I explore. I draw inspiration from nature and at times even feel in tune with it. Perhaps this has something to do with the meaning of my last name, Hensley. My name means "dweller in the woods frequented by wild birds." Interestingly, just the other day I was revising one of my papers in a nearby forest. I was halfway through my revisions when a bird pooped on my paper. I guess it shows that I am indeed a dweller in the woods frequented by wild birds. Perhaps the bird poop gave me some fertilizer to grow and nurture my ideas.

It is important to point out that one can develop a sense of place even when she travels often. Traveling can provide a person with a well-rounded portfolio of place-oriented knowledge. When this place-oriented knowledge is applied to one's homeland, a person is, at times, better equipped to "find [her] place and dig in" (Snyder in Orr, 2004a, p. 8). It is also important to note that a person who has not visited numerous places but knows her place intimately is not necessarily parochial.

Koyukon Perspective

There is an integrative quality associated with bioregional poiesis. When we have a strong sense of place, our worldview starts to bring things together instead of pulling them apart. Nelson (2002) discusses the ecological relationship of the Athabaskan, a large group of North American indigenous people. His essay entitled "Patriotism for the American Land" highlights the efforts of an Alaskan band of Athabaskan Indians called the Koyukon. The traditional "Koyukon villagers possess a remarkably intimate, voluminous, and sophisticated knowledge of their surrounding environment. They maintain complex ecological, economic, spiritual, ethical, personal, and social relationships with the natural world" (pp. 6–7). It is this depth of relationship that illustrates bioregional poiesis. Nelson notes that in the Koyukon view, "humans and nature comprise one great community, bound together through principles of moral reciprocity, respect, and restraint" (p. 7). This indigenous place-based philosophy illuminates the inextricability of the health of our bioregion and the lives that it sustains.

Through the eyes of the Koyukon we can piece together the possibilities for an eco-centric perspective that seeks union and ecological harmony. We begin to see the value of serving the interest of both our natural and social systems. Nelson (2002) adds that in Koyukon tradition, "the proper role of humankind is obedience toward the natural world and service toward the environment that gives...life" (p. 7). What does it mean to be obedient to the natural world? I propose that understanding the Koyukon notion of obedience to nature is crucial to living harmoniously with the land. It is a product of biophilia, a love of nature which emerges from compassion and attentiveness. Is it feasible that, without a love for nature, this intimacy and obedience would be possible?

I would argue that it is not. If we do not embrace the natural world in a meaningful way, we are unlikely to serve it in the form of stewardship.

Triple Bottom Line

Albert Schweitzer (1960) argues that we must position a "reverence for life" at the forefront of our conceptual schemas. When we embrace a reverence for life, we are likely to fight for the vitality of the biosphere, social solidarity, and economic responsibility. These three aspects: people, planet, and profit (Kakabadse & Kakabadse, 2003) are central to understanding the notion of sustainability. Sometimes these aspects are referred to as the triple bottom line of sustainable living. The triple bottom line is a framework for creating and measuring the success of sustainability programming. In the context of advocating for ecological sustainability, a reverence for life offers a transformative mode of thinking that can cultivate compassion. Compassion and reverence for life is different than the Westernized compulsion to control and dominate nature. Nelson (2002) argues that it is this close relationship to the land that encapsulates patriotism. He maintains that patriotism needs to view the "earth and myself of one mind. The measure of the land and the measure of our bodies are the same" (p. 7). Curriculum theory must precipitate a greater reverence for life. An eco-curriculum is one that is founded on compassion and viewing Earth's vitality as being inextricable from human well-being.

Healing and Connectedness

A paragon of the eco-curriculum I am theorizing about in this book is that of healing. That is a healing of our interpersonal and intrapersonal relationships, relationships with the land, and our overall relationship with the places in which we dwell. I believe that in the midst of the environmental crisis, curriculum theorists must serve as a community of healers committed to the restoration of ecological integrity. I argue that our places, our bioregions, and our subjectivity can serve as forms of eco-curriculum that can deepen our commitment to sustainable living. I theorize that an eco-curriculum can revitalize our relationship with the land. This shift towards a more integrative relationship with the land is one that can reinvigorate what the Spanish call *querencia* (Sale, 2000, p. ix).

Sale (2000) notes that querencia "implies not merely a 'love of home,' as the dictionaries say [but] a deep, quiet sense of inner well-being that comes from knowing a particular place of the earth" (p. ix). Getting to know a particular place of Earth takes some time. Some authors claim that it is a lifelong process to truly become attuned with a particular place (Berry, 1990; Snyder, 1995). Building the attentiveness to our surroundings can be transformative. Snyder believes that we can "now ask of education itself" to help develop "the sense of nativeness, of belonging to" our place (in Jardine, 2000, p. 11). Cultivating a sense of nativeness is a beautiful concept. Instead of pouring information into our students' heads we need to encourage them to explore their homeland, their backyards, to "find their places" and to "dig in" (Snyder, 1995). In spite of our reliance on the insipid mechanistically oriented, consumption-minded, traditional curriculum, an eco-curriculum advances a sense of place.

David Jardine (2000) notes that some people "are beginning to try to understand where they are, and what it would mean to live carefully and wisely, delicately in a place, in such a way that you can live there adequately and comfortably" (p. 11). Tapping into the wisdom of place-oriented knowledge is central to an eco-curriculum for sustainability. The wisdom of place is a valuable resource that can deepen our connection with past and future generations. Fox (2006) articulates a curriculum and pedagogy that is "wisdom-oriented and not just knowledge-oriented" (p. 9). Fox explores what he refers to as "Ancestral Wisdom Education." He argues that we need to return to the generational understanding of the indigenous people. An understanding of indigenous people begins with the knowledge of how they interacted with the land. From the context of living meaningfully in our unique places, we must learn from our ancestors. Ancestral wisdom is an interaction with the land that Berry describes as the "continuity of attention and devotion without which human life on the earth is impossible" (in Jardine, 2000, p. 20). Place-based wisdom is an endangered aspect of ecological education.

Instead of cultivating attentiveness to our unique places, today's carbon copy form of education is perpetuating generation after generation of humans who are ecologically out-of-touch. Because of an overemphasis on meeting pre-determined standards, today's educational model is not adequately equipping students with the wisdom to formulate solutions to the environmental crisis. Conversely, students are becoming more disenchanted with nature and less invested in their own learning process. In this era of fast food, sound bites, and instant communication we are shielded from the qualitative shift towards the slower form of attention and devotion necessary for affecting the restorative capacities of our next generation.

Environmental Mutuality

In the tradition of Pinar, I maintain that there needs to be a conversational component to the ecological healing process. Instead of outlining a unilateral, dogmatic agenda for advancing sustainability, I argue for a place-based, eco-contextualized interaction with our environment. It involves a dialogical relationship between generations, the land, and each other.

When it comes to forging solutions to the environmental crisis it is important to recognize the unifying properties of integral theory. Integral ecologists Esbjörn-Hargens and Zimmerman (2009) note that

> A premium is placed on solutions grounded in mutual understanding between divergent viewpoints and understandings. By cultivating the capacity to inhabit other perspectives and hold multiplicity, we will be able to respond more adequately than contemporary, less comprehensive approaches to the complex problems that currently face our planet. (p. 487)

Inhabiting other perspectives is valuable in the realm of rekindling our relationship with the natural world and emboldening our efforts towards sustainability. In this sense, we depart from our entrenched anthropocentric perspective and embrace a more pluralistic paradigm. This pluralistic design is what I refer to as an ecological worldview. A diverse range of epistemic possibilities are subsumed in an ecological worldview. As Dewey states, "The only truly general thought is generous thought" (in Garrison, 2001, p. 63). Dewey embodied this sentiment of generous thought throughout his scholarship. One of his hallmarks was his ability to adapt his conceptual schema to align with the nuances of virtually any area of inquiry. This is what I theorize that a bioregional poiesis can contribute to in students, a schema of divergent thinking that is pragmatic and ecologically grounded.

When a student develops the level of attunement with their bioregion that facilitates a healthy sense of place, they are more likely to understand the importance of how things interact. Accordingly, I argue that it is at this turning point, the point of acquiring a sense of place, that students depart from the mechanistic and fragmented thinking promulgated through traditional education. Subsequently, students can become more attuned to the importance of relationships. They begin to understand the relationships that make up our ecological inheritance and how important it is to nourish these relationships in compassionate ways. It is this attunement to place that enables us to recognize the importance of interactions at social and environmental levels.

The process of understanding eco-social relationships is central to the cultivation of the integrated perspective to which Esbjörn-Hargens and Zimmerman are referring. An ecologically oriented perspective is one that places value in cultivating the relationships that sustain us. Thinking ecologically enables us to see beyond the instant gratification of a fossil fuel economy—enabling us to consider the value of a wind and solar economy. Wind and solar economies are forms of enterprise that draw on the renewable forces of Earth. Instead of depriving fossil fuels, a solar economy and a wind economy enable a reconceptualization of how we can move forward and towards a carbon neutral society.

Sustainability as Facilitated Resilience

I posit that sustainability has to do with equipping a person, a group, or other living system with the necessary resources to respond to or adapt to extreme change. In this sense, sustainability is *facilitated resilience*. The term resilience comes from the discipline of ecology. It is a concept that deals with the capacity of living systems to respond to adverse or extreme situations. Resilience is at the very core of advancing sustainability. How can this notion of facilitated resilience advance our understanding of sustainability? There are many levels of insight that can be gleaned from this notion of facilitated resilience.

Without resilience a system will easily crumble under the smallest of stressors. Resilience implies a systematic readiness for the unknown. Walker et al. state that "Resilience is the capacity of a system to absorb disturbance" and to subsequently "reorganize while undergoing change, so as to still retain essentially the same function, structure, identity, and feedbacks" (in Hopkins, 2008, p. 54). The ability to reorganize while undergoing change is at the crux of resiliency. Resiliency means that one can roll with the punches in creative and salient ways. Hopkins notes that there are three ingredients necessary for a resilient system: diversity, modularity, and tightness of feedbacks (2008).

Diversity is an indicator of ecosystem and social community health. When there is a diversity of viewpoints within a social system there is greater capacity to solve problems. This is true, because in a diverse community with plurality of thought a number of approaches can be employed to respond to any given problem. When one approach does not work, it is easily replaced. According to Hopkins (2008) the "resilience of a system comes not only from the number of the species that make up that diversity, but also from the number of connections between them" (p. 55). The more connections that exist in a system creates a greater range of responsive opportunity to a variety of stressors. These connections offer a range of potential responses to a given stressor. Hopkins adds that diversity "also refers to the diversity of functions in our settlement (rather than just relying on one—say, tourism or mining) and a diversity of potential responses to challenges, leading to greater flexibility" (p. 55). Another meaning of diversity—in the context of resiliency—is that of diversity between systems.

There is a pragmatic function that is integral to system resiliency. What works for one system in a particular place often does not work for a similar system in a different location. Hopkins (2008) discusses the importance of each community formulating its own unique mode of operation. He states that "each community will assemble its own solutions, responses, and tools" (p. 55). Systems need to be localized so they can respond to the environmental stressors of the particular region in which they reside. The originality of a system's response helps it because "resilience-building is about working on small changes to lots of niches in the place, making lots of small interventions rather than a few large ones" (p. 55). This brings us to modularity.

Modularity deals with the way in which systems are connected and linked. Hopkins (2008) notes that the "over-networked nature of modern, highly connected systems allows shock to travel rapidly through them, with potentially disastrous effects" (p. 56). When structures are more modular, it means "that the parts of a system can more effectively self-organise in the event of a shock" (p. 56). This means that a modular system is better able to engage in auto-poiesis when confronted with system uncertainty. Hopkins (2008) illustrates this by providing an example, "as a result of the globalization of the food industry, animals and animal parts are moved around the world, leading to increased occurrences of diseases such as bird flu and foot-and-mouth disease" (p. 56). A more modular system is better able to draw its resources from the land base on which it is situated. This is an important idea because it deals with system self-reliance instead of depending on other systems. In essence, a modular system can meet its needs locally. Hopkins adds that

> [M]aximizing modularity with more internal connections reduces vulnerability to any disruptions of wider networks. Local food systems, local investment models, and so on, all add to this modularity, meaning that we engage with the wider world but from an ethic of networking and information sharing rather than of mutual dependence. (p. 56)

What does resiliency mean from an educational standpoint? I posit a three-fold answer: teach students about resiliency in natural systems, resiliency in social systems, and self-resiliency.

To teach students about resiliency in natural systems, we need to bring them outside. This could be as simple as a walk around the school's campus and exploring the interrelationships of the surrounding ecosystems. Even better, a trip to the local river—for a fresh water macroinvertebrate[11] study—can offer a more memorable and experiential sense of resilience. When there is more diversity in the macroinvertebrate population there is usually higher water quality and greater systemic resilience. Similarly, we can introduce social system resilience by drawing on the student's experiences in communities and groups. Classroom group problem solving activities can illustrate the importance of hearing all group members' opinions and advancing a more participatory form of problem solving. Processing these classroom activities can draw on the significance of resiliency. Self-resiliency is the ability to respond or cope with unanticipated stressors one encounters throughout their life. Humor and self-expression strategies are ways that self-resiliency can be built (Moore, 2006). Self-resilience involves resilience-based thinking.

How do we think in a way that is more resilient? Walker posits that there are three main concepts that define resilience thinking:

> The first is a recognition that complex adaptive systems are self-organizing. The second is a recognition that these systems are non-linear in their trajectories of change, which leads to their potential for multiple stability regimes, or multiple "basins" of attraction. The third is that systems go through adaptive cycles, cycles which describe a repeated process of growth, conservation, collapse and re-organization. (Walker in McDonald, 2007, p. 85)

Walker's description of resilience thinking mirrors Hopkins' (2008) discussion on resiliency. However, Walker's description departs from Hopkins' when he describes the stages of adaptive cycles inherent to maintaining a system's homeostasis. The concept of "multiple stability regimes" that Walker addresses is also an interesting semantically oriented point of departure. Earth is filled with multiple stability regimes and each ecosystem is therefore able to respond to stressors in a variety of ways. In the context of today's ecological crisis, there are a number of stability regimes that can be utilized. The trick is, within an educational context, to facilitate resilience.

---

11 Macroinvertebrates are small animals without backbones (Maryland Department of Natural Resources, 2004).

A system is more resilient when it maintains accessibility to its various forms of sustenance. For example, an oak tree relies on the sun to produce the nutrients it needs and water to facilitate the photosynthesis process. Without adequate supplies of water or sunshine the tree experiences stress. It is considered to be more resilient when it is able to adapt to this stress, find alternative sustenance, and perhaps slow down its metabolism until equilibrium is restored. A system that is flexible and able to sustain itself in a diversity of ways is more resilient. Resilience denotes a certain level of heartiness, a robustness that is capable of seeking out alternatives when its most vital link to survival is severed.

A system that has redundancies built into it is more resilient. By this, I mean that an area that has several different organisms that are able to do the same task will still be able to survive if some of its organisms are lost (because the other ones can step in and the area will still function). Ward states that "A resilient system is adaptable and diverse. It has redundancy built in. A resilient perspective acknowledges that change is constant and prediction difficult in a world that is complex and dynamic" (in Hopkins, 2008, p. 54). Adaptability and diversity are at the foundation of a resilient system. It is through adaptability that systems can respond in hearty ways to extreme stressors.

How can we facilitate resilience from an educational level? It starts with moving away from the carbon copy curriculum. As previously discussed, the carbon copy curriculum facilitates a monoculture of mind, duplication of old modes of thinking and doing, and reduces the capacity of a system to respond well to a stressor. Facilitating resilience from an educational perspective involves de-carbonizing a carbon copy curriculum. Advancing ecological attunement and facilitating alternatives to mainstream modes of consumption are at the core of facilitated resilience.

An eco-curriculum for sustainability facilitates resilience by emphasizing the value of the surrounding ecological and social communities. Eco-curriculum for sustainability advances the process of localizing the food, energy, and waste economy. Instead of importing food from several thousands of miles away and sending trash miles away from a community, an eco-curriculum for sustainability equips students with the knowledge necessary to eat locally and to understand that our contribution to the waste stream has far-reaching impacts. An eco-curriculum for sustainability facilitates resilience at many levels while inspiring and empowering individuals to modularize energy needs. It encourages students to draw from the abundance of the solar and wind economies. Coal-fired power plants can become history when we advance a systemic response to the ecological crisis. There is a great deal of possibility within the scope of embracing our places within the framework of advancing sustainability. In the next chapter I discuss the journey that is affiliated with trudging towards sustainability.

The Multidimensionality of Sustainability

The topics of eco-contextualization, bioregional poiesis, resilience, healing, compassion, aesthetics, and alternative energy serve as fundamental components to my discussion on advancing an eco-curriculum for sustainability. The broad scope of sustainability is what makes it such a lively and energetic concept. Situating our theorizing in our home ground enables us to "start small" and build a conceptual model that applies to several contexts. Theory allows us to forge viable alternatives to the mainstream modes of consumption and production. A place-based eco-curriculum is not limited in scope to any particular field. It is a transdisciplinary approach to mobilizing a more sustainable planet. In the next chapter, I explore qualitative dimensions of sustainability including spiritual and cosmological perspectives.

CHAPTER 6

Trudging Towards Sustainability

> No real public life is possible except among people who are engaged in the project of inhabiting a place.
>
> Kemmis in *LifePlace: Bioregional Thought and Practice*

THIS BOOK is committed to advancing sustainability within the field of curriculum studies. In this final chapter I take a discursive approach to understanding the possibilities for mobilizing a more enlivened educational discourse—a discourse committed to ecological revitalization. Accordingly, in this chapter, I explore the concept of trudging towards sustainability—denoting an arduous yet rewarding journey towards a greener and cleaner mode of human-Earth relations. This trudge recognizes that sustainability is an ongoing and multifaceted project. Within the realm of curriculum studies, I investigate the possibilities of de-carbonizing a carbon copy curriculum. Essentially, de-carbonizing entails a shift away from the fossil fuel driven economy into a "post-carbon" or a "carbon neutral" economy. In the realm of education, de-carbonizing involves teaching in a way that empowers and inspires students to seek out alternatives to the carbon dependent lives that characterize contemporary modes of Westernized consumption. Later in this chapter I unpack the ethereality of the trudge towards sustainability by recognizing that sustainability is a "prayerful act"[1] (Macdonald, 1995). Sustainability is a "prayerful act" because in essence it is an ethical imperative to take care of our planet.[2]

---

[1] James Macdonald (1995) argues that "curriculum theorizing is a prayerful act" and notes that educators need to profess "to reveal and justify from our own viewpoints what we believe and value" (p. 159; also in Collins & McNiff, 1999, p. 48). The act of expressing and professing what we believe and value, according to Macdonald, involves prayer. Later, I expand upon Macdonald's notion of prayer and study within the arena of ecological sustainability.

[2] When we see nature as a sacred place we can better appreciate it. Roderick Nash (1967) explores the implications of viewing the wilderness as a sanctuary and notes, "The logic [is] that if nature embodies moral law and spiritual truth, then wild nature provides the most direct link to the deity" (p. 268). Here, Nash helps to contextualize the spiritual possibilities associated with the outdoor world.

Responding to the current ecological crisis requires prayerful reverence. The "sustainability imperative"[3] (PC, Hunter Lovins, 2009) provokes a holistic commitment to the process of revitalizing Earth's capacity to respond in robust ways to the ever increasing stresses associated with the rapidly expanding human population (Orr, 2009). By theorizing about sustainability, we answer the ethical imperative associated with ecological restoration and find a way to best use our strengths in advancing sustainability collectively and individually. Sustainability is a sacred act because it involves working towards the restoration of our ecosphere—and protecting our Earth home is central to advancing our spiritual home.[4] This work involves diversity,[5] resilience, "complicated conversation" (Pinar, 2004), thinking ecologically, and a commitment to advancing environmental intelligence. Later in this chapter I posit that one throughline associated with the sustainability is wholeness. However, I recognize that sustainability is much more than wholeness; it is also found in the liminal space (the space in between "here" and "there"). This is the conversational aspect of sustainability—the interchange of ideas. For Hongyu Wang, conversation has to do with "the inter-space" (in Pinar, 2004, p. 159). Pinar adds that conversation "occurs at the boundaries and between spaces" (p. 159). In recognition that sustainability is a multifaceted project, all of the themes in this chapter fit within the theme of the trudge toward sustainability. Lastly, I offer concluding thoughts for the book and offer recommendations for further investigations into the scholarship of sustainability.

Trudging Towards Sustainability

A trudge is defined as a "long and difficult walk" (trudge, n.d.)—it involves a great deal of effort to trudge towards something. In the context of education, I suggest that we need to *trudge towards sustainability*.[6]

---

3   The sustainability imperative is the recognition that we must embrace a more sustainable lifestyle in order to prevent further loss of biological diversity and the destruction of vital resources. It is imperative to be more sustainable because the alternative, continuing as usual, will likely lead to ecological collapse which will compromise the habitability of the planet and the survival of all species.
4   We need a habitable planet in order to have a place to grow spiritually, physically, emotionally, and mentally.
5   Both unity in diversity and diversity in unity are themes that help to contextualize sustainability.
6   I adapted this title from William Ayers' (2006) chapter entitled "Trudge Toward Freedom: Educational Research in the Public Interest."

When I read William Ayers chapter, "Trudge Toward Freedom: Educational Research in the Public Interest," I was intrigued by the notion of a trudge. I realized that sustainability too is a trudge. Trudging towards sustainability is a simultaneously difficult and necessary journey. We need to embrace the centrality of our role as humans to advance ecological restoration. Embracing sustainable modes of living is intrinsically rewarding because it enables us to participate in the process of building ecological resilience. Sustainability is not a stagnate concept nor is it a fixed idea. Instead, it is a dynamic and robust course of action. One does not simply "attain" sustainability by living in an environmentally friendly way—it is not a possession. Instead, sustainability is a process towards which we must continually work. To borrow from Schubert (2009a), "the what and why" of sustainability must be "forever sought, never finalized, lest the term become brittle and crumble on the scrap pile of cliché" (p. 3). Working to understand the what and why of sustainability brings us to explore its contestedness. According to Ming Fang He[7] we must problematize the discussion pertaining to sustainability and recognize that there is a continual and dynamic fluidity associated with sustainability (PC, 2010).

If we look at it metaphorically, trudging towards sustainability is like navigating the challenging backcountry trail that demands tenacity and commitment. It is not the paved highway of flattened convenience. Trudging towards sustainability is not an enterprise that offers instant gratification; it is not simply about the destination. In some cases we might have to scale a colossal mountain to make the shift towards a sustainable lifestyle.

We cannot all approach sustainability in ways that are exactly the same—uniformity is not the answer. If we homogenize our response to the ecological crisis, we lose the breadth of possibility that we have as a human species. In other words, there is value in our uniqueness because each one of us has something different to contribute in confronting the quandary of anthropogenic ecological degradation. This gives legitimacy to my discussion on place-based education. I argue that we must draw from one's unique capacity to solve problems gained through lived experience. The process of developing a greater sense of self is one of the intrapersonal opportunities linked to bioregionalism. When we learn from the landscape of our lived experience and apply our distinctive set of

---

7 Ming Fang He is interested in the notion of sustainability as diversity and diversity as sustainability. She suggests that sustainability is much more than what most people think of it—it centers on the theme of diversity (PC, 2010).

strengths, interests, and fortitudes we can better work towards the resolution of environmental disequilibrium. If we all respond the same way to problems as large as global warming, we would lose the distinctiveness of our unique capacity to appropriately address the environmental crisis. Homogeneity precludes our ability to advance the project of ecological revitalization.[8]

Each one of us has something unique to bring to the sustainability movement. Our creativity enables us to formulate new ideas and strategies to address the environmental crisis. It is an expedition into new terrain that poses risks and challenges. How should we approach the backcountry mountain trek towards sustainability? Pirsig (1979) adds insight on this matter:

> [When climbing a mountain, the] reality of your own nature should determine the speed. If you become restless, speed up. If you become winded, slow down. You climb the mountain in an equilibrium between restlessness and exhaustion. Then, when you're no longer thinking ahead, each footstep isn't just a means to an end but a unique event in itself. This leaf has jagged edges. This rock looks loose. From this place the snow is less visible, even though closer. These are things you should notice anyway. To live only for some future goal is shallow. It's the sides of the mountain which sustain life, not the top. Here's where things grow. (p. 183)

Pirsig touches on many of the elements that are found on a trudge towards sustainability: balance, reflexivity, mindfulness, beauty, episodic connectivity and optimal experience. What I find most compelling about this passage from Pirsig is the notion that the mountainside, not the top, sustains life.

When I lived in the Cascade Mountains of southern Oregon, I remember looking up from the floor of the Rogue Valley and noting the abundance of life found on the side of the mountain. There was a scarcity of life on the top. I have noticed that there is a lack of mountaintop life on most of the mountains that I have hiked. Often, while hiking, the closer I get to the top the rockier and more barren the landscape becomes. We must draw sustenance from the journey itself. When education focuses on the outcome over the process it becomes merely a means to an end. Pinar adds that "sacrificing means to ends is not sustainable" (PC, 2010). It is not sustainable—from a perspective of cultivating an inquisitive mind—

---

8   Pinar suggests that the "standardization of subjectivity" is "one of the preconditions of the present ecological catastrophe" (e-mail, 2010). He asks, "If we as human subjectivities seem expendable and manipulable, why wouldn't nature be?"

to emphasize the educational outcome over the journey. In the realm of education, the compulsion to teach towards a test and hold the assessment score as the most important can be dangerous. We might overlook the learning process itself. In destination-oriented education, we miss out on the significant learning experiences that enable us to figure out who we are and where we are in this unpredictable world. What about educating students in a way that encourages ecological sustainability? Why does living sustainably involve trudging?

Since ecological sustainability is such a far-reaching concept the process of going green involves a lot of work. This is true because when we are living sustainably we need to be able to recognize reflexively how our choices, as humans, affect our ecological and social contexts. To be attentive to each of these contexts demands that we are flexible and adaptive—the living world is fluid. To build our ecological attunement we must embrace the richness of the natural world. As Dillard (1987) states, nature involves the "mystery of the continuous creation [which is affiliated with] the uncertainty of vision, the horror of the fixed...the intricacy of beauty, the pressure of fecundity, the elusiveness of the free" (p. 5). It is the mystery that Dillard describes that is found on the side of the mountain, it brings enchantment upon those who encounter the animated ecology of the natural world. According to Einstein, the "fairest thing we can experience is the mysterious" (in Schubert, 2009a, p. 2). We must return to the mysterious, which can provide a qualitative shift in consciousness that propels our wanderings and forays into greener living.

Recognizing the beauty and complexity of the polymorphous ecological and social characteristics in nature is something that requires time and study. We broaden our awareness and action from a self-centered acquisitive mindset to a broader eco-centric conception of participating in the world. The task of working towards sustainability requires tenacity, endurance, and strength. Education has the capacity to inspire and strengthen our inherent desire to protect the well-being of the planet. One of the major goals of education should be to enable people to live well in their places (Orr, 1992). Precipitating a form of education that helps people to live well in their place involves dramatic transformation. We must first overcome the mechanistic paradigm that is responsible for perpetuating a mode of education that is steeped in a conveyer belt mentality. This proposed transformation is an arduous journey, a trudge towards sustainability.

As I was walking last night under a starry night sky, the movement of trees in the wind got me thinking. The branches of the neighbors' large pine trees were swaying unhindered in the wintery wind. I started to realize that sustainability in its purest form is the freeing of the life processes towards reaching full potentiality. After reflecting on this notion of freeing the life processes I realized that this idea was Deweyian. I recalled an interesting statement that he had made. Dewey (1902) said that education is "freeing the life process for its own most adequate fulfillment" (p. 17). What does it mean to free the life processes? The task is much broader and deeper than working toward a single goal such as carbon neutrality. It entails ecological attentiveness to: the places that we inhabit, the communities we are a part of and the skills and strengths that we possess. In this sense, sustainability involves an arduous journey—a seeking—grounded in lively awareness and deliberate action. From the standpoint of education, the possibilities for cultivating a greener attitude toward Earth and toward others are bountiful. Even though there is a great deal of opportunity (from the standpoint of curriculum and pedagogy) it is not easy to infuse the steps at a systematic level. The exertion necessary to make education more ecologically sustainable involves patience and commitment.

Sustainability, Sacredness, and Prayer

Study...is a prayerful act.

Alan A. Block, *Talmud, Curriculum, and the Practical:*
Joseph Schwab and the Rabbis

American lives are ruled by speed and efficiency. We are inundated with instant messaging and acculturated to adhere to the idea that faster is better. James Gleick (1999) notes that we are barraged by what "instantaneity," which is an obsessive devotion to getting it, whatever *it* may be, done faster. We are ruled by speed—from instant coffee and instant replay to instant pancakes and instant relationships. What can be done to encourage people to slow down and enjoy life in the midst of the culturally driven need for speed? We can find inspiration in nature—an inspiration that builds our capacity to embrace the complexities of life, while problematizing our understanding. More particularly, we may find solace within wild places. These places have the capacity to embolden our spirit, provoke our thinking, and renew our sense of integrality. Wild places are spiritual sanctuaries that inspire creativity and reflexivity. The rivers, mountains, deserts and prairies call to us. The need to commune with wild places is a hardwired human necessity (Olson, 1956; Muir, 2001). The way that our culture is progressing, the rift between humans and nature is growing daily. Instead of going outside, people are desk-bound with computer-based jobs and lives.

A recent study (conducted by the Kaiser Family Foundation) indicates that the average young American now "spends practically every waking minute—except for time in school—using a smart phone, computer, television or other electronic device" (Lewin, 2010, n.p.). Youth aged 8 to 18 reportedly spend more than seven and a half hours per day with one of a variety of electronic devices (Lewin, 2010). It seems that the influence of electronic media has become an epidemic. Pinar suggests that "electronic media is undermining our sense of a natural world." He adds that it is important that we recognize that the natural world is also "an extension of our biological and psychic needs" (PC, 2010). Human connectivity to nature is interrupted by the addiction to electronic media. Our attention turns to electronic gadgetry for entertainment, education, communication, and more. I reference this media based human-nature disconnect because I have witnessed its impact.

When I was working as an outdoor educator for the Georgia Southern University botanical garden I noticed several situations that indicated the level in which electronic media influenced human-nature relationships. As I was leading a group of fourth graders on a field trip of the long leaf pine forest, one of the students looked around in awe at the tall conifers and then exclaimed "Wow! This is better than a video game." It was powerful to experience his nature-based awakening and it affirmed the significance of my research trajectory. The barrage of speed and technological gadgetry use that characterizes today's culture is not sustainable. The human tempo is getting replaced by the rhythm of whirring machinery and digital devices. What is this doing to our interest in spiritual connectivity and ecological stewardship? What can we do about it? I suggest that we turn to nature and recognize sustainability as a spiritual act.

When we recognize the importance of the relationships that sustain us, ecology takes on a deeper significance. When we study these relationships our worldview might be transformed. The potential transformation of perception associated with sustainability exists because of the visceral and intellectual comprehension of ecology that emerges from direct experiences with and in the natural world. I argue that it is crucial that we slow down and tap into a human rhythm—a cadence of inquisitive proportions. The importance of slowing down is heralded by Thomas Merton (2002), who insists that "We must slow down to a human tempo and we'll begin to have time to listen" (p. 75). It is time that we find the human tempo again—the pulse of *human speed* not *machine speed*. One aspect of the re-connecting that is inherent to an eco-curriculum for sustainability is tapping into the timescale by which our ancestors lived.

Synchronizing with the human tempo allows us to live in a way that is unhindered by the incessant chaos wrought by electronic organizers and digital watches. When we are connected to the organic and human rhythm, we can begin to listen to ourselves, others, nature, and to the lessons harvested from our lived experience. Incorporating the human tempo into our daily life is a form of re-wilding because we can begin to be more attentive. Madeleine Grumet notes that

> When we stay within a set of assumptions, our findings are domesticated, but when we undermine the divisions that separate public from private, individual from collective, and nature from culture, our work grows wild. (In Krall, 1994, p. vii)

We must let our work grow wild. Growing wild is what I am referring to by *re-wilding*—a return to our inherent ecologically derived sense of connectedness. Adapting from Grumet, I posit that we need to let our inquiries "cling to the shape of things, catching light from the sunset" (in Krall, 1994, p. vii) reflecting from Lake Superior. We must let ecology inform our practice as theorists, as educators and as human beings. This is at the very essence of re-wilding our educational discourse—to enliven the human tempo while harmonizing with the cyclical cadence of the natural world.

When we re-wild, we can return to optimal experience because we are able to dance to the beat of our own rhythm. In Maxine Greene's (2001) words, "we need to weave circles of quietness [and] of attentiveness [around] ourselves" in order to tap into our own rhythm (p. 75). Dewey referred to this moment of self-realization as a "moment of consummation" (in Greene, 2001, p. 75). Embracing the organic necessity of living on a human and ecological timescale is liberating and consummating. Moving beyond the distraction of an extrinsically dictated time scale allows us to give credence to the relationships that sustain us. Transforming from an isolationist to an ecological perspective is fundamental to embracing these life-giving relationships.

The late eco-theologian Thomas Berry urged that "[e]verything must be seen in its relationship to everything else" (2008, p. 55). We need to find ways that advance our attunement to the interrelationality of life. When we are aware of the fundamental interrelatedness between living systems we are better situated to live well on this planet. I believe there is no better way to do this than through immersion in nature. When we get outside and explore, we see ecology in action, up close and personal.

In nature we get to see how the health of an ecosystem is dependent on the sum of its parts. When one aspect of an ecosystem is removed, the system needs to respond to the disequilibrium and compensate for the missing piece. Once when I was hiking in the wilderness area of the Chequamegon National Forest in Wisconsin I saw ecological disequilibrium in action. The forest was showing signs of an oversized deer population. Overgrazing of the forest underbrush was evident. I remember wondering about why there were so many deer in that forest, more deer than I had seen anywhere else.

Richard Nelson's (1998) book *Heart and Blood: Living with Deer in America* gave me some insight on deer ecology. It turns out that the expanded number of hoofed mammals was a result of a missing top predator. In the 1980s when wolves were hunted in northern Wisconsin they came close to extinction. Wolves had previously served as the main predator of deer and helped to keep the deer population in check. When the wolf population became threatened (less than 80 wolves in the area) the population of deer subsequently increased exponentially (Wydeven, 2003). Luckily for wilderness enthusiasts and for the health of the forest, things have since equalized. A wolf recovery plan was enacted and the population of wolves has recovered. Our ecosphere exists within a fragile equilibrium, and when we get to see and experience how a small change in an ecosystem impacts the web of connections, we can gain a greater appreciation for the delicate balance of nature. An eco-curriculum for sustainability integrates the importance of gaining academic knowledge with that of becoming more attuned to the natural world and, more generally, to reality.[9]

It is impressive to see nature in action from microscopic to macroscopic levels. It is powerful to see systems of life interacting with one another at the microscopic level. When we view the vitality of these nurturing relationships as essential, we begin to see life as sacred. Instead of seeing the natural world as ordinary or mundane, it attains organismic[10] significance. When the biosphere is viewed as an organism,[11] it becomes enchantingly beautiful. Block (2004) posits that prayer

---

9 The idea of becoming more attuned, through academic knowledge, to reality and to the natural world is something that William Pinar shared with me in an e-mail (PC, March 13, 2010).

10 Organismic, "of or relating to or belonging to an organism" (organismic, n.d.).

11 Berry (2009) posits that "a number of scientists have noted the remarkable capacity of Earth for unified homeostatic adjustment to a diversity of outer conditions" (p. 103). The capacity for Earth to organismically respond to various

sacralizes the mundane. I submit that the acts that contribute to sustainability also *sacralize the mundane* and are, therefore, inherently sacred. By deliberately emphasizing biospheric well-being and venerating the processes that lead to ecological integrity, sustainability takes on a deeper significance.

Sustainability as a *Prayerful Act*

The act of thinking forwardly and recognizing how the choices we make today may affect future generations is a necessary part of sustainability. Forward thinking is a form of theorizing because it entails imagining what could be and what will be. Theorizing is working through conceptual and perceptual schemata to build a bridge from what is here now to what it can become. This is why theory in many ways is a form of practice. We do not theorize as curriculum scholars because we have nothing better to do with our time—we theorize because we realize the urgency in which we must work towards embracing a more comprehensive and more adequate perception of what we as humans are capable of doing to revitalize our relationships with each other and with the planet. Regarding theory, Van Manen says:

> Theorizing contributes to one's resourcefulness by directing the orienting questions toward the source itself; the source which gives life or spirit to (inspire) our pedagogic life. To theorize is to struggle to achieve one's limits, to find one's origins, one's grounding in that which makes our pedagogic life possible. (Van Manen in Macdonald & Macdonald, 1995, p. 183)

To direct orienting questions toward the source itself is a poignant description of our job as theorists. The essence of working to find one's limits and one's origins is embodied in theoretical practice. We work towards originality and organicity when theorizing around sustainability. To understand sustainability, it is important to explore what a system looks like when it is intact. We must theorize in a way that embraces the sacredness[12] and integrality of being alive in a time of epochal signifi-

---

changes is part of the Gaia hypothesis (see Lovelock, 1995, 2006). Gaia is a name taken from the Greek goddess of Earth. Berry notes that (2009) "the Gaia hypothesis suggests Earth is a self-regulating organism that has maintained the optimal temperature, atmosphere, and conditions for life" (p. 103). In short, the Gaia hypothesis views Earth as a single organism.

12 T.C. McLuhan (1994) tells us, "The idea of the sacred is founded upon a profound knowledge, understanding and conviction of the inherent sanctity of all things" (p.

cance. It is epochal in that we have the capacity to shift towards a more humane form of economic, social, and ecological sustainability. When we recognize the sanctity of life, we can then see that eco-stewardship and sustainability are sacred.

Treating Earth and its processes with reverence and attentiveness is a sacred act. I propose that sustainability and the theorizing pertaining to sustainability is not only sacred, but it is a "prayerful act." Prayer uplifts and recognizes the spiritual necessity and possibility of an eco-friendly action or process. Mathew Fox (2001) describes prayer as being *a radical response to life*. Similarly, sustainability is a radical response to the modern way of life. When we gain appreciation for the spiritual possibilities of fighting for sustainability and when we act on these convictions it becomes a *prayerful act*.[13] It becomes an act of faith and an act of hope. This form of prayer is not the conventional renouncement of the present in hopes of a better future (that is sometimes associated with religious prayer). Instead, the emphasis with sustainability as a form of prayer is on assuming a stance in the world (Block in Pinar, 2006a, p. 113). The contemplative theologian Henri Nouwen (1972) adds insight on prayer stating,

> It is impressive to see how prayer opens one's eyes to nature. Prayer makes men contemplative and attentive. In place of manipulating, the man who prays stands receptive before the world. He no longer grabs but caresses, he no longer bites, but kisses, he no longer examines but admires. To this man...nature can show itself completely renewed. (p. 24)

When we commune and fellowship with the natural world it is a prayerful act because it is more reverential. I relate to Nouwen's explanation of how prayer opens our attunement to the natural world. I too feel a greater connection to nature when praying. In the summer, when I plant tomatoes and get reacquainted with the soil, I become more attentive to the cycles of Earth. I pay attention to the balance between rain and sun.

---

376). When we recognize an inherent sanctity in all things we can better appreciate the natural world and our implicated role in facilitating ecological integrity.

13 James Macdonald (1995) posits that "[t]he act of theorizing is an act of faith, a religious act" (p. 181). Furthermore, theorizing "is the expression of belief...belief necessitates an act of the moral will based on faith" (p. 181). Therefore when we embrace a belief in the fundamental importance of biospheric integrity we embrace a moral will grounded in faith. This is a faith in the possibilities of the present and of what is yet to come. From an educational lens, Macdonald adds that "*Curriculum theorizing is a prayerful act*. It is an expression of the humanistic vision in life" (emphasis in original, p. 181).

Because it invokes the kind of care and awareness associated with prayer, I see gardening as a prayerful process.

Sustainability is a prayerful process because when we live in more environmentally friendly ways, we learn to bolster our relationship to the natural world. The sixth-century monk John Climacus said, prayer has the effect of "[holding] the world together" (in Norris, 1998, p. 58). This relationship is more contemplative and attentive because we must adopt a worldview that considers nature as an integral player in advancing human and non-human wellness. When we live sustainably we stop adhering to the industrial-minded alienation linked to co-opting and commoditizing our outdoor environment.

The ethereal beauty found in nature gives us a sense of the sublime. When we experience the sublime we are better positioned to encounter a proleptic moment. According to Slattery (2009), "a proleptic moment is any experience that transcends linear segmentation of time and creates a holistic understanding of the past, present, and future simultaneously" (n.p.). When we have a proleptic moment we experience a fullness of time in the past, present, and future (Slattery, 2009). When we work towards sustainability, I argue that we are more likely to experience this fullness of time because we are participating in the kind of prayer that embraces integrality. When living in a way that is environmentally friendly is seen as a sacred act we understand it as a timeless necessity. It is then that we might realize the possibilities of acting on behalf of the biosphere. There is an inherent hardwired human necessity to take care of the planet.[14] We must tap into our intuitive interest in promulgating biospheric wellness.

Those who participate in advancing ecological sustainability have decided to think critically about the ways of the world. In some cases, eco-advocates renounce commonly accepted practices entirely, based solely on the environmental implications. For example, some choose to never consume meat and live as vegetarians because of the environmental stress propounded by meat consumption.[15] It is important that we find

---

14 See Sigurd Olson's (2001) discussion on "racial memory" (p. 10). This is also addressed early in this book.

15 Meat consumption has a major impact on the environment. Meat that has been produced in conventional ways is non-sustainable. According to Bittman (2008) the proliferation of massive confined animal feeding and production operations are on the rise. He says, "These assembly-line meat factories consume enormous amounts of energy, pollute water supplies, generate significant greenhouse gases and require ever-increasing amounts of corn, soy and other grains"; it is "a de-

ways to think critically about the industrial mindedness of the world. Thomas Merton (1977) remarked that a monk "is someone who takes up a critical attitude toward the contemporary world and its structures" (p. vii). In this sense, those who struggle and fight for the well-being of Earth are monks. This is true because eco-advocates are taking a critical stance against mainstream consumerism. They challenge the very premise of the industrial individualism that guides Western living. The emphasis on the bottom line of the dollar sign is renounced. By focusing on sustainability, mainstream versions of success are challenged and critically examined. From the lens of sustainability, life is seen as something that is sacred and something that we must work to protect and serve from an environmental perspective. This notion of sacredness brings us back to the prayerful essence of participating in the sustainability movement.

Block says that "Study like prayer, is a way of being—it is an ethics" (in Pinar, 2006a, p. 109). I propose that *sustainability*, like prayer, is a way of being—it is an ethics (adapted from Block in Pinar, 2006a, p. 109). Sustainability, in its purest form, is a guiding principle that enables humans to live lastingly and lovingly on the planet. Block (2004) indicates that study is like prayer, suggesting that it is a spiritual discipline because it transforms the ordinary into extraordinary. He states that "In prayer and in study we acknowledge that our knowledge will never suffice and that what we undertake in the classroom is merely a hint of all that exists outside it" (in Pinar, 2006a, p. 114). When we let go of the fix-it-all obsession of humanity, we are better able to initiate the process of working towards the expansiveness of sustainability. From an ecological perspective, we need to cease from trying to "fix" everything as if the living world is a machine. This is a prayerful transition, to renew our faith in Earth to let nature regenerate and self-restore. Also, we need to get over our compulsion to know everything scientifically. When we view things in a traditional Cartesian scientific worldview, we cannot see them spiritually or aesthetically. By acknowledging that our immediate knowledge is limited and will never fully suffice, we can better participate in the project of educating our children and ourselves to advance the process of restoring ecological equilibrium.

Acknowledging the limitations of our knowledge means that we need to accept the dynamic quality and ever-changing character of contemporary life. This acceptance of the dynamic quality of life is not a rejection

---

pendency that has led to the destruction of vast swaths of the world's tropical rain forests" (n.p.).

of the value of the knowledge that has been accumulated through our lives and throughout the many generations of human life. Instead, acknowledging these limitations is the recognition of the fluid-like character of social and technological evolution. The rapidly changing landscape of humanity is mirrored by the swiftly changing landscape of the job market, politics, and industrialization. This is why it is important to equip today's youth with the problem-solving skills and critical-thinking capacity to address the unknown needs of the future.

In terms of thinking about environmental integrity, it is also important to build the ecological literacy and eco-political volition of students. Eco-literacy enables students to comprehend and respond to the needs of their home environment and home community in a way that is informed and pertinent to the given ecological context. Accordingly, it is important to cultivate a form of environmental understanding and political will that is able to adapt to the ever-changing social and ecological landscape.

Our role in advancing sustainability[16] needs to be an intentional act. If it is done well, our efforts towards regaining ecological integrity will embrace the unknown. As Guevara (1994) stated, a good education builds one's capacity to face the situations posed by life. We have to prepare our children for situations, challenges, and leadership roles for situations that we cannot predict. The uncertainty of what our future holds should serve as a powerful motivator. Perhaps it is when we face the ambiguities of the unknown that we grow the most. If this is the case, we should be growing rapidly, because we are facing a vastly unknown future.

Anthropogenic pollution creates and exacerbates biospheric uncertainty (Orr, 2009). It is impossible to entirely predict what the next manifestation of the ecological crisis will be. This is one of the roles that curriculum theory can take. We can theorize about what is to be, and work to strengthen our capacity to respond to these possibilities. We need to expand our capacity to recognize, withstand, and recover from the inevitable emergencies and storms that are yet to come. These environmental emergencies are disasters waiting to happen in the form of flooding, earthquakes, food shortages, and storms. Tornadoes and hurricanes are in the forecast, but we do not know when to expect them (Orr, 2009). As I write this, Washington, DC has just been blanketed in 30 inches of snow. It is an all time snowfall record for DC (for this time of year). Also, relief workers in Haiti are currently attempting to bring some semblance of normalization to the victims of one of the largest earth-

---

16 As discussed in a previous chapter, an eco-curriculum embraces the notion of being intentional about advancing sustainability.

quakes in the history of modern civilization. This happened just a few weeks ago, and over 200,000 people's lives were taken because of this natural disaster. It is not time to quibble about why these things are happening. Instead it is time to inspire, empower, and educate[17] citizens to initiate the trudge towards sustainability. I argue that an eco-curriculum for sustainability can help equip students for the severity of what is yet to come.

Possibilities for Sustainability

When we look at sustainability as a spiritual act, there is a paradigmatic shift that happens. Although there are certainly economic benefits that are tied to living green, when viewed as a spiritual act, sustainability can no longer be viewed as a mere business enterprise. Nor can it be viewed simply as a way to keep our natural resources in place for future use. There is much more to sustainability. As a spiritual act, sustainability is recognized as a mode of sacred intentionality, a communion with the biosphere. There is cosmological significance in seeing our actions as prayerful. When we participate in sustainability, there is a reconfiguration in the way that we see and interact with the industrial world. We are better able to critically question our modes of consumption and production. This is the case because we realize that whatever we make or consume leaves an impact. I refer to this as boomerang ecology.

Boomerang ecology is a term and concept that allows us to view the linkage between our choices and the effect that they have on the natural world. In this framework, we begin to realize that what we do to Earth will come back in some form, like a boomerang. From a collective perspective, one example of an ecological boomerang is the way that our reliance on combustion engines has resulted in global warming (Lynas, 2008; Monbiot, 2007). By spewing carbon into the atmosphere profusely for so many years, the boomerang is rapidly coming back to us (in the form of hotter summers, melting glaciers, etc.). Eco-boomerangs are the explicit eco-consequences to human-generated environmental degradation. The International Panel of Climate Change scientists have found a correlation between human-created climate change and cataclysmic storms. Storms such as tornadoes and hurricanes are a form of eco-boomerangs. Other examples are melting glaciers, depletion of our food reserves, and much more. Without a well orchestrated response to our industrial-

---

17 The orientation of inspiring, empowering, and educating is central to the mission statement of Young Harris College (Young Harris College, n.d.).

minded ecological dilemma, we are bound to be exposed to more ecological boomerangs. What are some potential strategies to respond to the destructive ecological boomerangs that we are releasing? I propose that we work towards *ecologizing, experientializing,* and *localizing.*

Ecologizing

To ecologize[18] is to cultivate knowledge and awareness of the connections that surround us. When we ecologize we look at the world through an ecocentric lens that appreciates and celebrates the unity and the diversity of the natural and cultural world. When we appreciate the connections that sustain us we are encouraged to find ways to learn more about them. Also, through ecological appreciation we will find ways to nurture sustainable interactions within our bioregion. This is true because appreciation leads to compassion which is integral to sustainability.[19] As Milbrath (1994) indicates, "Compassion is the core value that links our lives to the destiny of future generations" (p. 75). When we appreciate the significance of a healthy ecosystem we recognize the importance of caring for it—and we recognize the intergenerational importance of this work. When we see beyond the solipsistic lens that accompanies industrial thinking we can access a more cosmological viewpoint. Accordingly, there is a cosmological component to ecologizing. Cosmology is essentially a branch of study that views the universe as a large and ordered system while striving to understand the role of humans in the universe (cosmology, 2008). What does cosmology have to do with ecology? Thomas Berry tells us about the connection between cosmology and ecology. He states that

> [E]cology is [a] functioning cosmology. Ecology is the local expression of the cosmos; it is the small hoop that mirrors the large hoop. Accordingly, a cosmological viewpoint recognizes all living and non-living aspects of the universe as an integral whole. (Berry in Fox, 2006, p. 107)

This mentality of integrality enables us to strive for a more sustainable worldview. When we ecologize we recognize the importance of a unified vision that takes global and local ethics seriously. Like Block's conceptualization of study as a prayerful act, based on the fact that study is a way of being and an ethic, sustainability too is a way of being and an ethic.

---

18 I borrow the term *ecologize* from Morin (in Gadotti, 2008, p. 39).
19 As previously mentioned, Fox (2006) adds to this argument stating that "Compassion means justice. Another very current word for justice—and therefore compassion—is sustainability" (p. 123).

When we are able to harmonize our worldview with a more ecological perspective we are better able to recognize the significance of living environmentally friendly lifestyles. Hessel (2002) indicates that "Humanity now belongs to one interdependent household—the ecumenical earth community or *oikumene*—that needs to observe common ethical standards of sustainability, justice, and peace" (p. 593). Embracing this idea of oikumene is important from a spirituality and sustainability perspective. There is a prayerful aspect to ecumenical thinking because it is a *request* and a *petition* oriented towards advancing wholeness. Block (2004) posits that "because study is the equivalent of prayer...the school must be considered a sacred place" (p. 83; also in Pinar, 2006, p. 114). I adapt Block's statement and posit that—because *sustainability* is the equivalent of prayer—the *natural world* must be considered a sacred place. Ecologizing is also a sacred act, because it is the process of getting closer to the ethereality of the natural world.

I maintain that there is a religious aspect inherent to ecologizing. When we ecologize we are able to view the world through a more complete lens. I think of William Blake's poignant poetry:

> To see the world in a grain of sand
>
> And a heaven in a wildflower,
>
> Hold the universe in the palm of your hand
>
> And eternity in an hour. (William Blake in Braud, 1995, p. 64)

When was the last time that you experienced eternity in an hour or heaven in a wildflower? This change in perception indicates the phenomenological possibility and transformative capacity of nature. When I take students out for wilderness expeditions I am always happy to see the reactions to the beauty of places that appear to be untouched by man. In the Wind River Range of northwestern Wyoming the rugged terrain coupled with wildflowers had an enchanting quality. There is a spiritual and a religious component that is associated with the potential shift in our worldview that comes with seeing the world more ecologically.

Paul Tillich's conception of religion contributes to the discussion on spirituality, ecology, and sustainability. Tillich (1955) posited that religion is man's ultimate concern. Ecologizing becomes man's ultimate concern when it is recognized as essential to promoting the survivability of the planet. Without ecologizing we are bound to lives of continued fragmentation and specialization that result in larger carbon footprints[20] and more robotic regimentation. When we ecologize we are more likely to experience the sublime. As Einstein once said,

> The most beautiful thing we can experience is the mysterious. It is the source of all true art and all science. He to whom this emotion is a stranger, who can no longer pause to wonder and stand rapt in awe, is as good as dead: his eyes are closed. (Einstein in Emoto, 2004, p. 20)

The invocation from Einstein to embrace the mysterious is central to the notion of ecologizing because it touches on the value of connecting to the things that we are unable to see. To look at the world cosmologically, ecologically, and spiritually we need to have faith that living sustainably positively affects not only the visible, but the invisible as well. Ecologizing is enhanced through experientializing.

Experientializing

To experientialize is to restore and reclaim the centrality of lived experience into our epistemological assumptions. Experientializing recognizes the importance of learning directly from our experiences, with an emphasis on the academic facets of these experiences. Experience was the lynchpin for John Dewey's educational philosophy. Dykhuizen (1973) maintains that "one doctrine Dewey sought especially to clarify and establish was that reality is to be identified with experience" (p. 124). Dewey (1934) claims that everyday experience is of "irreducible importance" to philosophical method and proclaims the "value of the commonplace" (p. 249). Understanding the significance of everyday experience is fundamental to my argument surrounding the advancement of sustainability in education. It is through direct experience that we can cultivate the concern for Earth that will permeate through one's actions.

Direct experience enables us to gain intimacy with the subject matter. This is an intimacy that helps us to truly know what it means to learn in a way that is meaningful (see He et al., 2008). Dewey (1934) contends that philosophy's task is to create and promote "a response for concrete experience and its potentialities" (p. 249). In other words, philosophy should advance our capacity to learn from our experiences.

---

20 According to the Transition Network, "Every year of our lives since WWII (apart from the oil crises of the 70s) has been underpinned by more energy than the previous years" (2010b, n.p.). It is critical that we work towards less carbon intense lifestyles.

When we build our capacity to respond to the challenges that we face in life, we are on the pathway to learning from our experiences.

The importance of learning from our experiences is at the crux of Dewey's educational philosophy. That Dewey recognizes the inherent value of experience in the educational arena is the aspect of his theory that has drawn me to his work. Dewey (1929) asserts that "knowledge characterizes intelligently directed experience, as distinct from mere casual and uncritical experience" (p. v). When we move away from casual and uncritical experience we initiate what Dewey refers to as intelligently directed experience.

Intelligently directed experience is intertwined with the judgment that we gain through engaging in reflective inquiry. Reflective inquiry involves a process of undergoing an experience, processing the experience, and then integrating the new knowledge into our conceptual and perceptual schemata. From the standpoint of sustainability and bioregional education, it is essential that we honor the experiences that encourage us to be more intelligent ecological[21] stewards.[22] Dewey values the visceral propensity of experience to transform lives in an educational arena. Dewey later refers to fully completed experiences as "integrated experiences" (Dewey, 1934, p. 55). Integrated experiences contain a beginning, a continuous development, consummation, and an emotional satisfaction resulting from the experience's "movement toward intended fulfillment" (Dykhuizen, 1973, p. 259). In the realm of an eco-curriculum the intended fulfillment is to advance sustainability. Dewey condenses these components of educational experience into three stages and refers to them as "inception, development, fulfillment" (1934, p. 55). Accordingly, the experiential process has a beginning, middle, and an end.

---

21 In *What We Consume* John Huckle (1988) notes that we must teach in a way that helps us realize our impact. In particular, he urges us to educate about how our consumption habits are connected "to such environmental issues as deforestation in Amazonia, the draining of wetlands...and the debate over acid rain" (in N. Gough, 2003, p. 55).

22 Goleman (2009) discusses the importance of *ecological intelligence*, maintaining that "the more intelligent [we become] about the ecological impacts of how we live and how ecological intelligence, combined with marketplace transparency, can create a mechanism for positive change," which leads to a more sustainable world (p. 3). Ultimately Goleman argues that the impacts of our consumption habits are hidden and that we must learn to do a life cycle assessment of the products that we purchase. A life cycle assessment explores the "web of impacts" (p. 2) that an item has from when it is made, to when it is transported, and finally to when it is thrown away.

Although this process seems to be commonsensical, we must not overlook the significance of the experiential cycle. It is through direct experience that we can experience transformation (see Mezirow, 2000).

The transformative capacity that is available within an experience has diverse applications. Within experiential education there is a reflexive property pertaining to sustainability that can cultivate an ecological worldview. This ecological worldview is related to democracy and is propounded through direct experience. As Dewey indicates,

> Democracy as compared with other ways of life is the sole way of living which believes wholeheartedly in the process of experience as end and as means; as that which is capable of generating the science which is the sole dependable authority for the direction of further experience and which releases emotions, needs, and desires so as to call into being the things that have not existed in the past. For every way of life that fails in its democracy limits the contacts, the exchanges, the communications, the interactions by which experience is steadied while it is enlarged and enriched. (Dewey in Bernstein, 1985, pp. 49-50)

It follows that democracy is at the center of advancing sustainability. This is true because democracy advances the necessary contacts, exchanges, and communications inherent to mobilizing an ethic of sustainability and leads to integrated experiences. Integrated experiences in natural settings enable us to reverentially assume the role of ecological stewards. Stewardship is a form of democracy.

In Dewey's conceptualization of learning, it is crucial that democracy is in place in order for an "educative experience" to take place. Democracy enlarges the possibility for meaningful education to take place. In Dewey's words, "Since it is one that can have no end till experience itself comes to an end, the task of democracy is forever that of creation of a freer and more humane experience in which all share and to which all contribute" (Dewey in Bernstein, 1985, pp. 49-50). Again, in this sense democracy can enlarge and enliven the experiences that help us to be more human. In the context of sustainability, there is an opportunity to promote "freer and more humane experience" when there is a focus on reducing ecological exploitation and transforming the addiction to overconsumption. I posit that democracy should also extend to ecological attentiveness. It is an ecological attentiveness grounded in place.

To work towards intended fulfillment, an educational experience needs to be contextualized. Dewey posited that good education needs to be relevant. Learning from one's place is at the essence of relevancy.

When we learn from our localities we participate in a contextualization of our educational journey.

Localizing

> I believe that all education is local, if for no other reason than it concerns our children, our taxes, our community, our gifts, our time, [and] our learning.
>
> Mathew Fox, *The A.W.E. Project: Reinventing Education, Reinventing the Human*

To localize is to valorize the significance of living well within the places that we inhabit. Localizing is a shift in our sensual attunement that holistically embraces the totality of experiencing our bioregion. Sale (2000) suggests that to localize is to become a "dweller in the land" (p. 41). He posits that becoming a dweller in the land is the "alternative to the peril" of the "industrio-scientific paradigm" (p. 41). Forging alternatives to the industrial and mechanistic thinking that pervade our educational discourse is central to the process of localizing. Also, when we localize we build resiliency. Within the scope of this book I add that localizing needs to be grounded within the watersheds that align with our bioregions. A watershed is a more tangible delineation of a bioregion, and the waterways that compose our bioregions enable us to get ecological and hydrological feedback relatively quickly. If chemical levels are highly concentrated within the waterways that make up our bioregion, it will be reflected in water quality testing. Accordingly, healthy rivers and aquatic ecosystems in our watersheds serve as indicators to overall ecological health. This is one reason that I have selected a watershed-based model of bioregionalism to serve as one of the conceptual underpinnings of this book.

Localizing is a way to de-carbonize the carbon copy curriculum. Doing so will facilitate more robust human-Earth and human-human relationships thereby generating higher levels of resilience and positioning the scholarship of sustainability at the forefront of our intellectual excursions. Localizing draws on the scholarship of sustainability in both practice and theory because most literature related to sustainability emphasizes the value of developing a strong sense of place (Orr, 1992; Bowers, 2006; Jardine, 2000). Thusly, we work towards a praxis that embraces the theory and application of bioregional thinking and the possibility of place-based action. When we start from our own home we can generate ripples of stewardship that can travel through our neighborhoods. These ripples of stewardship are created through our personal efforts of living carbon neutral lifestyles, buying locally, consuming less and sharing more, and re-imagining the possibilities for a post-carbon world.

The process we have gone through to get to the point where we currently are, in terms of the advanced fossil fuel economy, has taken a great deal of innovative thinking. As the Transition Network posits, "we used immense amounts of creativity, ingenuity and adaptability on the way up the energy upslope, and...there's no reason for us not to do the same on the downslope" (Transition Network, 2010a, n.p.). Creativity, ingenuity, and adaptability are all accessible through an eco-curriculum for sustainability. We must embrace the "turning point" (Capra, 1982) that is surfacing in conjunction with the urgency to address the ecological crisis. This is why we must work towards an *ecological reconceptualization of education*[23] as we know it. The hope is to equip the next generation with the wisdom, passion, and talents necessary to engage in a radical de-carbonization of our industrial world. This does not require a full shift into continual primitive lifestyles or living in the trees—it is an approach that involves living for the trees. There is no prescriptive answer to all of our environmental woes...that is why we must work towards equipping the next generation with the heuristic tools to critically assess and creatively respond to the challenges that will occur at higher orders of magnitude beyond our current scope of imagination.

Connecting to Place

When we encounter sacred spaces we are able to connect to the universe with a more cosmological worldview. While studying the scholarship of sustainability, it is sometimes challenging for me to access a cosmological worldview. I have a tendency to get caught up thinking about all of the books that I want to read and thinking about the plethora of ideas that I have written about or discussed. However, in the midst of all this conceptual work, I miss out on spiritual connectedness. I relate to theologian Henri Nouwen's (1981) problem. He writes,

---

23 I believe that an *ecological reconceptualization of education* is necessary because the ways in which humans currently interact with the natural world are inadequate. We must stop educating in a way that equips students to become, as Orr (1994) posits, "more effective vandals of the earth" (p. 5). Unfortunately we are creating ecological vandals by promoting unceasing energy use and fossil fuel-centric thinking. The problems with ecological vandalism are well articulated by Orr (1994): "ecological vandalism undermines future prosperity and democracy alike" (p. 168).

> I have so many ideas I want to write about, so many books I want to read, so many skills I want to learn...and so many things I want to say to others now or later, that I do not SEE that God is all around me and that I am always trying to see what is ahead, overlooking him who is so close. (p. 223)

Nouwen recognizes that his cluttered life was lacking what he initially sought. Even though he devoted his life to studying and teaching about the word of God he was not able to participate in "the intimacy with God vital to his vocation" (Kirkus Reviews, n.d.). Nouwen[24] chose to move into a monastery so he could address this problem. For me, the wilderness serves as a monastery; it enables me to gain clarity and peace. I believe that encountering nature can facilitate a universal sense of interconnectivity. Also, nature helps us to develop a realization of the interdependence that exists between all living beings. Through nature immersion, we realize that we are not alone and that our communities are both local and global.

What does it mean to get into nature and reconnect? Answers to this question are as varied as the flora that make up a rainforest. However, there are overlapping experiential components pertaining to encountering the wild. A common theme that emerges from the narrative of nature-based excursions is that of feeling a deep sense of relatedness. Nature writer Sigurd Olson[25] describes a moment of connection he had in the wild:

---

24 I am intrigued by Henri Nouwen's writing, teaching, and life. At the age of 54, Nouwen took a leap in his spiritual walk and chose to move from being a well known theologian at Harvard Divinity School to living a non-competitive life with people who were handicapped. Nouwen (1997) devoted his life to serving as a pastor at a small community called the L'Arche Daybreak Institute in Toronto, Canada). At L'Arche, Nouwen (1997) devoted a large portion of his time to taking care of a particular resident named Adam. Nouwen's work is tremendously impacted by Thomas Merton (see Nouwen, 1972) with a focus on contemplative prayer and autobiographical spiritual work.

25 Sigurd Olson has had a significant influence on my scholarly thinking and writing. In particular, I am impressed with Olson's commitment to seeking out quiet and reflective places in nature—to cultivate a deeper sense of ecological community and a more refined sense of self. More specifically, his book entitled *Listening Point* (Olson, 1958) made a powerful contribution to sustainability discourse—with a focus on exploring wild places while learning the subtleties that make up these pristine chunks of land. Interestingly, the Sigurd Olson Environmental Institute is housed where I did my undergraduate work (Northland College).

The sun was trembling now on the edge of the ridge. It was alive, almost fluid and pulsating, and as I watched it sink I thought that I could feel the earth turning from it, actually feel its rotation. The silence of the wilderness, that sense of oneness which comes only when there are no distracting sights or sounds, when we listen with inward ears and see with inward eyes, when we feel and are aware with our entire beings rather than our senses. I thought as I sat there of the ancient admonition, "Be still and know that I am God," and knew that without stillness there can be no knowing, without divorcement from outside influences man cannot know what spirit means. (In Backes, 1997, p. 253)

When we enter the reflective space that allows us to listen with inward ears and to see with inward eyes, we gain a greater sense of connectedness. It is a spiritual and aesthetic atonement, a moment of ethereality. Today humans continue to wrap themselves in the chaos of industrialism and its related gadgetry. We need to take a breath and ask ourselves an important question: Is this the direction we need to be headed? Because, in idleness and in sweet silence is the opportunity for contemplation, reflection, and soul searching. It is through silence and idleness that our experiences are allowed to breathe.

When I spend time in the wilderness, I notice that my mind gets clearer the further that I get into the backcountry. There is something unexplainable that happens, an inexplicable qualitative shift in my thinking. The sound of the wind in the trees, the gentle movement of water through the stream, the smell of sun-baked pine needles in the mid-afternoon—they all coalesce in an organically orchestrated mixture of sensual connectivity. In the wilderness, mental clarity replaces clutter and a revitalizing sense of holistic centeredness takes over. We have the capacity to be encouraged and energized by nature. Why not go into the wilderness and get its good tidings? Nature is a powerful healer. Muir (1997) notes that "Nature's peace will flow into you as sunshine flows into trees.[26] The winds will blow their own freshness into you, and the storms their energy, while cares will drop off like autumn leaves" (p. 755). When I spend time playing, working, and traveling in the outdoors my cares

---

[26] I resonate with this quote from Muir for several reasons. First of all it is a quote that I read early in my undergraduate career as an outdoor educator. I would read it to my co-workers and to my students in the evening while sitting around the campfire underneath the stars. I am impressed with the way that John Muir spearheaded such a critical effort to set aside and preserve wild places in the form of National Parks. Muir was featured in several of the installments of Ken Burns' recent documentary entitled *The National Parks: America's Best Idea.*

drop off like autumn leaves. It is time, Ralph Waldo Emerson (2003) posits, that we "Leave this military practice [of over-regimentation] and adopt the pace of Nature. Her secret is patience" (p. 482). We need to cultivate and embolden our patience.

Nature operates on a different timescale than that of the industrialized world. This is why it is important to me to remove my watch when I enter the forest. For me, the wilderness is a sanctuary and a prayerful place of rediscovery. Instead of thinking about my work, I am able to become fully present in the backcountry. Wendell Berry (1987) believes in the nourishing and restorative capacity of encountering the wilderness. He states that "We need to go now and again into places where our work is disallowed, where our hopes and plans have no standing" (p. 147). When we enter the places where our work is banned, we get to enter more fully into the silence and solitude that can refresh our spirit. By exploring nature alone, with no preset agenda, we can become invigorated and recharged.

On a recent solo trip that I took in the mountains of north Georgia, I got to explore a place far from my home, where I did not have to think about my work. It was Blood Mountain located in the Chattahoochee National Forest. Blood Mountain is the highest point of the Appalachian Trail in Georgia. The purpose of this trip was to get my mind off of my job search and my book. On the trail there was no Internet access or cell phone reception. It was just me, my backpack, and the mountain. That night, I experienced the clearest night sky that I have ever seen in Georgia. On this solo trip, I noticed that nature's peace began to flow into me. At the end of my expedition I was better situated to carry on my job search and book work. I started out where I began but with a different perspective.

There are several benefits to intentional time spent alone in nature. These solo experiences can enhance our sense of feeling connected to place, to self, and to community (Bobilya, 2004). We are given the chance to partake in a deeper formulation of our unique self. We cultivate the development of a sense of self by developing the distinctive nuances of our identity. In the wilderness we can pray, play, scream, sing or just be present. Being present in nature has played an important part of my self-formulation. By spending time in the outdoors, I have realized that the wilderness is like a church for me. It is a place where I can give praise and pray. I get a strong sense of God's presence when I am in the wilderness. The contemplative theologian Thomas Merton (2002) posits that "In prayer we discover what we already have. You start where you are and you deepen what you already have, and you realize that you are already there" (p. 167). This is a cogent statement that Merton makes. In essence Merton is referring to the "Wizard of Oz" effect of prayer; we go on a journey to find our home and to figure out what we need. But, we come to realize that we already have what we need and that we already are living at "home." I like how Merton points out the simple necessities of a spiritual life. He makes complex ideas easy to understand. My dad[27] introduced me to Merton when I was in college, and I have been a huge fan ever since. When I go to a used book store I make it a point to look for his books. The connection in my mind between Merton and my father helps me to feel "at home" when I read books by the theologian.

The poet Mary Oliver (2006) urges us to keep our mind on what matters, our work, "which is mostly to stand still and to learn to be astonished" (p. 71). I believe that learning to be astonished is at the root of our spiritual work. When we experience the enchantment of a starlit night sky we can experience a transformation of spirit. It enlivens our comprehension of the expansive universe. We are better able to realize the implicated essence of our role on this planet.

Throughout my undergraduate years my close friend, Karen, and I were loud people. Still, we are both rather boisterous individuals with a passion to express ourselves. When we get together our interest in self expression is expanded. In college, a friend of ours once stated that we were quite possibly the only people who go into nature to have nature hear us. In graduate school and through my work as an outdoor professional, I began to learn a more gentle way to interact with nature. I started to listen to her secrets and embrace the possibilities of the outdoor world and began to be more and more astonished by nature.

There is sustenance to be found in the outdoors—spiritual, physical, mental, and emotional nourishment. John Muir (1997) observes that

---

27 My father introduced me to a wide range of authors. When I was a baby, my parents owned a Christian bookstore. It was the surplus from this bookstore that served as the foundation for my dad's diverse and eclectic library covering topics from ecology to prayer, from Buddhism to poetry and healing. Whenever our family was on a road trip, my father would make special stops at a variety of used bookstores. At first I did not like books or bookstores, but they started to grow on me. My sophomore year of my undergraduate program is when this love for books really hit me, and I have acquired hundreds of books since then. Again, it all goes back to my dad—he inspired me to inquire and encouraged me to pursue my dream of earning a doctoral degree. Although he died in June of 2007 his legacy lives on from his humor, his passion for contemplative prayer, and the intellectual curiosity that he instilled in his children.

"[e]verybody needs beauty as well as bread, places to play in and pray in where nature may heal and cheer and give strength to the body and soul" (p. 814). Immersing ourselves in nature can be just as important as eating. We are starving for encounters with the sacred. How do we encounter the sacred? For some it could be a short walk to a nearby city park at sunset, others may require a backcountry expedition in order to get away from the chaos of the work-a-day world. For me I like to go paddling on the Ogeechee River. A day of paddling helps my concerns and worries to drift away. I am able to think more clearly and to work harder after spending time on the river. We need to identify what blocks us from encountering the wild and take some steps to overcome these obstacles. When we are bound to routines that monopolize our creative energies and prevent us from cultivating a sense of connectedness we can become spiritually bankrupt. The quest for attaining "success" or "progress" can undermine the cultivation of our sense of place, sense of self, and sense of community. We are spiritual beings living in a fast paced and sometimes unforgiving world. As I previously stated, working towards a more sustainable planet can be a prayerful act. It is an intentional spiritual intercession, a petition for planetary well-being that is sparked by awareness and devotion.

De-carbonizing a Carbon Copy Curriculum

To de-carbonize means to transmute our dependence on fossil fuels. It is a move towards carbon neutrality that enables us to forge alternatives to the conventional reliance on oil, coal, and gas. To be carbon neutral is to be free from the processes that emit carbon into our atmosphere or to find ways to capture or offset all of the carbon that is released. In today's world it is rare to find people, products, or processes that, over a lifetime, do not add carbon to the atmosphere. Earlier in this book I argue that contemporary education approaches continue to perpetuate an unsustainable dependence on fossil fuel. Students are not being educated in ways that help them to imagine a life without fossil fuels—a post-carbon life. We are not teaching children to live well in their bioregions. We are not equipping students with the tools to forge alternatives to mainstream consumption and production habits. As a result, we continue to live carbon-intense lifestyles.

A person who lives a carbon intense lifestyle is more concerned about his own comfort than about taking care of his bioregion. One way that comfort has taken precedence over ecological stewardship is in automobile fuel efficiency standards. Through time vehicles are getting bigger and using a lot of gas. It has been over 20 years since the United States increased its fuel efficiency standards. The last time that federal fuel efficiency standards were raised for trucks and cars was in 1985 (Singer, 2002). With the rapid increase in fuel efficient technologies and the decrease in fuel production, it is important that we move towards higher fuel efficiency standards. The last increase in fuel efficiency standards was implemented in part as a result of President Jimmy Carter's efforts.[28] In contrast President George H.W. Bush exemplified a comfort-centered argument at the 1992 Earth Summit in Rio de Janeiro. After he was asked by representatives of several developing nations to position resource over-consumption mitigation as a top priority, he responded that "the American lifestyle is not up for negotiation" (in Singer, 2002, p. 2). For Bush, the focus of policy was on the economy because the financial well-being of Americans was priority. This money-centric mentality still pervades, as most people live comfortable lives without concern for the environment. Folks who overlook *living* green for *making* green typically do not think twice about driving instead of walking to the corner convenience store—just one block away—to pick up a newspaper. This person is not concerned about recycling or adding trash to the overstuffed landfills. These folks are sometimes referred to as "energy hogs" (Energy Hog, n.d). Energy hogs impetuously consume energy. They have a tendency to consume large quantities of gas and have a lead foot when they are driving. As long as an energy hog is meeting his needs, it does not matter to him how others are doing. I argue that education is generating more energy hogs.

The reliance on combustion engines and the energy produced through burning coal, gas, and oil epitomize a carbon copy curriculum. The existing transportation infrastructure in Westernized countries has become such a part of our culture it is hard to imagine a world without combustion engines. Fossil fuel based transportation is a way of life for most of us. How do we move beyond a curriculum that perpetuates carbon intensity? The process of confronting the carbon copy curriculum is what I refer to as *de-carbonizing*. De-carbonizing a carbon copy curriculum involves a shift in educational paradigms—a deliberate transition from a mechanical paradigm to a more organic paradigm. By organic I am referring to a spontaneous and natural form of educational discourse. It is a paradigm that differs from the norm in that it requires a funda-

---

[28] In a historically significant fireside chat held in the spring of 1977 Carter (wearing a cardigan sweater to make a point about keeping one's heat low) declared that the energy crisis was the moral equivalent of war.

mental change in how we choose to immerse students in various educational experiences. This shift in paradigms begins with the recognition that traditional educational approaches are inadequate when it comes to formulating solutions to the looming ecological crisis. In this section I outline the ways in which we can de-carbonize our educational efforts.

I argue that we must cultivate biophilia (Wilson, 1984) in our educational institutions. Fostering biophilia, the human tendency to love life, must start in our backyards. When education embraces a bioregional approach, students are reacquainted with the natural world. Also, in a bioregional approach, students get to encounter the "third places" (Oldenburg, 1989) that uniquely and distinctively represent the local community. Third place is a concept pertaining to community building. It refers to the social surroundings that are "separate from the two usual social environments of home and the work place" (Third Place, 2009). I encourage you, the reader, to take a moment and think about the third places and green spaces that you enjoy frequenting. What is it that brings you back to these places? What can we do to protect and to create more third spaces? Within the framework of the sustainability movement, third spaces are integral to developing a strong sense of community. Hopkins (Tools for Change, n.d.) says that to be sustainable we need to "unlock the collective genius of the community" (n.p.). Vibrant communities create and maintain a vital social presence that is informed by the cultural nuances of a particular place. In order to de-carbonize a carbon copy curriculum, we need to harness the unique possibility of our surrounding natural and social environments.

To advance an eco-curriculum for sustainability, I propose that we work to envision a curriculum that de-carbonizes our educational efforts. In an effort to mobilize de-carbonization, I propose that we slow down, unplug, reconnect, and re-imagine. I believe that following these steps can help our next generation to be more in tune with their bioregions, their communities, and themselves. Ultimately, we need to equip our youth with the knowledge, skills, and abilities to forge viable solutions to what could quite possibly be the greatest challenge humans have ever faced—the prospect of an anthropogenically generated ecological collapse. One manifestation of this challenge is the looming peak oil crisis. This is the point beyond which our oil production enters a terminal decline (Hopkins, 2008). To de-carbonize the carbon copy curriculum we need to build student capacity to withstand the inevitable conflict and social tension associated with peak oil.[29]

Slowing Down

To learn experientially takes time. Experiential education requires careful reflection and mindful responsiveness. Barry Lopez (2002) points out that "Firsthand knowledge is enormously time consuming to acquire; with its dallying and lack of end points, it is also out of phase with the short-term demands of modern life" (p. 31). We are in the midst of a quickening, in a fast-paced world that takes no prisoners. The indelibility of our compulsion for instant gratification, rapid transport, and fast food wears away at our souls. How can we sustain ourselves in the midst of a short-term and frenetically organized world? I believe we sustain ourselves by finding refuge, oases of hope, pockets of solitude, and through slowing down. Thus, I return to my first tenet of de-carbonizing our curriculum, that of slowing down.

I argue that when we slow down there are several benefits within an educational context. As mentioned above, when we slow down we create the space for experiential learning. It is a form of conceptual decompression, uncoiling, and it affords educators, students, and all other stakeholders the opportunity to relax and embrace the knowledge that is gained through day to day encounters with life. By slowing down,[30] we give ourselves breathing room, room to stretch out and to embrace uncertainty. As Dewey (1998) stated, "education is life" (p. 232), and as curriculum theorists, as teachers, and as students, we must embrace the bounty of experience-based education while cultivating a deeper commitment to learning from the nuances of our day to day encounters.

I propose that there is a *slowness imperative* imbedded in our need to forge a more sustainable educational response to the ecological crisis. Within the framework of the slowness imperative, our society will honor the fact that it takes quality time and quantity time to live in a way that is environmentally friendly. I posit that it is an imperative to slow down because if we keep at the pace we are going, our resource base will dissolve. It will dissolve at the rapidly growing pace which we embrace

---

29 Peak oil, also known as the tipping point for oil availability, is the point at which there is a sudden and rapid decline of available oil reserves (see Hopkins, 2008, p. 21).
30 See Honoré (2004) for an interesting discussion about the benefits of a slower-paced lifestyle.

through the globalized and fossil fuel oriented economy. Andrew Price (2009) discusses the necessity of slowing down. He states that "modernity's efficiency quest, in one instance after another, seems little more than an efficiency delusion" (p. 212). The current commitment to emphasizing speed in pedagogy and curriculum may appear to be efficient and effective from a superficial viewpoint. However, from a more critical standpoint, our compulsion to keep getting faster is not effective—it is a delusion. The speed compulsion does not cultivate harmonious learning or resilience; instead students are exposed to a mis-educative form of schooling, the kind that figuratively straightens one's river.

A modern culture example of an unhealthy reliance on efficiency in relationship making is speed dating. Speed dating is a process that involves several participants who get to meet a number of individuals of the opposite sex for a short amount of time. Within 30 seconds (or so) participants are supposed to decide if the other person is a compatible mate. Let us take a minute to explore a hypothetical situation. Imagine mandatory speed dating. What if it were required for all single people to attend a speed dating gathering? Let's take this scenario a step further; what if you were also required to select your lifelong partner in this short gathering? Does this not seem ludicrous to force someone to select a suitable lifelong partner in such a brief encounter? I propose that, metaphorically, this is what we are doing to today's youth. We do not give students the time to reflect upon and unpack their learning. We are not giving them the necessary space to explore, encounter, and understand their unique set of interests, skills, and abilities. Instead we are trying to fill students with "expert" derived information while pushing them to quickly pick out a career that can help them to attain "success" and "progress."

The goals for contemporary schooling are superficial and extrinsically derived. We have created a version of success and progress (Wessels, 2005) that is not sustainable. Orr (1991) recognizes education's unhealthy attachment to "success":

> There is a myth that the purpose of education is that of giving you the means for upward mobility and success. Thomas Merton once identified this as the "mass production of people literally unfit for anything except to take part in an elaborate and completely artificial charade." (p. 59)

According to Orr (1991), Merton proposed an unconventional way to view the role of education,

> ...His advice to students was to "be anything you like, be madmen, drunks, and bastards of every shape and form, but at all costs avoid one thing: suc-

cess." The plain fact is that the planet does not need more "successful" people. But it does desperately need more peacemakers, healers, restorers, storytellers, and lovers of every shape and form. It needs people who live well in their places. (p. 59)

How do we reconceptualize educational practice in a way that will create the necessary space for peacemakers, healers, restorers, storytellers, and lovers of every shape and form? Part of what we can do is to create more space for silence and solitude. It is in silence and solitude that we can begin to understand and respond to our true calling.

By slowing down and experiencing silence and solitude we have the potential to revolutionize our educational system. I once had a dream in which I had a supernatural ability to slow down the pace of the entire world with the push of a button. The button was located on a supernatural wristwatch that was the most sought after item in this particular dream world. It was a timepiece that had the extraordinary and somewhat mythical powers of slowing down the surrounding world. However, when the rest of the world would slow down, to the watch bearer, everything would look like it was in slow motion. This put the watch wearer at a distinct advantage because he was operating at a speed that was ten times faster than everyone and everything else on Earth. I share this story for two reasons: first to point out that the folks who "control" the world's pace and speed have a unique amount of power. Second, when we succumb to an imposed pace of life we are probably not even aware of it (like everyone in the dream who was not wearing the supernatural watch).

Sachs and George (1997) point out in their article entitled "Wasting Time Is an Ecological Virtue," the timescale that is "inherent to activities like...caring and hoping...cultivating friendship" and advancing ecological revitalization is "at odds with the speed of the economy" (p. 6). The frenetic pace of industrialism stifles our ability to respond to the very ecological degradation that we inadvertently generate through our everyday participation in the commercial world. Thackara and Schwarz point out that we "now live in a world dominated by speed—from CNN to super-fast computers, from MTV to high-speed travel, speed defines our products, our environment, our way of life and our imaginations" (in Sachs & George, 1997, p. 4). The idea of slowing down expressed by Sachs and George is well summarized in the statement that "slow is beautiful." When we are able to slow down and cultivate meaningful relationships within our communities, it is likely that we will be more attentive to the well-being of the natural world. This change in perception involves a qualitative paradigmatic shift.

Slowing down involves a shift in perception that requires a reconceptualization of our thinking. The transformation that is necessary for us to forge a more sustainable world involves a return to understanding our unique localities. This is a transformation that necessitates a form of education that does not rely solely on the existing mode of globalization, specialization, and efficiency which promulgates carbon emissions through traditional modes of consumption and production. Instead, I am proposing a form of curriculum that integrates the eco-social milieu of place-making into the "complicated conversation" (Pinar, 2004) that is necessary to advance the sustainability project. We need to return to our ancestrally derived wisdom that enables us to live carefully, wisely, and delicately in our places.

Slowness is the first step towards a post-petroleum, de-carbonized economy. When we slow down, we can walk and bike more and drive less. Less fossil fuel-based transportation means less carbon emissions. It also allows the walker or biker to experience the elements of nature. When I bike to my on-campus job I get to feel the wind, soak in some sun rays, and become more alert. I notice that the bike trip allows me to be in a better place to begin my work, and it prepares me to take on the challenges of the day.

Once, when I was a teenager, I developed an affinity for human powered travel and began to critique the Westernized reliance on automobile travel. For a while, every time my family got into the car, I would comment on how we were sitting in the "pod" and that we were distancing ourselves from the surrounding world. My twin brother, Caleb, would gladly participate in this banter. Reflecting back on this, I can see how it would have been annoying for my family, but I can also see that it was rather insightful.

Unplugging

The next step towards forging a de-carbonized curriculum is to unplug. By unplugging I am referring to the process of deliberately removing ourselves from the continual cascade and inundation of the digital media and the commercial, industrial, and technical world. For example, most of us always carry a cell phone, wear a watch, and cook with microwave ovens. Many of us sit behind a computer all day. We are so "plugged in" that we have lost an interest in aesthetics, craftsmanship, and cooking. Another way to "unplug" is to go off the grid. To go off the grid means to remove one's electrical hookup from the city power grid and to replace the energy source with a non-conventional, self-sustaining energy source—like solar or wind power.

I propose that we infuse more balance when it comes to technical gadgetry within our educational institutions (see Bowers, 2000). To seek out balance in our plugged-in world, I argue that it is important to occasionally unplug. That is, we must be deliberate about structuring time that enables us to: get away from the computer, turn off our cell phones, take off our watches, leave the television and get outside. A recent study (Maas, Verheij, de Vries, Spreeuwenberg, Schellevis, & Groenewegan, 2009) demonstrated that people who live in closer proximity to a "green living environment" are healthier and happier. Unplugging has mental, spiritual, and physical benefits. When we unplug we are better able to relax, unwind, and become centered. We are more likely to find silence, the kind of silence that enables us to grow spiritually, a contemplative silence. It is a powerful form of silence like the silence that Sigurd Olson encountered in the outdoors:

> Over all was the silence of the wilderness, that sense of oneness which comes only when there are no distracting sights or sounds, when we listen with inward ears and see with inward eyes, when we feel and are aware with our entire beings rather than our senses. (In Backes, 1992, p. 104)

Once we slow down and unplug, we are ready to reconnect cosmologically and bioregionally. One way to ensure that we can become unplugged is to take a backcountry expedition into the wilderness.

In the wilderness we are likely to go beyond cell phone range. We leave behind our computers due to the fact that there are no electrical outlets. In other words, we go "off-line" when we enter backcountry forests. We enter a primeval space that generates silence and solitude. It is here that we can listen with inward ears and see with inward eyes. In the wilderness we are given the opportunity to reconnect to ourselves and to nature. It is the reconnection that enables us to feel at peace and at one with our world and our life trajectory. We start to feel congruence between our dreams and our actions because we are given time to explore, seek, and pursue our talents and visions.

Reconnecting

To reconnect is to seek out wholeness and balance. Reconnecting is reuniting with our sense of place, sense of self, and sense of community. A transformative sustainability education paradigm is one that embraces connectedness and interconnectedness. Ecology, as previously stated, is the study of relationships within a particular environment. When students are enabled to reconnect, they are able to grasp a more ecological worldview. That is, students are able to participate with the world in a way that is livelier, more authentic, and more informed. Working towards livelier and more informed encounters with nature is at the essence of reconnecting. To reconnect is at the heart of an eco-curriculum for sustainability. Once we are reconnected, we can see the world through a more critical lens and we can begin to re-imagine a greener and cleaner planet. To re-imagine is to tap into the depths of our creativity and to reawaken our imagination and reengage our fullest selves. We can begin to re-imagine what a democratic community will look like and embrace a wiser form of environmentally grounded intelligence.

Complicated Sustainability and Integrality: Bringing It All Back Together

> The undefined pervasive quality of an experience is that which binds together all the defined elements.
>
> John Dewey, *Art as Experience*

> There is in all things...a hidden wholeness.
>
> Merton in *A Hidden Wholeness: The Journey Toward an Undivided Life: Welcoming the Soul and Weaving Community in a Wounded World*

We live in an abundant world. Almost everywhere that we look in nature we can find beauty and solace. The healthy ecosystems that we see in nature are the embodiment of wholeness. In this sense, wholeness is abundance, and strong relationships and communal diversity typically denote ecological health. In most cases, if we look closely, there is a hidden cornucopia of interconnectivity in nature. Let us consider the longleaf pine forest of southern Georgia. When a person walks into one of these forests, the profuse diversity of flora and fauna is immediately evident. At a smaller scale, one can find an abundance of nutrients in the soil. According to Wilson (2007), there are 4,000,000 bacteria in any given handful of healthy soil.

At the ground level in some longleaf pine forests you may find a pitcher plant bog. Pitcher plants are carnivorous plants, meaning that they eat bugs for survival. If one dissects a pitcher plant, she will most likely get to see a range of exoskeletons of diverse insect species that have been trapped in the tubular pitcher plant (Ray, 1999). The pitcher plant captures unsuspecting insects by luring them with an attractive odor, using gravity to make the bug slide to the bottom, and then presenting the bug with a cocktail of liquid. The liquid contains soporific enzymes. After awhile, this cocktail's chemicals begin to digest the bug, ultimately giving nutrients to the plant. After the process of liquid-based bug digestion, the exoskeleton of the insect is all that remains. This is the curriculum of the wild: the vastness of diversity, the breadth of vitality, the robust scenery, and the opportunity for self-discovery are all found in nature. A trip into the wilderness is much more than a mere outdoor excursion. It is an opportunity to break free from the monotony of the technological world. There is wisdom in the wild, a primordial wisdom that allows us to go deeper into an ecological mindset.

As an outdoor educator in southeastern Georgia, I have had the opportunity to introduce several students to pitcher plant bogs. To all, from preschoolers to college students, the wonder of these unique ecosystems is viscerally palpable. While growing up in Kansas I had no idea that tubular pitcher plants existed. The first time that I saw a pitcher plant was on Stockton Island in Lake Superior. Stockton Island's pitcher plants look more like a miniature catcher's mitt—they are much wider and shorter than southern Georgia tube-like pitcher plants. My favorite types of Georgian pitcher plants are the tube shaped *Sarracenia* variety. The tube shaped pitcher plants can grow up to three feet tall. I am intrigued by the morphology and functionality of these plants. They are essentially just one big modified leaf, which means that they operate like a standard plant leaf converting sunshine into sugar. But the fascinating thing about these plants is their ability to digest bugs for food. They need to eat bugs because the boggy soil they grow up in is low on nutrients.

In south Georgia, pitcher plants are able to thrive in the wet and acidic bog environment. A bog is described by Elizabeth Cox as a "low-lying area saturated with water [that] creates a hollow of decomposed vegetation in wet, spongy ground" (in Lopez & Gwartney, 2006, p. 40). Bogs are fascinating environmental features; when you walk on them you can sink into their wet and spongy soil. Cox notes that a bog is a "netherworld" with a "rank smell that lingers in the air," but bogs are certainly not dead (in Lopez & Gwartney, 2006, p. 40). Bogs are unique ecological systems that support life—they are "plant communities" (Cox in Lopez & Gwartney, 2006). I love guiding students through the Georgia Southern University botanical garden field site to the pitcher plant bog and allowing students to investigate these bug-eating plants. After I introduce the group to the plants and the bog I proceed to dissect a single plant to show how it does its work. Young and old alike are quick to exclaim that the pitcher plant and its contents are "gross" but they always glance at the bug remains—even if it is a furtive glance. It is experiences like these that draw me to the curriculum of the wild—enchanting, mysterious, primordial, and experiential.

I love digging in the dirt, stomping in mud puddles, sloshing through wet snow, and just playing in nature. What curriculum can be better than the curriculum of the wild? We must recognize that there are risks when we explore the natural world. The unpredictable bee sting, thunderstorm, poison ivy patch, attacks from alligators, and snake bites to name a few. However, these risks are inherent to outdoor travel. As the famous mountaineer and theologian Willi Unsoeld (1974) warned in his response to a worried parent's inquiry regarding the perils of outdoor adventure education, we (as outdoor educators) cannot guarantee the safety of a child, but we can guarantee the death of his soul if he lives in the bubble of predictability and protection that parents are trying to create. We grow through challenge and risk not comfort and conformity. We must abandon traditionally accepted modes of consumption-based living and strive for more environmentally integrated lives—this greening process can feel like risky business. But how do we move towards sustainability?

I argue that sustainability at all levels is best exemplified within the framework of integrity and wholeness.[31] When I think of wholeness, I think of the various wilderness areas that I have explored. From the deserts of the Southwest to the lush vegetation of the Cascade Mountains in the Northwest, to the prairie lands of Kansas and the swamps of the Okefenokee, there is much to experience in the out-of-doors. But why would we want to get outside when it is so comfortable inside? There is comfort in familiarity and predictability but what do we learn when we simply sit on the couch and watch television? It is all about balance. Why not become physically active once again?

---

31 Elaine Riley-Taylor (2002) notes that wholeness "emphasizes the importance of the whole and the interdependence of its parts" (p. 26). She suggests that wholeness should work towards the "recognition of the one and the many, a part-to-whole relation" (p. 26). Additionally, she indicates that there is a "sacred dimension to the notion of the interconnectivity of all things within a healthy and interdependent ecological balance" (p. 26). In this chapter, I work to build upon her conception of wholeness while advancing my notion of a bioregional eco-curriculum.

An Integrated Eco-curriculum for Sustainability

Wholeness is being in tune with the wind, sand and stars.

Henry Beston in *Reflections from the North Country*

Life delights in life.

William Blake in *The Outsider*

The capacity to feel more integrated and balanced is within all of us. Moving towards wholeness and integrality invokes the notion of integrity, which "means much more than adherence to a moral code: it means the state or quality of being entire, complete, and unbroken" (Palmer, 2004, p. 8). There is a bit of a dance involved in achieving the more complicated form of wholeness that involves recognition of both what we can impact and what is out of our hands. This choreography is a part of our lives that Merton referred to as "the general dance" (Palmer, 2004, p. 83). When students are encouraged to undergo ecological experiences, they are more likely to live more integrated lives and to develop an accurate sense of agency. Education should aim at teaching the general dance of life while restoring the hidden wholeness. Sustainability is much more than wholeness; it is multidimensional, embracing integrated thought and ecological attunement. Some refer to this process of restoring the hidden wholeness as holistic education.[32] For the purposes of this book I explore holism from the standpoint of ecological sustainability.

Holism is defined as a "theory that living matter or reality is made up of organic or unified wholes that are greater than the simple sum of their parts" (American Heritage Dictionary, in Riley-Taylor, 2002, p. 26). From an ecological context, holism embraces the belief that unity emerges through diversity and that diversity pivots around unity. Holism resonates with my educational philosophy because it embraces the uniqueness of each living being and promotes the use of mind, body, and spirit in the process of teaching and learning.

When I reflect on my educational experiences, the most significant learning events were the ones when I was most fully involved at all levels

---

32 Holistic education is a philosophy of education that embraces the integrality of mind, body, and spirit while emphasizing the development of a sense of self, sense of place, and sense of community within the context of values such as ecological stewardship, compassion, and peace (J. Miller, 1996, 2005, 2006; R. Miller, 1997, 2000). Scott Forbes (1996) argues that "holistic education reflects and responds more fully than conventional education to a new and increasingly accepted view of what it means to be [fully] human..." (n.p.).

emotionally, physically, and spiritually. In particular, I think of the student conservation crew that I worked on as a high school volunteer in the Ouachita Mountains of Arkansas during the summer of 1995. We learned about weather patterns by watching clouds roll in and about erosion by watching the way that the land responded to torrential downfalls. It is hard to get this depth of learning in any other way. Virtually every time that I enter the wilderness I experience a sense of wholeness. As Sigurd Olson (1976) states, "Wholeness is the sum total of wilderness experience; it is the ephemeral essence, the ultimate that puts one in tune with cosmic values" (p. 112). Nature immersion can be a gateway to a more adequate worldview. The simplicity and silence attainable in wilderness areas expands our frame of reference (Olson, 1976). Holism is embodied in nature systems—the natural world does not know anything but holism. I submit that holistic thinking enables us to embrace the lived and educational experience that has made us who we are today. When we look at our experiences through a lens of reductionism and fragmentation we are unable to see why we have become who we are.

Ecological holism posits that a diversity of roles within nature is necessary to maintain environmental integrity. In order to think and act more sustainably, it is important to view the world through the lens of holism. Olson (1976) posits that wholeness "is harmony and oneness, the very antithesis of fragmentation, emptiness, and frustration. It means being alive and aware of all about you and all that has ever been" (p. 112). When we are in tune with our surroundings and all of the process that has made us who we are, we recognize the dynamic interconnectivity inherent to life. Capra (1982) suggests that experiencing wholeness involves realizing the inherent interdependence and interrelatedness of living systems. Capra intimates that "All living beings...are organized in systems where each individual is part of the whole and embodies the whole in itself" (Medrick, 1987, p. 26). Recognizing the fundamental interconnectivity in life is associated with the ecological worldview.

Viewing the world in a holistic way helps us to realize that our actions impact other people and other non-human living beings. Our choices have far-reaching consequences. For example, the CO_2 that we release from our personal energy consumption (electricity, gas powered transportation etc.) habits adds to the greenhouse gases that create global warming. Global warming impacts some geographical locations more than others. Some coastal cities are already being affected by the rising water level related to global warming (Gore, 2009). Thus, our personal carbon emissions can generate problems that lead to environmental refugees—people who are forced out of their homes because of rising ocean levels. Once we recognize the connections between our actions and the suffering of others we are more likely to work towards a more ecologically viable way of life.

Ecological thinking looks at the integrality of the relationships that enable us to live comfortably on this planet. As Jon Miller notes, "Nature at its core is interrelated and dynamic. We can see this dynamism and connectedness in the atom, organic systems, the biosphere, and universe itself" (in O'Sullivan, 1999, p. 64). Once we recognize the holism that surrounds us and we appreciate the holistic continuity between the multiplicities of our life experiences, I believe we will be better situated to live sustainably.

Comprehending the depth of interconnectivity that weaves the natural world together is at times a challenge. We are conditioned to avoid nature and trained to insulate ourselves from the outside world. Understanding the depth of nature-human connectivity involves living and thinking like a native. Gary Snyder states that living like a native entails "Thinking in terms of the whole fabric of living" and understanding how one affects this fabric (in Jardine, 2000, p. 11). As previously discussed, appreciating the delicate balance in nature begins when we experience it firsthand.

Experiencing nature in a way that is both authentic and meaningful presupposes a slowing down to a more humane and ecological pace. It involves moving away from the rapidly accelerating technozoic world.

> Understood in this earthy, intergenerational way, education has the opportunity, perhaps the obligation, to slow down the pace of attention, to broaden out its own work into the longstanding patterns and places we inhabit and which inhabit us. It has the opportunity, perhaps the obligation, to take on a mood not unlike ecological mindfulness. (Jardine, 2000, p. 11)

The beauty of an eco-curriculum for sustainability is that it advances our ability to appreciate the abundance of relationships that enable us to live comfortably on this planet.

Parting Thoughts

In this book I have made several proposals for reconceptualizing curriculum in a way that instantiates sustainability. These proposals included *ecologizing, experientializing,* and *localizing.* Ecologizing is the process of honoring, appreciating, cultivating, and venerating the relationships that sustain us. When we ecologize we celebrate the complex network of interconnectivity that sustains our world. Honoring these relationships is something that is readily advanced within my conceptualization of re-infusing experience into our learning endeavors. Experientializing, in this sense, is repositioning academic study and active inquiry into the framework of education. Academic study, when done right, is fundamentally experiential because it provokes the inquiry process. Within the framework of curriculum studies, academic knowledge that is gained through studying various texts, is central to intellectual, spiritual, and emotional growth. Accordingly, experientializing is a holistic re-attunement to the web of life that can facilitate wholeness. Wholeness within the framework of experiential learning occurs because students are engaged in minds on, hands on, and hearts on activities. Learning through experience, both intellectually and kinesthetically, involves getting reacquainted with our surroundings.

Localizing is a process of returning to our immediate environmental and cultural milieus. By returning to our immediate milieus we embrace the depth and breadth of learning that is accessible in our own backyards and our bioregions. This type of learning gleans wisdom from nature and gains insight into human problems by studying how nature takes care of complex tasks in ways that are elegant and simple (see Benyus, 1998). To localize is a pragmatic approach to addressing the most pressing of environmental issues.

Also, in this book I argued for the necessity of slowing down, unplugging, and reconnecting. Slowing down is essential to returning to the human pace, not the economic and consumption race. By slowing down, we are more likely to take the time to appreciate the mystery and enchantment of the natural world. Slowing down is complemented by unplugging, which allows us to listen to our own thoughts and experience the world without the urgency associated with cell phones, computers, and other gadgetry. Ultimately, through unplugging and slowing down we can take the time to reconnect to ourselves, our place, and our communities. I write about these three components in the context of sustainability because I believe that it is essential that we make dramatic changes in our education systems quickly (see Fullan, 2005). These changes need to be built around a paradigm of ecological sustainability.

An eco-curriculum for sustainability is a holistic and transformative approach to education. This book explores the complicated conversation associated with greening, leaning, and cleaning the human environmental impact. This study employs the discourse of revitalization necessary for creating a more socially just and ecologically sound world. Thus, the theme of sustainability is woven throughout the fabric of the entire book. Working towards sustainability involves striving for wholeness, which can bring about an ecologically oriented change in our thinking, our passions, and our actions. In this work, I sought to help the reader realize that attentiveness to building eco-literacy is given credence in an eco-curriculum along with cultivating epistemological curiosity. The ultimate aim is to help advance eco-social solidarity and vitality at all levels. This book does not provide a "one-size-fits-all" approach to curriculum; instead, the hope is to offer a heuristic for "learning our way out" (see Milbrath, 1989) of the ecological crisis. In this book, I have explored the unique cultural and ecological nuances, particularities, and value of place. Accordingly, bioregional eco-curriculum and place-based education are both recognized as crucial features to infusing sustainable discourse and transformative approaches into teaching, researching, studying, and learning.

I submit that we need to reformulate our curriculum by returning to the local. As the Post Carbon Institute (2010) argues, "Complex, interconnected issues must be dealt with rapidly and effectively if we are to achieve a resilient future" (n.d). A big part of building resilience is the process of restoring our attunement to our surroundings, an attunement that is integral to a deeper sense of place. We can embrace the regions in which we live and the places that surround us to ground our curriculum. Our bioregions can serve as integrating contexts for learning. This book attempts to add symmetry in the intersections between place, curriculum, watershed study, and ecological sustainability. The far-reaching terrain of curriculum studies has enabled me to compose this discursive inquiry that has the capacity to guide future investigations associated with sustainability.

In this book I utilized an ecological worldview as my theoretical framework which emphasized the interconnectedness, interdependence, and interrelatedness that exists in the fluid inquiry associated with expounding an eco-curriculum for sustainability. This research is both timely and urgent in that we have arrived at an era that demands intentional, collaborative, and coordinated efforts towards mobilizing sustainability. Participatory democracy is essential in our effort to establish ecological renewal. I argue that the field of curriculum studies is positioned to harmonize the widespread efforts and energy necessary to make this world a more habitable and compassionate place to live.

Where to Go from Here

The possibilities for sustainability within the landscape of curriculum studies are bountiful. It is exciting to think about the numerous directions that the scholarship of sustainability can take. Sustainability studies are now an official major at a number of higher education institutions.[33] The intersections between sustainability studies and curriculum studies are abundant. Both fields of inquiry are interdisciplinary, both are committed to advancing participatory democracy, and both fields recognize the urgency in which a response needs to be formulated to the ecological crisis. As curriculum theorists, we have the capacity to help transform the future of our planet. We can help make Earth become a more habitable and robust place to live. This is true because of the amount of intellectual terrain that falls within our jurisdiction—we are not limited to a fenced-off field of inquiry. It is the work of curriculum theorists that is at the forefront of forging greater international solidarity (see Trueit et al., 2003; Pinar, 2003) and promoting intellectual curiosity within the framework of autobiography.

I posit that curriculum theorists are a community of healers. In this sense, curriculum theorists are charged with the task of restoring the balance. Theorists do not use the tools of the codified, atomistic, and mechanistic approach that characterize contemporary education. This restoration of balance invokes a return to the "pattern that connects" (Bateson, 1972) as a guiding force in our theory and our practice. When we appreciate the pattern that connects, we recognize the holistic forces that sustain life. An understanding of the cosmos enables us to unlock the doors of mechanism and enter into a deeper and more meaningful organic relationship with the ecosystem of life. This relational knowledge cultivates a more vital coexistence with human and non-human life. It is here, at the intersection of human-centered and biology-centered thinking, that restoration of balance can emerge.

From an ecological lens, it is crucial that curriculum theorists embrace humanization as a step towards sustainability. Humanization is the process of becoming more fully human and more fully alive. Thus, humanization can precipitate the development of a greater sense of self. Humanization involves a form of self-literacy and eco-literacy—a form of literacy that enables one to "read the world" and subsequently to "read the word" (Freire & Macedo, 1987). It facilitates the comprehension of one's place from an internal and external perspective. An ability to read the text of one's passions, motivations, and desires as well as the forces

---

[33] Examples of higher education institutions with sustainability studies programs include: the University of New Mexico, University of Texas, University of Florida, UC Berkeley, University of Massachusetts, and Arizona State University.

that obscure the humanization process helps one encounter the unitive quality (see May, 1987) of the pattern which connects (Bateson, 1972).

Within the intellectual realm, unity is represented by the theoretical spaces in which intersections occur, where ideas merge, transform, and take on new qualities. Achieving a "common-unity" takes work. Humans must recognize that a community of both human and non-human beings inhabits this planet. Non-human members of the biosphere depend on our reverence and respect for their survival. It is important to point out that virtually all of Earth's species would still survive without humans (see Weisman, 2007). Also, it is important to note that it is possible for human and non-human life to harmoniously and sustainably co-exist on this planet. This is at the foundation of what I believe that the scholarship of sustainability can offer—to further advance the field of curriculum studies and curriculum theory. The scholarship of sustainability advances the cultivation of an ecologically oriented worldview and an unfaltering commitment to intergenerational equality and bioregional sensitive lifestyles.

My recommendations for future scholarship pertaining to sustainability and curriculum studies include: exploring the possibilities for transformation in the framework of nature immersion, expounding upon the theoretical possibilities for expeditionary-oriented educational approaches founded in advancing ecological literacy and watershed awareness, investigating the possibilities of space[34] in curriculum and sustainability, and identifying how the theoretical landscape of bioregions provide a wonderful backdrop for eco-aesthetic[35] ruminations. There is a great deal of topography available for exploration within the framework of curriculum studies and sustainability. It is my hope that this book has helped to open doors for further inquiry into this dynamic, engaging, eclectic, and organic field of scholarship.

We do not have all of the solutions to the ecological crisis. Also, we do not know for certain when (or if) all of the glaciers will melt away or when (or if) our planet's average temperature will be increased by 2

---

34 Space is much broader in scope than place—it encompasses the spiritual, emotional, physical, social, and much more (PC, Ming Fang He, 2010). An investigation of space is beyond the scope of this book.

35 By eco-aesthetic I am referring to the notion of an ecologically oriented aesthetics. This is an aesthetics that embraces the natural world in an attempt to further contextualize environmental sustainability.

degrees Celsius.[36] It is in this space of uncertainty that curriculum theorizing becomes even more important. It is imperative that we theorize about how we can educate towards a more adequate way of being in this world. We need a more sustainable perceptual framework that will nurture ecological integrity and revitalization. As I mentioned before, this process of trudging towards sustainability is crucial—it is our chance as a human species to step up to the challenge of reconceptualizing our role on this planet and reconceptualizing the role of education. I posit that advancing environmentally sensitive thinking is not something that needs to be imposed on people—it can be reawakened through encounters with the natural world. We can move forward in playful, intentional, and organic ways. These organic approaches can open intellectual doorways and inspire both present and future generations to embrace the possibilities of living green while moving away from the fossil-fuel-powered economic machine.

---

36 A 2-degree Celsius increase in global average temperatures would have disastrous effects on the planet, including rising sea levels, food shortages, species extinction, a radical increase in disease carrying organisms, and much more (see Gore, 2006).

References

350.org. (n.d). 350 science. *350.org*. Retrieved March 1, 2010, from http://www.350.org/about/science.

Abbey, E. (1982). *Down the river*. New York: Dutton.

———. (1990). *Desert solitaire: A season in the wilderness*. New York: Simon & Schuster.

Abowitz, K. K. (2000). A pragmatist revisioning of resistance theory. *American Educational Research Journal, 37*(4), 877–907.

Ackerman, D. (1997). *The rarest of the rare: Vanishing animals, timeless worlds*. New York: Vintage.

Aoki, T. T. (2005). *Curriculum in a new key*. (W. Pinar & R. L. Irwin, Eds.). Mahwah, NJ: Lawrence Erlbaum.

Apostle Islands. (n.d.). In *Wikipedia*. Retrieved from http://en.wikipedia.org/wiki/Apostle_Islands.

Aridjis, H. (2008). Foreword. In P. Corcoran, J. Wohlpart, & B. Hollingshead. *A voice for Earth: American writers respond to the Earth Charter*. Athens: University of Georgia Press. xi–xii.

Aubrey, R. (1984). Reform in schooling: Four proposals on an educational quest. *Journal of Counseling & Development. 63*(4), 204.

Ayers, W. (2006). Trudge toward freedom: Educational research in the public interest. In G. Ladson-Billings & W. F. Tate (Eds.), *Education research in the public interest: Social justice, action, and policy* (pp. 81–97). New York: Teachers College Press.

———. (2009, November, 3). Diving into life: Writing into contradictions. Georgia Southern University Lecture.

Backes, D. (1992). *The wilderness companion*. Minocqua, WI: NorthWord Press.

———. (1997). *A wilderness within: The life of Sigurd F. Olson*. Minneapolis: University of Minnesota Press.

Bateson, G. (1972). *Steps to an ecology of mind*. New York: Ballantine Books.

———. (1979). *Mind and nature: A necessary unity*. New York: Dutton.

Bawden, R. (2004). Sustainability as emergence: The need for engaged discourse. Peter Blaze Corcoran & Arjen E. J. Wals (Eds.), *Higher education and the challenge of sustainability: Problems, promise, and practice*, 21–32. Dordrecht: Kluwer Academic.

Ben-Eli, M. (n.d.). *Sustainability: The five core principles*. Retrieved December 3, 2008, from http://bfi-internal.org/sustainability/principles.

Benyus, J. M. (1998). *Biomimicry: Innovation inspired by nature*. New York: Quill.

Bergea, O., Karlsson, R., Hedlund-Åström, A., Jacobsson, P., & Luttropp, C. (2006). Education for sustainability as a transformative learning process: A pedagogical experiment in Eco-Design doctoral education. *Journal of Cleaner Production, 14*(15–16), 1431–1442.

Bernstein, R. J. (1985). Dewey, democracy: The task ahead of us. In J. Rajchman & C. West (Eds.), *Post-analytic philosophy* (pp. 48–59). New York: Columbia University Press.

Bernstein, R. (2002). The origins of Totalitarianism: Not history, but politics. *Social Researcher, 69*(2), 381–395.

Berry, T. (1978). *The new story.* Teilhard studies, no. 1. Chambersburg, PA: Published for the American Teilhard Association for the Future of Man by ANIMA Books.

———. (1990). *The dream of the earth.* San Francisco: Sierra Club Books.

———. (1999). *The great work: Our way into the future.* New York: Bell Tower.

———. (2006). *Evening thoughts: Reflecting on Earth as sacred community.* (M. E. Tucker, Ed.). San Francisco: Sierra Club Books.

———. (2008). Thomas Berry Interview. In D. Jensen. *How shall I live my life?: On liberating the earth from civilization* (pp. 39–56). Oakland, CA: PM Press.

———. (2009). *The sacred universe: Earth, spirituality, and religion in the twenty-first century.* New York: Columbia University Press.

Berry, W. (1987). *Home economics: Fourteen essays.* San Francisco: North Point Press.

———. (1989, June). Latest thinking: True integration. *Mother Jones Magazine,* 16–19.

———. (1997). *The unsettling of America: Culture & agriculture.* San Francisco: Sierra Club Books.

———. (2001). *Life is a miracle: An essay against modern superstition.* Washington, DC: Counterpoint.

Bisson, C. A. (2009). Philosophical influences in outdoor, adventure, and experiential education. In B. Stremba & C. A. Bisson (Eds.), *Teaching adventure education theory: Best practices* (pp. 110–121). Champaign, IL: Human Kinetics.

Bittman, M. (2008, January 27). Rethinking the meat-guzzler. *The New York Times.* Retrieved from http://www.nytimes.com/2008/01/27/weekinreview/27bittman.html.

Blake, W. (1926). *The prophetic writings of William Blake.* Oxford: The Clarendon Press.

Block, A. A. (2004). *Talmud, curriculum, and the practical: Joseph Schwab and the Rabbis.* New York: Peter Lang.

Blockstein, D. E. & Greene, J. (Eds.). (2003). National Council for Science and the Environment (NCSE). *Recommendations for education for a sustainable and secure future.* Washington, DC: NCSE. Available: http://www.ncseonline.org/2003conference/2003Report.pdf

Bobbitt, F. (n.d.) Franklin Bobbitt (1876–1956)—Social efficiency movement, Bobbitt's contribution. *StateUniversity.com*. Retrieved March 9, 2010, from http://education.stateuniversity.com/pages/1794/Bobbitt-Franklin-1876-1956.html.

Bobilya, A. J. (2004). *An investigation of the solo in a wilderness experience program* (Unpublished dissertation). Minneapolis, MN: University of Minnesota.

Bourne, S. (2005). The environmental science of drinking water. *Environmental Health Perspectives, 113*(12), 858.

Bowers, C. A. (1993). *Education, cultural myths, and the ecological crisis: Toward deep changes.* Albany: State University of New York Press.

———. (1995). *Educating for an ecologically sustainable culture: Re-thinking moral education, creativity, intelligence, and other modern orthodoxies.* Albany: State University of New York Press.

———. (1997). *The culture of denial: Why the environmental movement needs a strategy for reforming universities and public schools.* SUNY series in environmental public policy. Albany: State University of New York Press.

———. (2000). *Let them eat data: How computers affect education, cultural diversity, and the prospects of ecological sustainability.* Athens: University of Georgia Press.

———. (2001a). *Educating for eco-justice and community.* Athens: University of Georgia Press.

———. (2001b). How language limits our understanding of environmental education. *Environmental Education Research, 7*(2), 141–151.

———. (2002). Greening the university curriculum. Retrieved from http://www.cabowers.net/pdf/greeningUniversityCurr.pdf.

———. (2003). *Mindful conservatism: Rethinking the ideological and educational basis of an ecologically sustainable future.* Lanham, MD: Rowman & Littlefield.

———. (2006). *Revitalizing the commons: Cultural and educational sites of resistance and affirmation.* Lanham, MD: Lexington Books.

Bowers, C. A., & Flinders, D. J. (1990). *Responsive teaching: An ecological approach to classroom patterns of language, culture, and thought.* Advances in contemporary educational thought series, v. 4. New York: Teachers College Press.

Braud, W. G. (1995). An experience of timelessness. *Exceptional Human Experience, 13*(1), 64–66.

Broswimmer, F. J. (2002). *Ecocide: A short history of the mass extinction of species.* London: Pluto Press.

Caine, R. N., Caine, M. G., McClintic, C. L., & Klimek, K. J. (2004). *12 brain/mind learning principles in action: The fieldbook for making connections, teaching, and the human brain.* Thousand Oaks, CA: Corwin Press.

Callicott, J. B. (1989). *In defense of the land ethic.* Albany, NY: SUNY Press.

———. (2001). Aldo Leopold, 1887–1948. In J. Palmer, D. E. Cooper, & P. B. Corcoran (Eds.), *Fifty key thinkers on the environment* (pp. 175–180). London: Routledge.

Campbell, J. (2001). *Creating our common future: Educating for unity in diversity.* New York: Berghahn Books.

Capra, F. (1982). *The turning point: Science, society, and the rising culture.* New York: Simon and Schuster.

———. (1996). *The web of life: A new scientific understanding of living systems.* New York: Anchor Books.

———. (2002). *The hidden connections: Integrating the biological, cognitive, and social dimensions of life into a science of sustainability.* New York: Doubleday.

———. (2005). Preface: How nature sustains the web of life. In M. Stone & Z. Barlow (Eds.), *Ecological literacy* (pp. xiii–xv). San Francisco: Sierra Club Books.

Capra, F., & Steindl-Rast, D. (1991). *Belonging to the universe: Explorations on the frontiers of science and spirituality* (1st ed.). San Francisco, CA: HarperSanFrancisco.

Carlson, D. (1998). Who am I? Gay identity and a democratic politics of the self. In W. Pinar (ed.), *Queer theory in education* (pp. 107–119). Mahwah, NJ: L. Erlbaum Associates.

Carlson, J. (2009). *Never finished—just begun: A narrative history of L.B. Sharp and outdoor education.* Edina, MN: Beavers Pond Press.

Carolina Sandhills National Wildlife Refuge. (2009, June 3). The longleaf pine/wiregrass ecosystem. *U.S. Fish & Wildlife Service Carolina Sandhills National Wildlife Refuge.* Retrieved January 25, 2010, from http://www.fws.gov/carolinasandhills/longleaf.html.

Carson, R. (1962). *Silent spring.* London: Hamilton.

———. (1965). *The sense of wonder.* New York: Harper Collins Publishers.

Carver, B. (2004). Nineteenth-century American jewelry. In *Heilbrunn timeline of art history.* New York: The Metropolitan Museum of Art. Retrieved November 9, 2009, from http://www.metmuseum.org/toah/hd/ajew/hd_ajew.htm.

Casas, M. (2003). *Cries for social efficiency in the pedagogical arenas of the early twentieth century and the early 1960s.* Retrieved from: ERIC database 11/9/06. ED479761.

Casemore, B. (2008). *The autobiographical demand of place: Curriculum inquiry in the American South.* New York: Peter Lang.

Casey, E. S. (1993). *Getting back into place: Toward a renewed understanding of the place-world.* Studies in Continental Thought. Bloomington: Indiana University Press.

———. (1997/1999). *The fate of place: A philosophical history*. A centennial book. California: University of California Press.
Center for Ecoliteracy (Organization). (n.d.). Education for sustainability competencies. *The Cloud Institute for Sustainability Education*. Retrieved December 5, 2008, from http://www.ecoliteracy.org/education/competencies.html.
Chabot, L., & Wavle, E. (2005). Sustainability: A context for achieving positive growth and viability. In H. A. Thompson (Ed.), *Currents and convergence: Navigating the rivers of change* (pp. 61–68). Minneapolis, MN: Association of College & Research Libraries. Retrieved from http://books.google.com.
Chawla, L., & Escalante, M. (2007, November). Student gains from place-based education. Retrieved January 15, 2008, from http://www.foresthistory.org/education/Curriculum/StudentGains-Chawla.pdf.
Cirillo, J. (2008). About the Sustainable Schools Project. *Sustainable Schools Project*. Retrieved April 6, 2009, from http://www.sustainableschoolsproject.org/about.
Clark, S. (1994). Review: Monocultures of the Mind: Perspectives on Biodiversity and Biotechnology. *International Affairs, 70*(2), 337–339.
Clifford, P., & Friesen, S. (1994). *Choosing to be healers*. Presented at the JCT Conference on Curriculum Theory and Classroom Practice, Banff, Alberta.
Cloud Institute. (n.d.). The Cloud Institute. *The Cloud Institute for Sustainability Education*. Retrieved March 15, 2010, from http://www.sustain-abilityed.org/.
Cobb, J. B. (1988). Ecology, science, and religion: Toward a postmodern worldview. In D. R. Griffin (Ed.), *The Reenchantment of science* (pp. 99–114). New York: SUNY Press.
Collins, Ú. M., & McNiff, J. (1999). *Rethinking pastoral care*. New York: Routledge.
convergent thinking. (n.d.). *WordNet Search*. Retrieved September 21, 2009, from Wordnet.princeton.edu website: http://wordnetweb.princeton.edu/perl/webwn?s=convergent%20thinking.
Corcoran, P. B. (2004). What if? The educational possibilities of the Earth Charter. *Educational Studies, 36*(1), 108–117.
Corcoran, P. B., & Wals, A. E. (Eds.). (2004). *Higher education and the challenge of sustainability: Problems, promise, and practice*. Dordrecht: Kluwer Academic.
Corcoran, P. B., Wohlpart, J., & Hollingshead, B. P. (2008). *A voice for Earth: American writers respond to the Earth Charter*. Athens: University of Georgia Press.
cosmology. (2008). Definitions of anthropological terms. *Definitions of anthropological terms*. Anthropology resources, Oregon State University. Retrieved March 1, 2010, from http://oregonstate.edu/instruct/anth370/gloss.html.

Cottrell, D. P. (1964). Review: A short review. [Review of the book Education and the Foundations of Human Freedom by George S. Counts]. *The Journal of Higher Education, 35*(4), 238.

Counts, G. (1930). *The American road to culture.* New York: John Day Company.

———. (1978). *Dare the school build a new social order?* Carbondale: Southern Illinois University Press.

———. (2009, July 27). *Wikipedia.* Retrieved September 16, 2009, from http://en.wikipedia.org/wiki/George_Counts#cite_ref-8.

Coupe, L. (Ed.). (2000). *The green studies reader.* New York: Routledge.

Crede, J. (2009). *Nature immersion: A model of sustainability education.* Unpublished Ph.D. Book, Prescott College.

Csikszentmihalyi, M. (1975). *Beyond boredom and anxiety.* San Francisco: Jossey-Bass.

———. (1990). *Flow: The psychology of optimal experience.* New York: Harper & Row.

———. (1996). *Creativity: Flow and the psychology of discovery and invention.* New York: Harper Collins Publishers.

———. (1997a). Flow and education. *The NAMTA Journal, 22*(2), 3–35

———. (1997b). *Finding flow: The psychology of engagement with everyday life.* MasterMinds. New York: BasicBooks.

Daniel, J. (2007). A world in favor of rootlessness. In B. H. Lopez, *The future of nature: Writing on a human ecology from Orion magazine.* Minneapolis, MN: Milkweed Editions, 160–166.

David W. Orr: Some like it hot—but lots more don't: The changing climate of US politics. (2008). Retrieved from http://www.youtube.com/watch?v=Boie5ugiTA4&feature=youtube_gdata.

Davison, A. (2001). *Technology and the contested meanings of sustainability.* New York: State University of New York Press.

Dean, A. (1995). *Peace of mind: Daily meditations for easing stress.* New York: Bantam Books.

Decade of Education for Sustainable Development [DESD]. (n.d). *ESD Toolkit.* Retrieved September 24, 2009, from http://www.esdtoolkit.org/discussion/default.htm.

Dewey, J. (1902/1990). *The school and society: And the child and the curriculum.* Chicago: University of Chicago Press.

———. (1916). *Democracy and education.* New York: The Macmillan Company.

———. (1929). *Experience and nature.* New York: Norton.

———. (1931). *The way out of educational confusion.* Cambridge, MA: Harvard University Press.

———. (1933, April 23). Dewey outlines utopian schools. *New York Times,* p. 7.

———. (1934). *A common faith.* New Haven: Yale University Press.

———. (1938/2005). *Art as experience.* New York: Perigee.

———. (1938). *Experience and education.* New York: Macmillan.

———. (1989). *The later works, 1925–1953.* (J. A. Boydston, Ed.). Carbondale, IL: SIU Press. Retrieved from http://books.google.com.

———. (1990). *The school and society and the child and the curriculum.* Chicago: University of Chicago Press.

———. (1998). *The essential Dewey: Pragmatism, education, democracy.* (L. Hickman & T.M. Alexander, Eds.). Bloomington, IN: Indiana University Press.

Diamond, J. M. (2005). *Collapse: How societies choose to fail or succeed.* New York: Viking.

Dillard, A. (1987/1990). *Pilgrim at Tinker Creek; An American childhood.* New York: Quality Paperback Book Club.

———. (1988). *Teaching a stone to talk: Expeditions and encounters.* New York: Harper & Row.

divergent thinking. (n.d.). Word Net. In *WordNet Search—3.0.* Princeton. Retrieved from http://wordnetweb.princeton.edu/perl/webwn?s=divergent %20thinking.

Dobson, A. (1996). Environmental sustainabilities: An analysis and a typology. *Environmental Politics, 5*(3), 401–428.

Doerr, M. (2004). *Currere and the environmental autobiography: A phenomenological approach to the teaching of ecology.* New York: Peter Lang.

Doll, M. A. (2000). *Like letters in running water: A mythopoetics of curriculum.* Lawrence Erlbaum Associates.

Doll, W. E. (1993). *Post-modern perspective on curriculum.* New York: Teachers College Press.

Dykhuizen, G. (1973). *The life and mind of John Dewey.* Carbondale, IL: Southern Illinois University Press.

Earth Charter Associates. (n.d.). What is the Earth Charter? Retrieved February 18, 2010, from http://www.earthcharterinaction.org/content/pages/What-is-the-Earth-Charter%3F.html.

Earth Charter International Secretariat. (2000). *The Earth Charter briefing book.* San Jose, Costa Rica: Earth Charter Commission.

Edgerton, S. H. (1996). *Translating the curriculum: Multiculturalism into cultural studies.* New York: Routledge.

Edwards, A. R. (2005). *The sustainability revolution: Portrait of a paradigm shift.* Gabriola, BC: New Society.

Elgin, D. (1993). *Voluntary simplicity: Toward a way of life that is outwardly simple, inwardly rich.* New York: Quill.

Emerson, R. W. (2003). *Selected Writings of Ralph Waldo Emerson.* (W. Gilman & C. Johnson, Eds.). Signet Classic.

Emoto, M. (2004). Healing with water. *The Journal of Alternative & Complementary Medicine, 10*(1), 19–21.

Energy Hog. (n.d.). Retrieved February 3, 2010, from http://www.energyhog.org/adult/adults.htm.

Environmental Protection Agency. (1997, August). EPA energy conservation. US EPA. Retrieved September 21, 2009, from http://www.epa.gov/reg5rcra/wptdiv/p2pages/energy.pdf.

———. (2008a). Introduction to the Clean Water Act. *EPA.gov.* Retrieved February 15, 2010, from http://www.epa.gov/watertrain/cwa/.

———. (2008b). History of the Clean Air Act. *EPA.gov.* Retrieved February 15, 2010, from http://www.epa.gov/air/caa/caa_history.html.

Esbjörn-Hargens, S., & Zimmerman, M. (2009). *Integral ecology: Uniting multiple perspectives on the natural world* (1st ed.). Boston: Integral Books.

Esteva, G., & Prakash, M. S. (1998). *Grassroots post-modernism: Remaking the soil of cultures.* New York: Palgrave Macmillan.

Evans, K. G. (2000). Reclaiming John Dewey. *Administration & Society, 32*(3), 308–328.

Fenn, N. (n.d.). Joseph Campbell's ten commandments of reading myths. *Bemy Astrologer.* Retrieved March 9, 2010, from http://www.bemyastrologer.com/myths.html.

Fien, J. (1993). *Environmental education: A pathway to sustainability.* Geelong, Vic.: Deakin University.

Filho, W. L. (2000). Dealing with misconceptions on the concept of sustainability. *International Journal of Sustainability in Higher Education, 1*(1), 9–19.

Forbes, S. H. (1996). Values in holistic education. Presented at the Third Annual Conference on 'Education, Spirituality and the Whole Child,' Roehampton Institute London. Retrieved from http://www.putnampit.com/holistic.html.

Fox, M. (1979). *A spirituality named compassion and the healing of the global village, Humpty Dumpty and us.* Minneapolis: Winston Press.

———. (2001). *Prayer: A radical response to life.* New York: Putnam.

———. (2006). *The A.W.E. project: Reinventing education, reinventing the human.* Kelowna, BC: Copper House

Franklin, B. (1999). Review essay: The state of curriculum history. *History of Education, 23*(4), 459–476.

Frederico, C. M., Cloud, J. P., Byrne, J., & Wheeler, K. A. (2002). Kindergarten through twelfth-grade. In J. C. Dernbach (Ed.), *Stumbling toward sustainability* (pp. 607–623). Washington, D.C.: Environmental Law Institute.

Freire, P. (1970/2000). *Pedagogy of the oppressed.* New York.

———. (2004). *Pedagogy of indignation.* Boulder: Paradigm

Freire, P., & Macedo, D. P. (1987). *Literacy: Reading the word & the world.* Critical studies in education series. South Hadley, Mass: Bergin & Garvey.

———. (1995). A dialogue: Culture, language, and race. *Harvard Educational Review, 65*(3).

———. (1999). Pedagogy, language, and race: A Dialogue. In J. Leach & B. Moon (eds.), *Learners and pedagogy*. London; Thousand Oaks, CA: P. Chapman Pub. in association with Open University, 46–58.

Fromm, E. (1973/1992). *The anatomy of human destructiveness*. New York: Holt, Rinehart and Winston.

Fullan, M. (2005). *Leadership & sustainability: System thinkers in action*. Thousand Oaks, CA: Corwin Press.

Gadotti, M. (2008). Education for sustainability: A critical contribution to the Decade of Education for Sustainable Development. *Green Theory & Praxis: The Journal of Ecopedagogy*, *4*(1), 15–64. Retrieved from http://greentheory andpraxis.ecopedagogy.org/index.php/journal/article/viewArticle/38.

Garrison, J. (2001). Assaying the possibilities of spiritual education: Toward a curriculum of poetic creation. *Journal of Curriculum Theorizing*, *17*(1), 63–70.

———. (Ed.), (2008). *Reconstructing democracy, recontextualizing Dewey: Pragmatism and interactive constructivism in the twenty-first century*. Albany, NY: State University of New York Press.

Glanville, W. E. (1911). A modern view of the hereafter. *The Biblical World*, *37*(2), 107–114.

Gleick, J. (1999). *Faster: The acceleration of just about everything*. New York: Pantheon Books.

Goldsmith, E. (1998). *The way: An ecological world-view*. Athens, GA: University of Georgia Press.

Goleman, D. (1995). *Emotional intelligence*. New York: Bantam Books.

———. (2003). *Destructive emotions: How can we overcome them?* New York: Bantam Books.

———. (2009). *Ecological intelligence: How knowing the hidden impacts of what we buy can change everything*. New York: Broadway Books.

Good, R.L. (1998). *Sustainable living and learning: The connection among paradigms, educational theories, and praxis*. Unpublished doctoral book: Pennsylvania State University.

Goodwin, B. (2007). *Nature's due: Healing our fragmented culture*. Edinburgh: Floris.

Gookin, J. (1999). *NOLS wilderness educator notebook*. Lander, WY: National Outdoor Leadership School.

Gorbachev, M. (n.d.). Green Cross International. Retrieved April 3, 2009, from http://www.gci.ch/.

Gore, A. (2006). *An inconvenient truth: The planetary emergency of global warming and what we can do about it*. New York: Rodale Press.

———. (2009). *Our choice: A plan to solve the climate crisis*. New York: Melcher Media.

Gough, A. G. (1993). Towards a socially critical environmental education: Water quality studies in a coastal school. *Journal of Curriculum Studies, 25*(4), 301–316.

———. (1997). *Education and the environment: Policy, trends and the problems on marginalisation*. Australian Education Review, no. 39. Melbourne: Australian Council for Educational Research.

———. (2005). Sustainable schools: Renovating educational processes. *Applied Environmental Education & Communication, 4*(4), 339–351.

Gough, A., & Gough, N. (2004). Environmental education research in southern Africa: Dilemmas of interpretation. *Environmental Education Research, 10*(3), 409–424.

———. (in press). Environmental education. In C. Kridel (Ed.), *The SAGE Encyclopedia of Curriculum Studies*. New York: Sage Publications.

Gough, A. G., & Robottom, I. (1993). Towards a socially critical environmental education: Water quality studies in a coastal school. *Journal of Curriculum Studies, 25*(4), 301–316.

Gough, N. (1989). From epistemology to ecopolitics: Renewing a paradigm for curriculum. *Journal of Curriculum Studies, 21*(3), 225–241.

———. (1994). Playing at catastrophe: Ecopolitical education after poststructuralism. *Educational Theory, 44*(2), 189–210.

———. (1999). Rethinking the subject: (De)constructing human agency in environmental education research. *Environmental Education Research, 5*(1), 35.

———. (2003). Thinking globally in environmental education: Implications for internationalizing curriculum inquiry. In W. Pinar (Ed.), *International handbook of curriculum research* (pp. 53–72). Mahwah, NJ: Lawrence Erlbaum Associates.

———. (2006). Sustainable development in learning, leadership and the law: A review essay. *Australian Journal of Environmental Education, 22*, 115–121.

———. (2009). Ecology, ecocriticism, and learning: How do places become 'pedagogical'? *TCI (Transnational Curriculum Inquiry), 5*(1), 71.

———. (n.d.). Weather incorporated: Environmental education, postmodern identities, and technocultural constructions of nature. *Canadian Journal of Environmental Education (CJEE), 2*(1–1997). Retrieved from http://cjee.lakeheadu.ca/index.php/cjee/article/viewFile/359/336.

Gove, P. B. (1984). Merriam-Webster's dictionary of synonyms. In *Synonyms: A dictionary of discriminated synonyms with antonyms and analogous and contrasted words*. Springfield, MA: Merriam-Webster.

Grant, G. P. (1986). *Technology and justice*. Toronto: Anansi.

Gray-Donald, J., & Selby, D. (Eds.). (2008). *Green frontiers: Environmental educators dancing away from mechanism*. Rotterdam: Sense Publishers.

Greene, M. (1995). *Releasing the imagination: Essays on education, the arts, and social change*. The Jossey-Bass education series. San Francisco: Jossey-Bass.

———. (2001). *Variations on a blue guitar: The Lincoln Center Institute lectures on aesthetic education.* New York: Teachers College Press.

Gruenewald, D. A. (2003). Foundations of place: A multidisciplinary framework for place-conscious education. *American Educational Research Journal, 40*(3), 619–654.

Gruenewald, D. A., & Smith, G. A. (Eds.). (2008). *Place-based education in the global age: Local diversity.* New York: Lawrence Erlbaum Associates.

Guevara, C. E. (1994). *Bolivian diary.* New York: Path Finder.

Guruswamy, L. D., & McNeely, J. A. (eds.). (1998). *Protection of global biodiversity: Converging strategies.* Durham, NC: Duke University Press.

Hartsfield, L. (2009). [Book review] The origins of modern environmental thought. *Green Theory & Praxis: The Journal of Ecopedagogy, 5*(1), 264–269.

Hawken, P. (2007). *Blessed unrest: How the largest movement in the world came into being, and why no one saw it coming.* New York: Viking.

He, M. F., Connelly, F. M., & Phillion, J. A. (Eds.). (2008). *The SAGE handbook of curriculum and instruction.* Los Angeles: Sage Publications.

Heidegger, M. (2001). *Poetry, language, thought.* New York: Perennial Classics.

Hessel, D. T. (2002). Sustainability as a religious and ethical concern. In J. C. Dernbach (Ed.), *Stumbling toward sustainability* (pp. 593–606). Washington, D.C.: Environmental Law Institute.

Hewitt, R. (2007). *Dewey and power: Renewing the democratic faith.* Rotterdam: Sense Publishers.

Heylighen, F., & Joslyn, C. (1992). What is systems theory? *Principia Cybernetica Web.* Retrieved March 6, 2010, from http://pespmc1.vub.ac.be/ SYSTHEOR.html.

Honoré, C. (2004). *In praise of slowness: How a worldwide movement is challenging the cult of speed.* San Francisco: HarperSanFrancisco.

Hopkins, R. (2008/2009). *The transition handbook: From oil dependency to local resilience.* Totnes, England: Chelsea Green. Retrieved from http://books.google.com/books?id=Vb2IHRGiIYIC&printsec=frontcover&dq=9781900322188&cd=1#v=onepage&q=&f=false

Huckle, J. (1988). *What we consume: The teachers' handbook.* Surrey, England: WWF in conjunction with Richmond Pub.

Huebner, D. E. (1999). *The lure of the transcendent: Collected essays by Dwayne E. Huebner.* (W. Pinar & V. Hillis, Eds.). New York: Routledge.

Hug, J. (1998). *Learning and teaching for an ecological sense of place: Toward environmental science education praxis* (Unpublished Book). Pennsylvania State University.

Hunt, J. S. (1995). Dewey's philosophical method and its influence on his philosophy of education. In K. Warren, M. Sakofs, & J. Hunt (Eds.), *The theory of experiential education* (pp. 23–32). Dubuque, IA: Kendall/Hunt.

Hutchison, D. (1998). *Growing up green: Education for ecological renewal.* New York: Teachers College Press.

IAACS. (n.d.). Mission. *International Association for the Advancement of Curriculum Studies*. Retrieved February 21, 2010, from http://www.iaacs.org/.

Iihardt, B. L., Verry, E. S., & Palik, B. J. (2000). Defining riparian areas. In E. S. Verry, J. W. Hornbeck, & C. A. Dolloff (Eds.), *Riparian management in forests of the continental Eastern United States* (pp. 23–42). Boca Raton, FL: CRC Press.

industrialism. (n.d.). *WordNet Search—3.0*. Retrieved February 23, 2010, from http://wordnetweb.princeton.edu/perl/webwn?s=industrialism.

integrality. (n.d.). *Dictionary.com unabridged*. Retrieved February 19, 2010, from Dictionary.com website: http://dictionary.reference.com/browse/integrality.

Inyo. (2001). *Why channelizing a river is never a good idea*. Retrieved March 12, 2010, from http://everything2.com/title/Why+channelizing+a+river+is+never+a+good+idea.

Ivanko, J. D., & Kivirist, L. (2004). *Rural renaissance: Renewing the quest for the good life*. Gabriola Island, BC: New Society.

Jardine, D. W. (2000). *"Under the tough old stars": Ecopedagogical essays*. Brandon, VT: Foundation for Educational Renewal.

Jardine, D. W., Friesen, S., & Clifford, P. (2006). *Curriculum in abundance*. Studies in curriculum theory. Mahwah, NJ: Lawrence Erlbaum Associates.

Jardine, D. W., LaGrange, A., & Everest, B. (2004). "In these shoes is the silent call of the earth": Meditations on curriculum integration, conceptual violence, and the ecologies of community and place. In D. J. Flinders & S. J. Thornton (Eds.), *The Curriculum Studies Reader* (pp. 323–329). New York: Routledge.

Jensen, D. (1995). *Listening to the land: Conversations about nature, culture, and Eros*. San Francisco: Sierra Club Books.

———. (2006). *Endgame* (1st ed.). New York: Seven Stories Press.

———. (2008). *How shall I live my life?: On liberating the earth from civilization*. Oakland, CA: PM Press.

Jensen, D., & Draffan, G. (2003). *Strangely like war: The global assault on forests*. Politics of the living. White River Junction, VT: Chelsea Green.

Jensen, D., & McBay, A. (2009). *What we leave behind*. New York: Seven Stories Press.

Jones, K. A. R. (2001). *Retracing the Savannah River portion of John Muir's thousand mile walk: An interpretive regional study suggesting curriculum for sustainability*. Doctoral Thesis (Ed.D.), Georgia Southern University.

Jucker, R. (n.d.). [Book Review of Bowers] Mindful conservatism. Rethinking the ideological and educational basis of an ecologically sustainable future. *C.A. Bowers*. Retrieved from http://www.cabowers.net/pdf/MindfulConservReview.pdf.

Jung, C. G. (2001). *The earth has a soul: The nature writings of C.G. Jung*. (M. Sabini, Ed.). Berkeley, CA: North Atlantic Books.

Kahn, R. V. (2008). From education for sustainable development to ecopedagogy: Sustaining capitalism or sustaining life? *Green Theory & Praxis: The Journal of Ecopedagogy,* 4(1), 1–14. Retrieved from http://greentheoryandpraxis.eco pedagogy.org/index.php/journal/article/viewArticle/37.

———. (2010). *Critical pedagogy, ecoliteracy, & planetary crisis: The ecopedagogy movement.* New York: Peter Lang.

Kakabadse, N. K., & Kakabadse, A. (2003). Polylogue as a platform for governance: Integrating people, the planet, profit and posterity. *Corporate Governance, 3*(1), 5–39.

Keystone species. (2010). *Wikipedia.* Retrieved February 22, 2010, from http://en.wikipedia.org/wiki/Keystone_species.

Kimmins, J. P. (1999). Biodiversity, beauty and the "beast": Are beautiful forests sustainable, are sustainable forests beautiful, and is "small" always ecologically desirable? *Forestry Chronicle, 75*(6), 1–11.

Kincheloe, J. L., & Pinar, W. (Eds.). (1991). *Curriculum as social psychoanalysis.* Albany, NY: SUNY Press.

Kirkman, K. (2004, May 14). New Georgia Encyclopedia: Upper Coastal Plain. *The new Georgia encyclopedia.* Retrieved February 2, 2010, from http://www.georgiaencyclopedia.org/nge/Article.jsp?id=h-2129.

Kirkus Reviews. (n.d). [book review] The Genesee diary. Retrieved February 3, 2010, from http://books.google.com/books

Kliebard, H. (1995). *The struggle for the American curriculum 1893–1958 (2nd ed).* New York: Routledge.

Klohr, P. (1971). The greening of curriculum, *Educational Leadership.* 455–457.

Knox, E. L. (n.d.). Medieval Society. Retrieved November 9, 2009, from http://www.boisestate.edu/courses/westciv/medsoc/23.shtml.

Krall, F. R. (1994). *Ecotone: Wayfaring on the margins.* Albany: State University of New York Press.

Krulwich, R. (2009). *Episode 1: Global warming, it's all about carbon.* Retrieved from http://www.youtube.com/watch?v=ypbb9Zi5Tao&feature=youtube_gdata.

Laarman, J. G. (1996). Ecological resistance movements: The global emergence of radical and popular environmentalism. *Environmental History, 1*(3), 103–104.

Leddy, T. (2006, September 29). Dewey's aesthetics. Retrieved November 30, 2009, from http://plato.stanford.edu/entries/dewey-aesthetics/#HavExp.

Lehman, H. (1998). John Leslie, the end of the world: The science and ethics of human extinction. *Journal of Agricultural and Environmental Ethics, 11*(1), 63–65.

Lemons, J., Westra, L., & Goodland, R. (1998). *Ecological sustainability and integrity.* Springer.

Lenz, Richard. J. (2008). Longstreet Highroad guide to the Georgia Coast and the Okefenokee. Retrieved from http://www.sherpaguides.com/georgia/coast/northern_coast/ogeechee_river.html.

Leopold, A. (1989). *A Sand County almanac.* Oxford: Oxford University Press.

Lewin, T. (2010, January 20). If your kids are awake, they're probably online. *The New York Times*. Retrieved February 4, 2010, from http://www.nytimes.com/2010/01/20/education/20wired.html.

literalism. (n.d.). *Dictionary.com Unabridged*. Retrieved February 23, 2010, from Dictionary.com website: http://dictionary.reference.com/browse/literalism

Lohan, T. (Ed.). (2008). *Water consciousness: How we all have to change to protect our most critical resource*. San Francisco: Watershed Media.

Lohan, T., & Lohan, E. (2008). Water neutral: New technology and green design. In T. Lohan (Ed.), *Water consciousness: How we all have to change to protect our most critical resource* (pp. 146–160). San Francisco: Watershed Media.

Lopez, B. (2002). The naturalist. In *Patriotism and the American land* (pp. 23–36). Orion Society.

Lopez, B., & Gwartney, D. (Eds.). (2006). *Home ground: Language for an American landscape*. San Antonio: Trinity University Press.

Louv, R. (2005). *Last child in the woods: Saving our children from nature-deficit disorder*. Chapel Hill, NC: Algonquin Books of Chapel Hill.

Lovelock, J. (1995). *Gaia: A new look at life on Earth*. Oxford: Oxford University Press.

———. (2006). *The revenge of Gaia: Earth's climate in crisis and the fate of humanity*. New York: Basic Books.

Luckner, J. L., & Nadler, R. S. (1997). *Processing the experience: Strategies to enhance and generalize learning*. Dubuque, IA: Kendall/Hunt.

Lydon, A. T. (1992). *Cosmology and curriculum: A vision for an Ecozoic Age*. Doctoral Book, Louisiana State University, Baton Rouge, LA.

Lynas, M. (2008). *Six degrees: Our future on a hotter planet*. Washington, DC: National Geographic.

Maas, J., Verheij, R. A., de Vries, S., Spreeuwenberg, P., Schellevis, F. G., & Groenewegen, P. P. (2009). Morbidity is related to a green living environment. *British Medical Journal, (63)*, 967–973.

Macdonald, J. B., & Macdonald, B. J. (Eds.). (1995). *Theory as a prayerful act: The collected essays of James B. Macdonald*. New York: Peter Lang.

Macy, J. (1998). *Coming back to life: Practices to reconnect our lives, our world*. Gabriola Island, BC: New Society Publishers.

Maffi, L. (2001). *On biocultural diversity: Linking language, knowledge, and the environment*. Washington, DC: Smithsonian Institution Press.

Marsden, W. E. (1971). Environmental studies courses in colleges in education. *Journal of Curriculum Studies, 3*(2), 163–178.

Martin, L. (2006). Carbon neutral: What does it mean? *eejits' guides*. Retrieved February 9, 2010, from http://www.eejitsguides.com/environment/carbon-neutral.html.

Martusewicz, R. A. (2001). *Seeking passage: Post-structuralism, pedagogy, ethics*. New York: Teachers College Press.

———. (2005). Eros in the commons: Educating for eco-ethical consciousness in a poetics of place. *Ethics, Place & Environment, 8*(3), 331–348.

Maryland Department of Natural Resources. (2004). Freshwater benthic macroinvertebrates. *Maryland Department of Natural Resources.* Retrieved February 22, 2010, from http://www.dnr.state.md.us/streams/pubs/freshwater.html.

Matheny, J. G. (2007). Reducing the risk of human extinction. *An International Journal, 27*(5), 1335–1344.

May, G. G. (1987). *Will and spirit: A contemplative psychology.* San Francisco: Harper & Row.

McDonald, T. (2007). Resilience thinking: Interview with Brian Walker. *Ecological Management & Restoration, 8*(2), 85–91.

McGinnis, M. (Ed.). (1999). *Bioregionalism.* New York: Routledge.

McKibben, B. (2008). *The Bill McKibben reader: Pieces from an active life.* New York: Henry Holt.

McLennan, J. F. (2004). *The philosophy of sustainable design: The future of architecture.* Kansas City, MO: Ecotone Publishing. Retrieved from http://books.google.com/books.

McLuhan, T. C. (1994). *The way of the earth: Encounters with nature in ancient and contemporary thought.* New York: Simon & Schuster.

Meadows, D. H. (1972). *The limits to growth; A report for the Club of Rome's project on the predicament of mankind.* New York: Universe Books.

Meadows, D. H., Randers, J., & Meadows, D. L. (2004). *The limits to growth: The 30-year update.* White River Junction, VT: Chelsea Green Publishing Company.

Medina, J. (2009). Creating history: Exploring the past and future of adventure education. In B. Stremba & C. A. Bisson (Eds.), *Teaching adventure education theory: Best practices* (pp. 78–80). Champaign, IL: Human Kinetics.

Medrick, F. (1987). *The new age wilderness leader: A rationale and experiential model for training* (Ed.D., Book). Greeley, CO: University of Northern Colorado.

Merton, T. (1968). *Zen and the birds of appetite.* New York: New Directions.

———. (1977). *The monastic journey.* (P. Hart, Ed.). Mission, KS: Andrews & McMeel.

———. (2002). *Seeds.* Boston: Shambhala.

Mezirow, J. (2000). *Learning as transformation: Critical perspectives on a theory in progress.* San Francisco: Jossey-Bass.

Mihelcic, J. R. (2008, January 4). Sustainable future. In G. Douglas (Ed.), *The encyclopedia of Earth.* Retrieved September 22, 2009, from http://www.eoearth.org/article/Sustainable_future.

Milbrath, L. W. (1989). *Envisioning a sustainable society: Learning our way out.* Albany, NY: State University of New York Press.

Miller, J. (1996). *The holistic curriculum.* Toronto: OISE Press.

———. (2005). *Holistic learning and spirituality in education: Breaking new ground.* State University of New York Press.

———. (2006). *Educating for wisdom and compassion: Creating conditions for timeless learning.* Corwin Press.

Miller, R. (1997). *What are schools for?* Brandon, VT: Holistic Education Press. Retrieved from https://great-ideas.org/SchoolsSample.pdf.

———. (2000). Education and the evolution of the cosmos. *Caring for new life: Essays on holistic education.* Retrieved from http://www.ctr4process.org/publications/SeminarPapers/232Miller.doc.

Monbiot, G. (2007). *Heat: How to stop the planet from burning.* Cambridge, MA: South End Press.

Moore, D. (2006). A guide to personal resilience. *Self growth: The online self improvement encyclopedia.* Retrieved February 22, 2010, from http://www.selfgrowth.com/articles/Moore77.html.

Morris, M. (2001). Curriculum as ecological text: A rat, a snake, a dove. *Journal of Curriculum Theorizing, 17*(3), 3–8.

———. (2002). Ecological consciousness and curriculum. *Journal of Curriculum Studies, 34*(5), 571–588.

———. (2008). *Teaching through the ill body: A spiritual and aesthetic approach to pedagogy and illness.* Rotterdam: Sense.

Morrison, R. (1995). *Ecological democracy.* Boston: South End Press.

Mueller, M. (2008). Ecojustice as ecological literacy is much more than being "green!", *Educational Studies, 44*(2), 155–166.

Mueller-Worster, A., & Ebersole, M. (2005). Place and standards-based teacher preparation courses. In *Annual meeting of the North American Association for Environmental Education Proceedings* (pp. 1–10). Presented at the annual meeting of the North American Association for Environmental Education, University of Hawai'i at Hilo.

Muir, J. (1997). *Nature writings.* New York: Library of America.

———. (2001). *The wilderness world of John Muir.* (E. W. Teale, Ed.). New York: Houghton Mifflin Harcourt.

Nash, R. (1967). *Wilderness and the American mind.* New Haven: Yale University Press.

NCSE [National Conference on Science & the Environment]. (2003). *Recommendations for education for a sustainable and secure future: A report of the third national conference on science, policy, and the environment.* Washington, DC: NCSE. Retrieved April 6, 2009, from http://www.ncseonline.org/NCSE conference/2003conference/2003report.pdf.

Nelson, R. (1998). *Heart and blood: Living with deer in America.* New York: Vintage.

———. (2002). Patriots for the American land. In *Patriotism and the American land* (pp. 1–21). Great Barrington, MA: Orion Society.

Ng-A-Fook, N. (2007). *An indigenous curriculum of place: The United Houma Nation's contentious relationship with Louisiana's educational institutions.* Complicated conversation, v. 25. New York: Peter Lang.

Nicol, R. (2002). Outdoor environmental education in the United Kingdom: A conceptual framework of epistemological diversity and its educational implications. *Canadian Journal of Environmental Education, 7*(2), Spring. 207–223.

NIES. (2010). Introduction: The Earth Day story and Gaylord Nelson. *Gaylord Nelson and Earth Day.* Retrieved February 15, 2010, from http://www.nelsonearthday.net/earth-day/index.htm.

Norris, K. (1998). *Amazing grace: A vocabulary of faith.* New York: Riverhead Books.

Northland College. (n.d.). Outdoor Orientation. *Northland College.* Retrieved February 2, 2010, from http://www.northland.edu/student-life-opportunities-outdoor-orientation.htm.

Nouwen, H. (1972). *Pray to live. Thomas Merton: A contemplative critic.* Notre Dame, IN: Fides Publishers.

———. (1981). *The Genesee diary.* Garden City, NY: Image Books.

———. (1997). *Adam, God's beloved.* Maryknoll, NY: Orbis Books.

Nussbaum, M. (1996). Introduction: Cosmopolitan emotions? In *For love of country: Debating the limits of patriotism* (pp. ix–xiv). Boston: Beacon Press.

Oldenburg, R. (1989). *The great good place: Cafés, coffee shops, community centers, beauty parlors, general stores, bars, hangouts, and how they get you through the day.* New York: Paragon House.

Oliver, M. (2005). *New and selected poems.* Boston: Beacon Press.

———. (2006). *Thirst.* Boston: Beacon Press.

Olson, S. F. (1956/1997). *The singing wilderness.* New York: Knopf.

———. (1958). *Listening point* (1st ed.). New York: Knopf.

———. (1976). *Reflections from the North Country* (1st ed.). New York: Knopf.

———. (1998). *Open horizons.* Minneapolis, MN: U of Minnesota Press.

———. (2001). *The meaning of wilderness: Essential articles and speeches.* (D. Backes, Ed.). Minneapolis: University of Minnesota Press.

organismic. (n.d.). Wordnet search. In *WordNet Search—3.0.* Retrieved from http://wordnetweb.princeton.edu/perl/webwn?s=organismic.

Orr, D. (1991). What is education for? *In Context: A quarterly of Humane Sustainable Culture,* 52–60. Retrieved from http://www.context.org/ICLIB/IC27/Orr.htm.

———. (1992). *Ecological literacy: Education and the transition to a postmodern world.* SUNY series in constructive postmodern thought. Albany: State University of New York Press.

———. (1994). *Earth in mind: On education, environment, and the human prospect.* Washington, DC: Island Press.

———. (2001). Foreword. In S. Sterling, *Sustainable education: Re-visioning learning and change* (pp. 7–9). Totnes, UK: Green Books for the Schumacher Society.

———. (2003). Walking north on a southbound train. *Conservation Biology,* (17), 348–351.

———. (2004a). *Earth in mind: On education, environment, and the human prospect.* Washington, DC: Island Press.

———. (2004b). *The last refuge: Patriotism, politics, and the environment in an age of terror.* Washington: Island Press.

———. (2005). Place as pedagogy. In M. Stone & Z. Barlow (Eds.), *Ecological literacy* (pp. 85–95). Bioneers series. San Francisco: Sierra Club Books.

———. (2009). *Down to the wire: Confronting climate collapse* (1st ed.). New York: Oxford University Press.

O'Sullivan, E. (1999). *Transformative learning: Educational vision for the 21st century.* London: Zed Books.

———. (1999). *Transformative learning: Educational vision for the 21st century.* London: Zed Books.

———. (2007). Giving nature its due. *Resurgence,* (245). Retrieved from http://www.resurgence.org/magazine/article75-Giving-Nature-its-Due.html.

———. (2008). The reenchantment of the natural world: Education with the needs of the planet in mind. In J. Gray-Donald, & D. Selby (Eds.), *Green frontiers: Environmental educators dancing away from mechanism.* Rotterdam: Sense. 132–141.

Outdoor education minor. (2009). *SUNY College at Oneonta.* College. Retrieved March 12, 2010, from http://www.oneonta.edu/academics/physed/Outdoor%20Education%20minor.asp.

Palmer, P. J. (1998). *The courage to teach: Exploring the inner landscape of a teacher's life.* San Francisco, CA: Jossey-Bass.

———. (2004). *A hidden wholeness: The journey toward an undivided life: Welcoming the soul and weaving community in a wounded world* (1st ed.). San Francisco, CA: Jossey-Bass.

Partridge, E. (n.d). Anthropocentrism. *The online gadfly.* Retrieved April 27, 2009, from: http://gadfly.igc.org/e-ethics/ee-topic.htm#anthro.

PCSD. (n.d.). *President's Council on Sustainable Development.* Home Page for the President's Council on Sustainable Development (PCSD). Retrieved September 1, 2009, from http://clinton2.nara.gov/PCSD/.

Pearce, F. (2005). Where have all the wild rivers gone? *New Scientist, 186* (2496), 10.

Phillips, C. (n.d.). Trail design and maintenance. *Foresthill Trails Alliance.* Retrieved February 21, 2010, from http://www.foothill.net/fta/work/maintnotes.html.

Pinar, W. F. (1978). The reconceptualization of curriculum studies. *Journal of Curriculum Studies, 10*(3), 205–214.

———. (1997). The reconceptualization of curriculum studies. In D. J. Flinders & S. J. Thornton (Eds.), *The curriculum studies reader* (pp. 149–157). New York: Routledge.

———. (1999). *Contemporary curriculum discourses: Twenty years of JCT.* New York: Peter Lang.

———. (2001). *The gender of racial politics and violence in America: Lynching, prison rape, and the crisis of masculinity.* New York: Peter Lang.

———. (2003). *International handbook of curriculum research.* Mahwah, NJ: Erlbaum.

———. (2004). *What is curriculum theory?* Mahwah, NJ: L. Erlbaum Associates.

———. (2006a). *The synoptic text today and other essays: Curriculum development after the reconceptualization.* New York: Peter Lang.

———. (2006b). *Race, religion and a curriculum of reparation.* New York: Palgrave Macmillan.

———. (2007a). *Intellectual advancement through disciplinarity: Verticality and horizontality in curriculum studies.* Rotterdam: Sense.

———. (2007b). Introduction: A queer conversation, toward sustainability. In Nelson Rodriguez and W. F. Pinar (Eds.), *Queering straight teachers* (pp. 1–12). New York: Peter Lang.

———. (2009a). The unaddressed 'I' of ideology critique. *Power and Education, 1*(2), 189–200.

———. (2009b). *The worldliness of a cosmopolitan education: Passionate lives in public service.* New York: Routledge.

Pinar, W., & Grumet, M. R. (1976). *Toward a poor curriculum.* Dubuque, IA: Kendall/Hunt.

Pinar, W. F., Reynolds, W. M., Slattery, P., & Taubman, P. M. (1995/2004). *Understanding curriculum: An introduction to the study of historical and contemporary curriculum discourses.* New York: Counterpoints.

Pinto, J. P. (2006). *Journey to wholeness.* Mumbai: St. Pauls.

Pirsig, R. M. (1979). *Zen and the art of motorcycle maintenance.* New York: Morrow Quill Paperbacks.

Pool, C. R. (1997). Maximizing learning: A conversation with Renate Nummela Caine. *Educational Leadership, 54*, 11–15.

Porritt, J. (1990). Introduction, in P. Martin, *First steps to sustainability: The school curriculum and the environment.* Godalming, UK: WWF-UK.

Post Carbon Institute. (2010). Issues. *Post carbon institute.* Retrieved March 4, 2010, from http://www.postcarbon.org/.

Prakash, M. S. (1994). From global thinking to local thinking: Reasons to go beyond globalization toward localization. *Holistic Education Review, 7*(4), 50–6.

———. (1995). Whose ecological perspective? Bringing ecology down to earth. In W. Kohli (Ed.), *Critical conversations in philosophy of education* (pp. 324–339). Retrieved September 21, 2009, from http://books.google.com/books.

———. (1998). *Escaping education: Living as learning within grassroots cultures.* New York: Peter Lang.

Prandoni, M. (2009, November 18). Know your lifeboat: An interview with permaculturist Brock Dolman. *EcoHearth: Come home to the earth.* Retrieved February 1, 2010, from http://ecohearth.com/eco-zine/eco-heroes/1088-know-your-lifeboat-an-interview-with-permaculturist-brock-dolman.html.

Price, A. (2009). *Slow-tech: Manifesto for an overwound world.* London: Atlantic.

Project WILD. (1992). *Aquatic Project WILD: Aquatic education activity guide.* Boulder, CO: Project WILD.

Ramljak, S. (2010). Crafting a new world. *Utne Reader.* Retrieved from http://www.utne.com/print-article.aspx?id=2147486003.

Rawlins, C. L. (1993). *Sky's witness: A year in the Wind River Range.* New York: Holt.

Ray, J. (1999). *Ecology of a cracker childhood.* Minneapolis: Milkweed Editions.

———. (2008). Hope for democracy. In P. Corcoran, J. Wohlpart, & P. Hollingshead (Eds), *A voice for Earth: American writers respond to the Earth Charter* (pp. 113-126). Athens: University of Georgia Press.

Rea, D. W. (2000). Optimal motivation for talent development. *Journal for the Education of the Gifted, 23*(2), 187–216.

Reason, P. (2007). Thinking about sustainability. *Perspective, school of management house journal* (July). Retrieved April 27, 2009, from http://people.bath.ac.uk/mnspwr/Papers/Perspective.pdf.

Reed, F. (1990). Indicators for monitoring biodiversity: A hierarchical approach. *Conservation Biology, 4*(4), 355–364.

Reynolds, W. M. (2003). *Curriculum: A river runs through it.* New York: Peter Lang.

Richter, W. (1945). *Re-Educating Germany.* Chicago, IL: University of Chicago.

Riley-Taylor, E. (2002). *Ecology, spirituality & education: Curriculum for relational knowing.* New York: Peter Lang.

Rilke, R. M. (1993). *Rilke on love and other difficulties: Translations and considerations of Rainer Maria Rilke* (John J. Mood, Trans.). New York: Norton.

riparian zone. (n.d.). *Wikipedia.* Retrieved March 11, 2010, from http://en.wikipedia.org/wiki/Riparian.

Rogers, E. K., Kostigen, T. & Kostigen, T. M. (2007). *The green book: The everyday guide to saving the planet one simple step at a time.* New York: Random House.

Rossman, P. (n.d.). *The future of higher education: Exploring and creating the future in virtual space.* Retrieved March 5, 2009, from http://ecolecon.missouri.edu/globalresearch/chapters/1-PREF.html.

Sabini, M. (2001). Introduction. In C. G. Jung. *The earth has a soul: The nature writings of C.G. Jung* (pp. 1–24). Berkeley, CA: North Atlantic Books.

Sachs, W., & George, S. (1997). Wasting time is an ecological virtue. *New Perspectives Quarterly, 14*(Winter), 4–9.

Sale, K. (2000). *Dwellers in the land.* Athens, GA: University of Georgia Press.

Sanders, S. R. (2008). Wilderness as a Sabbath for the land. In P. B. Corcoran, J. Wohlpart, & B. P. Hollingshead (Eds.), *A voice for Earth: American writers respond to the Earth Charter* (pp. 80–89). Athens, GA: University of Georgia Press.

Sanger, M. (1997). Sense of place and education. *Journal of Environmental Education, 29*(1), 4.

Santone, S. (2007). *The cloud institute for sustainable education.* Retrieved November 27, 2008, from www.sustainabilityed.org/what/education_for_sustainability/what_is_sustainability.html.

Sargent, P. (1945/1976). *Between two wars: The failure of education, 1920–1940.* Boston: P. Sargent.

Scherer, M. (2002). Do students care about learning? A conversation with Mihaly Csikszentmihalyi. *Educational Leadership, 60*(1). 12–17.

Schiller, F. (1965/2004). *On the aesthetic education of man.* Mineola, NY: Dover Publications.

Schubert, W. H. (1986/1997). *Curriculum: Perspective, paradigm, and possibility.* Upper Saddle River, NJ: Prentice-Hall, Inc.

———. (2002). *Curriculum books: The first hundred years.* New York: Peter Lang.

———. (2006). Teaching John Dewey as a utopian pragmatist while learning from my students. *Education and Culture, 22*(1), 78–83. Retrieved July 17, 2009, from http://muse.jhu.edu/journals/education_and_culture/v022/22.1schubert.html.

———. (2009a). *Love, justice and education: John Dewey and the utopians.* Charlotte, NC: IAP.

———. (2009b). Currere and disciplinarity in curriculum studies: Possibilities for education research. In J. Henderson & K. Kesson. Curriculum Disciplinarity and Education Research: Advancing a Scholarly and Professional Agenda, *Educational Researcher, 38*(2), 136–140.

Schumacher, E. F. (1973). *Small is beautiful: A study of economics as if people mattered.* London: Abacus.

Schweitzer, A. (1960). *The philosophy of civilization.* New York: MacMillan.

Seed, J. (Ed.). (1988). *Thinking like a mountain: Towards a council of all beings.* Philadelphia, PA: New Society.

Selby, D. (2008). The firm and shaky ground of education for sustainable development. In J. Gray-Donald & D. Selby (Eds.), *Green frontiers: Environmental educators dancing away from mechanism* (pp. 59-75). Rotterdam: Sense Publishers.

Seligman, M. E., & Csikszentmihalyi, M. (2000). Positive psychology: An introduction. *American Psychologist, 55*(1), 5–14.

Seuss, T. G. (1971). *The Lorax.* New York: Random House

Shepard, P. (2003). *Where we belong: Beyond abstraction in perceiving nature.* (F. Shepard, Ed.). Athens, GA: University of Georgia Press.

Sherman, E. (1991, Fall). Book reviews. *Teachers College Record, 93*(1), 184. Retrieved April 19, 2008, from Sociological Collection database.

Shernoff, D. J., Csikszentmihalyi, M., Schneider, B., & Shernoff, E. S. (2003). Student engagement in high school classrooms from the perspective of Flow Theory. *School Psychology Quarterly, 18*(2), 158–176.

Shiva, V. (1993). *Monocultures of the mind: Perspectives on biodiversity and biotechnology.* London: Zed Books.

———. (2004, May). Turning scarcity into abundance. *yes! Supporting you in building a just and sustainable world.* Retrieved October 7, 2009, from http://www.yesmagazine.org/issues/whose-water/turning-scarcity-into-abundance.

———. (2005). *Earth democracy: Justice, sustainability, and peace.* Cambridge, MA: South End Press.

———. (2008). *Soil not oil: Environmental justice in a time of climate crisis.* Cambridge, MA: South End Press.

Shoaf, R. A. (2001). *Chaucer's body.* Gainesville, FL: University Press of Florida.

Shorb, T. (2009). *The butterfly curriculum: Learning to help heal the community of all beings.* Unpublished PhD Book, Prescott College.

Singer, P. (2002). *One world: The ethics of globalization.* New Haven: Yale University Press.

Slattery, P. (1995). A postmodern vision of time and learning: A response to the national education commission. *Harvard Educational Review, 65*(4), 612–633. Retrieved September 1, 2009, from http://www.coe.tamu.edu/~pslattery/documents/prison.pdf.

———. (2006/2009). *Annotated glossary for curriculum development in the postmodern era, 2nd ed. [unpublished manuscript].* College Station, TX: Texas A&M.

Slattery, P., & Edgerton, S. H. (2009). Advancing a curriculum of place for justice and sustainability: American association for the advancement of curriculum studies presidential address. *Journal of the American Association for the Advancement of Curriculum Studies, 5.* Retrieved from http://www.uwstout.edu/soe/jaaacs/Vol5/Presidential_Address.htm.

Smith, G. A., & Williams, D. R. (1999). *Ecological education in action: On weaving education, culture, and the environment.* Albany, NY: State University of New York Press.

Snyder, G. (1995). *A place in space: Ethics, aesthetics, and watersheds.* Washington, DC: Counterpoint.

Spencer, H. (1860). *Education: Intellectual, moral, and physical*. New York: D. Appleton and Company.

Spring, J. (1986). *The American school 1642–1985*. New York: Longman.

Steen, S. (2008). Bastions of mechanism-castle built on sand. In J. Gray-Donald & D. Selby (Eds.), *Green frontiers: Environmental educators dancing away from mechanism*. Rotterdam: Sense, 228–240.

Steier, F., & Jorgenson, J. (n.d.). Patterns that connect: A thematic Foreword. *Cybernetics & Human Knowing, 12*(1–2), 5–10. Retrieved from http://www.imprint.co.uk/books/Bateson_Intro.pdf.

Sterling, S. (2001). *Sustainable education: Re-vision learning and change*. Bristol, UK: Green Books.

———. (2004a). Higher education, sustainability, and the role of systemic learning. In P.B. Corcoran & A.E.J. Wals (Eds.), *Higher education and the challenge of sustainability: Problems, promise, and practice*, 49–70. Dordrecht: Kluwer Academic.

———. (2004b). *Whole systems thinking as a basis for paradigm change in education: Explorations in the context of sustainability*. Book, University of Bath (United Kingdom. Retrieved February 4, 2009, from http://proquest.umi.com.libez.lib.georgiasouthern.edu/pqdweb?did=920921591&Fmt=7&clientId=30291&RQT=309&VName=PQD.

Sterling, S. & EDET Group (1992). *Good Earth-keeping: Education, training and awareness for a sustainable future*. Environment and Development Education and Training Group, UNEP-UK, London.

Stewart, M. (2000). *Follow your dreams gift book: You can if you think you can*. Center City, MN: Hazelden.

Stone, M., & Barlow, Z. (Eds.). (2005). *Ecological literacy: Educating our children for a sustainable world* (1st ed.). San Francisco: Sierra Club Books.

Surian, N. (2003). River channelization (Abstract). In B. A. Stewart & T. Howell (Eds.), *Encyclopedia of water science*. New York: Marcel Dekker.

sustainability. (n.d.). Glossary. *Glenelg Hopkins Catchment Management Authority—Glossary*. Retrieved March 15, 2010, from http://www.glenelg-hopkins.vic.gov.au/?id=glossary.

Taubman, P. (2009). *Teaching by numbers: Deconstructing the discourse of standards and accountability in education*. New York: Routledge.

Thayer, R. L. (2003). *LifePlace: Bioregional thought and practice*. Berkeley: University of California Press.

Third Place. (2009, November 21). *Wikipedia, the free encyclopedia*. Retrieved February 3, 2010, from http://en.wikipedia.org/wiki/Third_place.

Thompson, S. (2008). Environmental justice in education: Drinking deeply from the well of sustainability. In J. Gray-Donald & D. Selby (Eds.), *Green frontiers: Environmental educators dancing away from mechanism* (pp. 36–58). Rotterdam: Sense Publishers.

Tillich, P. (1955). *Biblical religion and the search for ultimate reality.* Chicago: University of Chicago Press.

Tools for Change. (n.d.). Upcoming events. *Tools for change: Bringing history, heart, spirit, values, and vision into the center of public life.* Retrieved March 4, 2010, from http://toolsforchange.org/pages/UPCOMING.html.

Transition Network. (2010a). What is a transition initiative? *Transition network.* Retrieved March 2, 2010, from http://transitionnetwork.org/community/support/what-transition-initiative.

———. (2010b). 12 ingredients. *Transition Network.* Retrieved March 2, 2010, from http://www.transitionnetwork.org/community/support/12-ingredients.

Triche, S. (2002). *Reconceiving curriculum: An historical approach.* Unpublished doctoral book, Baton Rouge: Louisiana State University.

trudge (n.d.). *WordNetWeb.Princeton.edu/perl/webwn.* Retrieved March 7, 2010, from http://www.google.com/firefox?client=firefox-a&rls=org.mozilla:en-US:official.

Trueit, D., Doll, W. E., Wang, H. & Pinar, W. (eds.) (2003). *The internationalization of curriculum studies: Selected proceedings from the LSU conference 2000.* New York: Peter Lang.

UNESCO. (n.d.). Education for sustainable development. Retrieved March 6, 2010, from http://www.unesco.org/en/esd/.

———. (1972). *The Stockholm Declaration,* Stockholm: UNESCO.

———. (2005). *UNDESD (2005–2014): International implementation scheme* (p. 31). Implementation Scheme, Paris, France: UNESCO. Retrieved September 24, 2009, from http://unesdoc.unesco.org/images/0014/001486/148654e.pdf.

Unsoeld, W. (1974). *Spiritual values in wilderness.* Paper presented at the Association for Experiential Education Conference, Estes Park, CO.

Van Doren, M. (1965). *Liberal education* (6th ed.). Boston, MA: Beacon Press.

Van Kannel-Ray, N. (2006). Guiding principles and emerging practices for environmentally sustainable education. In B. S. Stern (Ed.), *Curriculum and teaching dialogue* (Vol. 8, pp. 113–123). Charlotte, NC: Information Age Publishing. Retrieved from EBSCO Host Electronic Database.

Vitousek, P. M., Mooney, H. A., Lubchenco, J., & Melillo, J. M. (1997). Human domination of Earth's ecosystems. *Science, 277*(5325), 494.

Wackernagel, M., & Rees, W. E. (1996). *Our ecological footprint: Reducing human impact on the earth.* Gabriola Island, BC: New Society.

Wals, A. E. J. (Ed.). (2007). *Social learning towards a sustainable world: Principles, perspectives, and praxis.* The Netherlands: Wageningen Academic.

Water cycle. (2010). *Wikipedia.* Retrieved February 14, 2010, from http://en.wikipedia.org/wiki/Hydrologic_cycle.

Weisman, A. (2007). *The world without us.* New York: St. Martin's Press.

———. (2008). *Gaviotas: A village to reinvent the world.* White River Junction, VT: Chelsea Green Publishing.

Wensing, E., & Torre, C. (2009). The ecology of education: Knowledge systems for sustainable development and sustainability. *Journal of Teacher Education for Sustainability, 11*(1), 3–17.

Wessels, T. (1997/2005). *Reading the forested landscape: A natural history of New England* (1st ed.). Woodstock, VT: New York: Countryman Press.

———. (2006). *The myth of progress: Toward a sustainable future.* Burlington, VT: University of Vermont Press.

Whitehead, A. N. (1997): *Science and the modern world.* New York: Simon and Schuster.

Whitney, K. (2001). Greening by place: Sustaining cultures, ecologies, communities. *Journal of Women & Religion 19,* 11–25.

Why Now? (n.d.). *Smart Meme: Changing the story.* Retrieved April 26, 2009, from http://smartmeme.org/article.php?id=289.

Wilber, K. (Ed.). (1982). *The holographic paradigm and other paradoxes: Exploring the leading edge of science* (1st ed.). Boulder: Shambhala.

Wild. (n.d.). GALILEO: Oxford English Dictionary (OED) (2nd Edition): Text (2nd ed.). Oxford.

Williams, T. T. (2001). *Red: Passion and patience in the desert.* New York: Pantheon Books.

———. (2008a). *Finding beauty in a broken world.* New York: Pantheon Books.

———. (2008b). Taking the globe to our bosom. In P. Corcoran, J. Wohlpart, & P. Hollingshead. *A voice for Earth: American writers respond to the Earth Charter* (pp. xiii–xviii). Athens: University of Georgia Press.

Wilson, C. (1964). *The outsider.* London: Gollancz.

Wilson, E. O. (1984). *Biophilia.* Cambridge, MA: Harvard University Press.

———. (2007). [Video Recording] Saving life on Earth. www.*TED.com*. Retrieved February 25, 2010, from http://www.ted.com/talks/e_o_wilson_on_saving_life_on_earth.html.

World Commission on Environment and Development [WCED]. (1987). *Our common future.* Oxford paperbacks. Oxford: Oxford University Press.

Wright, T. S. A. (2002). Definitions and frameworks for environmental sustainability in higher education. *International Journal of Sustainability in Higher Education, 3*(3), 203–220.

Wydeven, A. (2003). Northern Wisconsin: Northwoods Wolf Report. *Wolf Report.* Retrieved February 5, 2010, from http://www.northernwisconsin.com/wolfreport.htm.

Young Harris College. (n.d.). Mission, Goals, Values and Vision Statements—Young Harris College. Retrieved April 3, 2010, from http://www.yhc.edu/about-yhc/mission-goals-values-and-vision-statements.aspx.

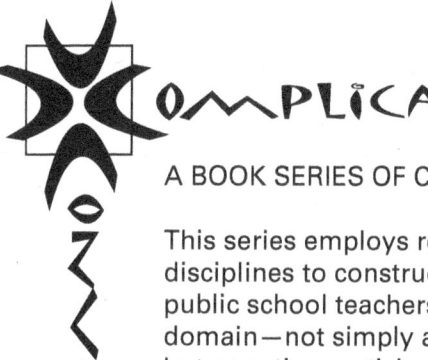

Complicated Conversation

A BOOK SERIES OF CURRICULUM STUDIES

This series employs research completed in various disciplines to construct textbooks that will enable public school teachers to reoccupy a vacated public domain—not simply as "consumers" of knowledge, but as active participants in a "complicated conversation" that they themselves will lead. In drawing promiscuously but critically from various academic disciplines and from popular culture, this series will attempt to create a conceptual montage for the teacher who understands that positionality as aspiring to reconstruct a "public" space. Complicated Conversation works to resuscitate the progressive project—an educational project in which self-realization and democratization are inevitably intertwined; its task as the new century begins is nothing less than the intellectual formation of a public sphere in education.

The series editor is

> Dr. William F. Pinar
> Department of Curriculum Studies
> 2125 Main Mall
> Faculty of Education
> University of British Columbia
> Vancouver, British Columbia V6T 1Z4
> CANADA

To order other books in this series, please contact our Customer Service Department:

> (800) 770-LANG (within the U.S.)
> (212) 647-7706 (outside the U.S.)
> (212) 647-7707 FAX

Or browse online by series:

> www.peterlang.com